THE FOUR SEASONS OF MARY LAVIN

The Arts Council
An Chomhairle Ealaíon

First published in 1998 by
Marino Books
16 Hume Street Dublin 2
Tel: (01) 661 5299; Fax: (01) 661 8583;
e.mail: books@marino.ie

Trade enquiries to CMD Distribution
55A Spruce Avenue
Stillorgan Industrial Park Blackrock
County Dublin
Tel: (01) 294 2556; Fax: (01) 294 2564

© Leah Levenson 1998

ISBN 1 86023 066 0

10 9 8 7 6 5 4 3 2 1

A CIP record for this title is available
from the British Library

Cover design by
Penhouse Design Group
Printed in Ireland by ColourBooks
Baldoyle Industrial Estate, Dublin 13

THE FOUR SEASONS OF MARY LAVIN

LEAH LEVENSON

For Mary's girls: Valdi, Elizabeth and Caroline

Contents

PREFACE

Mary Lavin's place in literature is well documented and her ability as a master of the short story form firmly established. Articles, reviews, and introductions to her collections of short stories, as well as three critical studies of her work published since 1975, make that clear. But the saga of the events and the people that helped to shape her personality, the influences which contributed to the development of Mary Lavin as a writer, and the impact she made upon the period in which she lived had yet to be told. *The Four Seasons of Mary Lavin* is designed to fill that gap.

Mary Lavin was born in East Walpole, Massachusetts, of Irish parents, and she knew Ireland only as a visitor for the first nine years of her life. When, therefore, at the age of nine, she and her mother left the States and settled in Ireland permanently, she was able to view Irish life through the eyes of an American child: one who had a great love for and curiosity about people, as well as remarkable insight. An only child, a beautiful mother whose values Mary Lavin grew to deplore, and a father who adored her and was ambitious for her, all contributed to the development of her personality. Important as well was her participation in the life of the wealthy East Walpole Bird family by whom her father was employed, and later her exposure to the lifestyle of Lord Dunsany, who became her mentor.

It was to Athenry, a small town in the west of Ireland and her mother's home-town, that Mary Lavin and her mother went when first they returned to Ireland, and they lived there for some nine months. Those months contributed greatly to the development of the incipient writer. As she has said, when she began to write she found herself casting her characters in the shape of the people in Athenry. 'I used them as prototypes for people like them that I had met elsewhere.' Those early Athenry experiences provided the basis for a pattern that was followed throughout her writing career.

Mary Lavin's work encompasses a fifty-year period: a period during which the literary climate in Ireland went from what the Irish novelist and short story writer Mervyn Wall called the Dark Ages to the fairly enlightened one of today; a period in the history of Ireland that saw social change for the intellectual, the writer and the artist. Through her deeds and her writings Mary Lavin helped considerably to mould that period. There were very few women who were receiving recognition in Ireland when Mary Lavin was writing. She, however, earned a reputation not only in Ireland but internationally. She managed at the same time to raise three daughters single-handedly. As a young widow, she supported herself and her family by her writings and, by example, she led the way for other women in her field. She said in one of her many interviews that she hoped to do the impossible: 'to put things before my work and still make my work good'. And she proved that she could.

Much has been written about O'Flaherty, O'Faolain and O'Connor, and Mary Lavin's name has often been linked with theirs. But her subject matter is not the politics of Ireland or the 'Troubles', as theirs so often was. She believed herself to be 'of a different generation', was of a different background and brought a fresh perspective to the country and its people. Declan Kiberd, in his literary history of modern Ireland, *Inventing Ireland*, described the difference in this fashion: 'Her touch was ever light and easy. She had no desire to dig society up by its roots, rather she worked to hold it true to its own nobler imperatives.' And as the novelist and short story writer Evelyn Conlon expressed it in her introduction to the 1996 reissue of *Tales from Bective Bridge*, she 'examined the wars of relationships rather than those of countries'.

Mary Lavin also played a significant role in the development of a number of young aspiring writers and artists. In the early 1960s she established a salon – unique in Dublin – where those young people were always sure of a warm reception and assistance. They were drawn to her salon – the Mews, as her home was called – by her personality, her magnetism, and by her ability to make budding writers feel that their work and their lives were of much more significance than hers. There are successful writers in Ireland and in the United States who can testify to the value of her encouragement. Writers already successful, such as Frank O'Connor and Benedict Kiely also delighted in visiting the Mews and spending time in her company.

The importance of Mary Lavin's work has been acknowledged by such major literary figures as William Trevor, Seamus Heaney, V. S. Pritchett, Frank O'Connor, Kay Boyle, Eudora Welty, Maeve Binchy and Benedict Kiely. As William Trevor wrote in a tribute to Mary Lavin's stories shortly after her death: 'Another renowned practitioner of the art – Elizabeth Bowen – described the modern storyteller's task as revealing the hidden significance of "the small event", and in this Lavin succeeded superbly well.'

I have discussed many of Mary Lavin's stories at great length. Because of their semi-autobiographical nature, it has been possible – and indeed necessary – to use them to fill in details of her life, since they reflect it so well. In all cases, I have striven to make the distinction between fact and fiction clear.

Leah Levenson
Worcester, MA
November 1997

ACKNOWLEDGEMENTS

Without the assistance of Elizabeth Walsh Peavoy, Mary Lavin's daughter, this biography would have been well-nigh impossible. She placed at my disposal her time, so many of the letters to and from her mother, and her recollections and reflections. Her sisters, Valentine and Caroline, have also been extremely helpful, and I am deeply grateful to them for their wholehearted support and their willingness to give me full access to the Lavin papers and photographs without in any way curbing my freedom to deal with the material as I saw fit.

Certain family members in addition to Mary Lavin's daughters have talked with me and shared their memories of her: Eoghan and Adam Peavoy and Kathleen MacMahon, Mary Lavin's grandchildren; Diarmuid Peavoy, Desmond MacMahon and James Ryan, her sons-in-law; Michael Walshe Jr, William Walsh's nephew, and Florence Walsh, his niece; and Eileen and Augustine O'Toole, Mary Lavin's cousins. I thank them all.

A biography such as this, although one individual remains responsible, becomes a collective effort. I list with my thanks the many people – Mary Lavin's friends and colleagues – who have taken the time to talk or to correspond with me: Dr Robert Gillen, Alex Medlicott, Margaret MacCurtain, Thomas Kilroy, Lorna Reynolds, Sam Stephenson, Fr F. X. Martin, Maura and Maurice Harmon, Nuala O'Faolain, the Hon. Edward Plunkett, Desmond O'Grady, Patrick Shanley, Elizabeth Shannon, Benedict Kiely, the late Augustine Martin, Mervyn Wall, Garret FitzGerald, Cormac O'Malley, John Beary, Tom MacIntyre, Hazel Douglas, Elizabeth Cullinan, Zack Bowen, Richard F. Peterson, Maeve Binchy, Seamus Heaney, William Trevor, Fr Peter L'Estrange, William Maxwell, Ann Waldron, Anne Francis Cavanaugh,

Maureen Murphy, Norman D. Stevens, Joan and Jack Cahill, Liam O'Heagharty, Elizabeth Cottrell and Sister Esther Brady.

Finally, I am greatly indebted to my friend Angela Von Laue, who read the manuscript in its early stages and who offered extremely helpful editorial suggestions. If I have inadvertently omitted anyone from this list, I offer my apologies and my thanks.

I

SPRING

CHAPTER 1

Mary Lavin was born of Irish parents in East Walpole, Massachusetts, where her father, Tom Lavin, was gainfully and happily employed. She might have spent more than the first nine years of her life there had her mother, Nora Mahon, not disliked life in the United States so thoroughly that she could scarcely wait to escape. As a matter of fact, Mary's parents had very little in common except their nationality.

Nora Mahon was the daughter of a prosperous merchant in Athenry, County Galway, a small, walled, twelfth-century market town in the west of Ireland. The Mahon establishment, on Cross Street, was housed in the most impressive building in town and dealt in such diverse and essential items as coal, tea, spirits and grain. Patrick Mahon, her father, also acted as agent for the Cunard and White Star Steamship Lines. Indeed, the business was the mainstay of Athenry. Everyone knew and respected the Mahons, and the attractive Mahon daughters were much in demand.

Conversely, little is known of Tom Lavin's antecedents or of his life in Frenchpark, the poverty-stricken, Irish-speaking area in County Roscommon where he was born. From time to time over the years, however, he gave his daughter 'scraps of information', as she said. His great friend as a boy, he told her, was a young Protestant named Douglas Hyde, an Anglo-Irish rectory child in Frenchpark. This was the Douglas Hyde who became a passionate advocate of the revival of Gaelic, the founder of the Gaelic League, and, in 1938, the first President of the Irish Free State. Tom Lavin spoke Irish as a boy, he once said, but later could remember only the Hail Mary.

A controversy with his teacher in the one-room school-house in Frenchpark ended Tom Lavin's schooling and hastened his departure at a very early age from the town: he may not yet have been sixteen. He escaped to Dublin, then moved to Liverpool. From there he went to Scotland, and then to Yorkshire. He found employment wherever he went: in Scotland in the potato fields, in Yorkshire in the hop fields. Finally – the date is unknown but the year may have been 1890 – he arrived in New York City.

His descendants tell a story, possibly apocryphal, that in New York he boarded a train for Boston: a logical destination for an Irishman then as now. In Walpole, some thirteen miles from Boston, the train was stalled because of snowdrifts on the tracks and that was as far as Tom got. On the station platform that day he met Charles S. Bird, owner of a large and prosperous mill and the town's major employer. Tom, far from shy, struck up a conversation with Mr Bird. 'I could clear that track single-handed,' he bragged. At which point Mr Bird handed him a shovel. Before the train left Walpole, Tom, handsome, sturdy, and with a winning personality, had been hired to help with the raising of Bird's prize Guernsey cattle and the care of his horses at Endean, the family estate.

Whether or not this was the accident that brought Mr Bird and Tom Lavin together, one thing is certain. It was a fortuitous meeting. Charlie Bird was a decent, kind, appreciative employer and Tom Lavin was devoted, intelligent and hard-working. He continued to work for the Bird family, both in the States and in Ireland, until his death.

His meeting with his future wife was equally accidental. In August 1908 Tom Lavin – by then an indispensable part of the Bird family – boarded the SS *Franconia* to go to Ireland to purchase horses for Mr Bird. One of his fellow passengers was Nora Mahon. She had, since September of the previous year, been visiting her granduncle, the Reverend James Dermody, in Waltham, Massachusetts, where he was pastor of the Roman Catholic church. The Reverend Dermody's claim to fame, at least in the eyes of the Mahon family, was that his brother was the first American soldier to be killed in the Spanish-American war (1898).

Nora's visit seems to have had a definite objective. Even though the Mahon establishment did a brisk business, Patrick Mahon, Nora's father and a kindly gentleman, was not a good businessman and half the town was in his debt. With twelve children to support, there was very little money to spare. As the story has been told countless times by family members, Delia Mahon (née Higgins), Nora's mother, a woman of great determination, had convinced Nora that, as the eldest daughter, it was her duty to make way for her younger sisters. Getting married was the best way to do it but, in her mother's estimation, there was no one in Athenry good enough for Nora – or for any of her daughters for that matter. Consequently, Nora was sent to the States to find a suitable husband. The visit had not been a success. She had been unhappy in Waltham, had met no eligible candidate, and was returning home when Tom Lavin met her.

For Tom, struck by her classic beauty and her general air of refinement, it was love at first sight. Nora, on the other hand, always claimed that she had taken an instant dislike to him and had made clear that she was not interested in his advances. Yet it is difficult to believe that she was not flattered by the persistent courtship of this handsome, black-haired, blue-eyed older man, with his outgoing and engaging temperament.

The game of quoits was what finally brought them together. Two chivalrous elderly gentlemen had taken it upon themselves to look after the young Irish girl travelling alone. They arranged to have her at their table, placed her deckchair between theirs, promenaded the deck with her, and played quoits with her regularly. When one day one of the gentlemen – her partner – had to pause to rest, Tom, waging a fierce campaign to win Nora and usually to be found in her vicinity, stepped in. He and Nora won the match handily and from then on he was her partner.

By the time they reached Ireland and landed at Queenstown, now Cobh, Tom had decided this was the woman he intended to marry. Nora, however, continued to insist that she was uninterested. But Tom did not give up. As Mary Lavin told the story in an interview some years later, after a correspondence conducted more ardently by Tom than by Nora, he sent her a diamond ring and money for her passage back to the States to marry him.

It is not clear how reluctant Nora Mahon was to take the final step in what appears to have been a fairly one-sided courtship. At any rate, on the fifth day of July in the year 1911, Thomas Lavin, teamster, and Nora Mahon, at home, were joined together in holy matrimony in the parochial house in Waltham. The marriage was solemnized by Fr F. S. Millard.

Apparently neither participant was particularly concerned with accuracy when supplying data for the marriage licence. Nora gave her name as Lolo and her age as twenty-six. Her birth certificate, however, states that Nora Teresa Mahon was born on the seventh day of April 1881 and she would, therefore, have been thirty years old when she married. As for her name, Lolo was the pet name by which, according to her cousin Eileen Daly O'Toole, she was always known. Why she used it on an official document is puzzling. She also used Miss Lolo T. Mahon on their quite formal wedding announcements. Tom, who gave his age as thirty-nine on the licence, was not sure of the date of his birth but was undoubtedly older than that. In 1936 he had applied for a permit to visit England and attempted to obtain a birth certificate from the Custom House. Authorities there informed him that all records had been destroyed in a fire. He persisted, however, and finally one of the officials – 'a very decent man', according to Tom – found an entry which corresponded with whatever known facts were available. He accepted that as his birth certificate but always said firmly that he did not believe it was his. When he died in 1945 Mary Lavin was of the opinion that he was in his quite late seventies.

From the start, Nora had been scornful of Tom Lavin's

occupation, his background and his friends. Marriage did not change her attitude. The newlyweds rented a flat in a two-family house on Washington Street in East Walpole: a house which was owned by Tom's employer and was part of the Bird estate. Theirs was a large and pleasant flat and Tom was well able to provide every comfort for his wife but Nora made no secret of the fact that she hated living in East Walpole and was homesick and unhappy. Almost immediately, she insisted on going back to Athenry to visit her family. Within a few months, however, she was pregnant and both her doctor and the Cunard Line discouraged her from travelling in that condition.

Mary Josephine Lavin, the couple's first and only child, was born on 10 June 1912. (Her father's middle name, Joseph, was the source for the Josephine.) In June 1913, as soon as Mary was weaned, Nora succeeded in persuading her husband to let her go back to Athenry: just for a visit, she said. A year later he had to go over to bring them back. Mary Lavin always believed that at that time her mother's intention had been to remain only long enough to pack her things and go back to Ireland to stay. Perhaps that was so, but the difficulties of travel during World War I forced her to remain in East Walpole. 'What with passport and political difficulties, she was detained in America for another seven years, before we returned to Ireland for good when I was nine,' Mary wrote later.

During his bachelor days, Tom, highly eligible thanks to his position with the Bird family, had had a fine time in East Walpole. His employer, like so many mill owners, made a practice of bringing over from Ireland poor, uneducated girls to work as maids and housekeepers, and young men to work in the mill. Those young men and women constituted Tom's social circle. He enjoyed drinking with the men and dating the women. When, as often happened, his friends married, he was always a welcome guest in their homes.

The picture changed when he married Nora. She was

firm in her resolution not to settle into East Walpole life. She did not intend to socialize with his friends. Her parents had always had servants and, as she did not hesitate to state, the wives of Tom's chums were the kind her mother would have hired. They would have waited on her in Athenry. She would certainly not have granted them her friendship. So she refused invitations to their homes in order to ensure that she would not have to invite them to hers. From all accounts, Tom took her attitude fairly calmly. As a matter of fact, he seemed to accept her estimate of her worth and, to a certain extent, glory in her aloofness. He continued to drink with his friends and to visit their homes, but he did it alone.

Mary liked the town and her father's friends. In her estimation, the town of East Walpole was a fine place in which to grow up and the Bird estate a superb playground. It was vast, with Endean – the family home built in 1839 – high on a hill overlooking lawns with lofty, aged trees sloping down to the shores of the Neponsett River, and with a view of the mills across the river. Behind the Lavins' house, and part of the Bird estate, was a wooded area. There Mary wandered for hours and there, too, she developed a love of nature and a knowledge of flowers that never left her. She always remembered the excitement of finding a yellow violet. 'I knew all about blue and white violets, but a yellow violet seemed very exotic to me.'

Many years later Mary was asked by the poet Eavan Boland how she felt about being an only child. She had not thought much about it when she was young, she said. She was alone but never lonely. Indeed, she had enjoyed solitude. It was only as she grew old and her mother grew older that she began to think of being an only child as 'the greatest curse that could befall anyone', for she was destined to care for an aged parent with no one to share the responsibility. As she talked with Boland, the thought occurred to her that perhaps she could, at least to a certain extent, trace her ability as a writer to those days of isolation when she filled a vacuum with imaginary people.

Mary shared her love of nature, as well as her enjoyment of his friends, with her father. But her devotion to the written word, developed early, was foreign to him. She had no recollection of his reading anything but newspapers. There were no books in the house except Pears *Cyclopaedia*, which she read over and over again. Her mother, however, was an avid reader and, thanks to her, Mary was introduced to and made full use of the local library. Nora's taste ran to romantic novels set in the Victorian era and Miss Childs, the librarian, soon learned what books to set aside for her. Mary Lavin never forgot Miss Childs, who, when Mary had exhausted the children's section of the small library, allowed her to take books from the adult section – under her supervision, of course. Miss Childs introduced her to *The House of Seven Gables* and to Longfellow's *Hiawatha*. She memorized much of the latter and would walk through the woods reciting loudly.

Though Mary's recollections of those years in East Walpole were understandably vague, trips she made to the States as an adult revived some of them. When, on a visit to a rural area in New England, she heard the kittiwakes and crickets, she recalled hearing those sounds as a child. When in Ohio the snow began to fall, she realized that 'that side of winter was absolutely without parallel in my Irish life'. And when she experienced a New England winter with its brisk, cold days and beautiful white snow, she grew nostalgic and thought of a Christmas present her father had given her when she was a little girl. It was a sled: a blue sled with a little pink rose painted on the seat. He would tie a rope around his waist, tie it to the sled, and pull her along in the snow, to her great delight. And he had bought her ice skates as well.

A great many of her memories of childhood revolve around her father and his love for her. Once he had dared her to walk, after dark, up the road from their house and through the wooded area as far as the entrance of the Bird home. When she came back to report her success, Tom said: 'You didn't think I was going to let you do that on your own, girlie.' He had followed her all the way. 'I loved my father very, very dearly. I think that he was well worth loving because I still meet people who tell me what an extraordinary person he was,' Mary wrote many years later. Over the years, she cherished the letters her father wrote her. As she looked back on the three years of her parents' courtship, she searched for letters that he must have written to her mother during that period and longed to see them. Her mother saved quite unimportant things and yet Mary could find no letters. Because she was well aware of her father's difficulty with spelling and grammar, she wondered if possibly they had been destroyed for that reason. It seemed to her that such a gesture would have been in keeping with her mother's pretentiousness.

When Mary reached school age, she was enrolled in the Bird School on Washington Street, the street on which the Lavins lived. In her day it was a wooden structure which housed students in grades one to four. Over the years there were additions and in the early 1930s it was replaced by a brick structure and renamed the Bird Elementary School. Although books were Mary's constant companions, she was not a loner by any means. As she said later, 'I enjoyed solitude but I was also gregarious, and I had great fun at school with my companions.' She made friends easily and liked her classmates. She visited their homes and, unlike her mother, found her friends' mothers a fun-loving, kind-hearted lot.

Life in East Walpole must have been dreary for Nora. She managed to fill her days with her romantic novels and her embroidery, at which she was highly skilled, but she must have been alone a great deal. That her isolation was of her own making could not have made it any easier. Consequently, she lived a great deal in her Athenry past. When, therefore, Mary was old enough to show an interest, Nora entertained her – and herself – with tales of her Athenry days. Those stories had an indelible effect on Mary and are woven into her own stories. She saw that clearly when much later she wrote:

> I always assume that any gifts I have inherited came from my father because of the real depth and power of his emotion. He was such a strong person and yet, looking back on it, I think that I may be unjust to my mother, because I thought of her as a rather giddy little person, full of stories. She was always telling me stories of her own childhood . . . There was simply nothing she forgot about her childhood and later, when I came to write, I think I drew on *her* memories. Her memories seemed to become more real than my own.

One story that Nora told her daughter more than once had all the elements of the kind of Victorian novel she liked to read. As Mary retold it in 'Tom', a story written in the 1970s about her father – and one which she said later was close to fact – one day, when Nora and one of her sisters were gathering daffodils in a field beyond the town ramparts, the land agent in charge of the area came by. He did not reprimand them and that same evening came into the Mahon shop ostensibly to buy a drink but actually, Nora was sure, to see her. Every evening thereafter he would come in for his one glass of port and Nora would stay in the shop to chat until closing time. With him she could discuss literature, she emphasized, presumably drawing a distinction between the land agent and Tom Lavin. Her sisters, she said, were furious because, though all of them could play the piano, she was the best – as she appeared to be in all her stories – and they needed her in the parlour. Why didn't she take him into the parlour, Mary wanted to know. Was it because he was so much older? No, it was because he was a Protestant.

No further explanation was needed.

The evenings spent with the agent continued and then one day, when Nora was polishing the glass for his port wine, it broke in her hand. She had a scar that ran almost all the way around her finger to prove it. She was proud of the fact that the handkerchief he tore to shreds to bind her wound was silk and monogrammed.

The climax of the story never failed to thrill little Mary. Two days after Nora left Ireland to visit her granduncle in Waltham, the agent was found one morning face down in a ditch where there was only half a foot of water. He could not have been drunk, Nora insisted, because he never took more than one glass of port. There must have been a fair amount of truth in this undoubtedly heavily embroidered story for years later, when Mary was in Athenry, she heard one of her aunts talk of the man and refer to his death as suicide. Possibly Nora's attachment to the Protestant land agent was one of the reasons she was shipped off to the States to find a husband of the proper religious persuasion.

Nora had a hundred recollections of summer evenings when she and her sisters strolled around the rampart walls that enclosed the small town. Every story had the same 'tinkle of laughter . . . and the same innocent pretence of surprise when the girls met their beaux taking the air in the same place at the same time'. As Mary wrote later, her mother could have reduced the stories of all the winter evenings she talked about to just one story 'of one evening in one parlour, my mother at the piano, with her sisters in a half-circle around her singing high and the beaux in an outer ring singing strong and low'. But, Mary wrote, her mother, in her stories, 'never discarded duplicates'.

The picture that emerges in Nora's stories of herself as a young girl is not in many respects an attractive one. She was always called 'Miss Imperious', she often said, and appeared to consider this a great source of pride.

In October 1921, when Mary was nine years old, her

father finally gave in to his wife's pleading. He booked passage for her and Mary on the SS *Winefriedian*, drew some of his savings out of the Boston State Street Trust Company, told her to buy a house in Dublin, and promised to join them when she had done so. She was to live with her family in Athenry while she was searching.

As she would do throughout her stories, Mary wove her memories of the evening before she and her mother left for Ireland into 'Lemonade' published in 1961 in Lavin's *The Great Wave and Other Stories*. 'Lemonade' is told through the eyes of the young daughter, called Maudie. The parlour is crowded with her father's friends and he is in his element, opening bottle after bottle of whiskey under the disapproving eyes of his wife, and telling stories. Apparently a pact has been made: her mother is to pretend that she is going home just for a visit. No one, not even little Maudie, is to know of her plan to stay, or his plan to join her. Every indication from later accounts of what really happened at that time in the Lavins' marriage is that not even young Mary knew that their stay in Ireland was not to be merely temporary. The reason for this ruse may have been that Tom Lavin was protecting his job, or perhaps neither of the Lavins felt completely sure of the future of their marriage.

Mary dated her 'tremendous passion' for the sea from about the time that she and her mother set sail for Ireland: a passion she considered an emotional one, linked to her father. As she saw him drive away from the ship in his beach wagon, 'it was a lonely feeling'.

Travelling across the Atlantic ocean brought home the vastness of the gulf between my father and me; and all the time the sea was entering into my feelings as a powerful emotion. Later, when I stood on the beach in Galway, I had no interest in sandcastles. I just stood there, spellbound by that great stretch of water which separated me from my father.

25

But, though leaving her father was a wrench, she was looking forward to meeting the family she had heard so much about over the years. She wanted to get to know all the beautiful aunts. She already knew Minnie, the aunt next to Nora in age. Minnie, like Nora, had been sent off to the States when she fell in love with a poor shop assistant. Ostensibly she was going over because Nora, then pregnant, needed her help and she was to return home after the baby was born and Nora was fully recovered. But, unlike Nora, she liked life in East Walpole, where she was in great demand with the young Irish lads. When Tom saw how happily she was settling in, he got her a job in the office of the mill and each week invested a good part of her salary for her. Not until five years later did she return to Ireland: by then she was the owner of a magnificent car, and a rich woman by Irish standards. Later accounts indicate, however, that she never did get over her love for the poor shop assistant, a fact which intrigued Mary.

There were still the remaining aunts for Mary to meet: Nan, Kathleen and Queenie (Eugenia). The aunt Mary was particularly eager to see was Kathleen. She had always longed to have a sister so she had decided to pick an imaginary one from among the aunts. Kathleen was the one she had chosen after careful study of the photos, of which her mother possessed scores. They were kept under her parents' bed in a cardboard box from Moon's High Class Drapery in Galway. All her sisters were beautiful, Nora claimed, and Mary could see that they were indeed a handsome lot. Their dresses, of course, added considerably to their beauty. As Mary described them later in her 'A Bevy of Aunts', those dresses were 'bewitching'. The skirts were as ample as 'full blown roses'. The bodices were tight. Beading and hand-tucks at the necks and at the waists added touches of glamour to the soft shades of the dresses themselves.

The favourite locale for picture-taking seemed to be the Mahon back parlour. Mary could scarcely contain her excitement at the thought of seeing that glamorous room where the young people had gathered in the evening for singing. It was a spacious room, Nora told her daughter, and judging by the clutter shown in the pictures it would have had to be. It contained the grand piano, a davenport and a love-seat, and bric-a-brac covered every available surface. During that period, the landed gentry were closing their houses and auctioning off the contents. Delia, Nora's mother, was an inveterate auction-goer and apparently she had been unable to resist bargains.

As Mary's mother described it, in the rear of the house was a cobbled yard leading to sheds and warehouses and then an iron gate that led to the garden. The garden would be wild and overgrown, Mary knew, because her mother had assured her that it was so large that it simply had to be neglected. Every summer the grass was cut around an old apple tree and there Mary's grandmother had her tea on the fine days.

When, after their long journey from the States, they reached Athenry, Mary was in for quite a shock and so was her mother. Nora had been in fairly close touch with the Athenry family through letters, but either the letters were deceptive or she had not wanted to believe what they told her. One brother, Vincent – the photographer in the family – had died in 1918 during the influenza epidemic raging in every country. Another, Joseph, had been killed in the war. Her mother, while not completely bedridden, seldom made the effort to leave her room. Her sister Nan had eloped with someone her mother considered unsuitable and she and her husband were living in Dublin. Queenie had made a marriage her mother approved of but was living in Galway. Nora's brothers Harry and Leo had taken over the management of the store. And, to Nora's considerable distress, the only help in the house was a young schoolgirl who came in for a few hours each afternoon.

Much that Mary saw in the Athenry household bore no

resemblance to her preconceptions, but the store was just as she had pictured it. It was large, with old wooden counters, and so full of merchandise that it looked like a warehouse. There was even a bar where the locals could sit and sip their Guinness while they waited to have their orders for grass seed, meal and grain filled. It was what in those days was referred to as an emporium.

It is impossible, of course, to know exactly what Nora's plans for the future were when she returned to Athenry. She continued to refer to her stay in Ireland as a visit and Mary accepted that since her mother did not enrol her in the local school. And, though Tom had instructed her to buy a house, she did not seem to be in any great hurry to go searching for one. One thing is clear, however. Her brothers Harry and Leo made no attempt to conceal the fact that they expected her stay to be a short one.

The move to Athenry was a genuine culture shock in more than one area for the nine-year-old Mary Lavin. The school she had attended in East Walpole had given her an excellent basic education and she had emerged a voracious reader of quite good literature. In Athenry she found her tastes considerably more developed than those of her peers. Like most children, she had no desire to appear different, so she prudently kept silent and began reading on their level.

It was the attitude towards religion in Athenry that was undoubtedly the greatest surprise. She had come to Ireland, she said, at a time when 'Catholicism was Catholicism as Rome never knew it'. It had been a shock. Previously, she had never seen a nun and had only seen a priest at the altar. In East Walpole the Catholics went to Mass in the local movie house. After the last performance on Saturday night, the screen was removed and, in preparation for Sunday Mass, an altar set up. The priest came in from out of town and if, on occasion, he was unable to make it, the children had full permission to attend either the Greek Orthodox or the Polish church. 'Religion never gave me any bother in my years in

East Walpole,' Mary noted.

There was no such light-hearted attendance in Athenry, however. 'Religion (and one religion at that) was all-pervasive. Everyone was rushing off not just to Mass but to Benediction and the Stations of the Cross.' In this area Mary made her own kind of adjustment. She visited the church just about as often as everyone else did. She had discovered that she could have a great time playing there when there was no service under way. It was 'an absolutely wonderful place to play – among the pews and in the confessionals, running in and out behind the statues and shrines'.

There was also in Athenry a whole new concept of sin, which she was sure she had not had as a child in the States. 'In America there were transgressions, but there were not sins and people did not go burrowing into your conscience.' Understandably, this divergence in the two attitudes towards religion created a certain amount of confusion in the nine-year-old. She was concerned for a time about what sins she might inadvertently have been committing and she had attacks of remorse. But, as she grew older, she came to terms with the problem. As she explained it later:

> It seems to me that religion is like a place – where one is born. I didn't feel that I had to throw away everything: I kept a few basic beliefs. In fact that era gave me a great sense of conscience – something I believe in absolutely. I find it hard to understand some Irish writers who claim that their lives were destroyed by some little sex exploits or imagined sins when they were children. I find it hard to understand that they were so brittle.

For eight months Mary led a carefree existence in Athenry. For the East Walpole woods she had loved, she substituted people. A sturdily built, round-faced little girl, with an enchanting smile and bright eyes, 'the Yank', as she was known to the townspeople, was a celebrity. Because she had been so much alone and so much in the company of adults, and possibly because of her extensive reading, she was old for her years. She talked and she listened. She saw that period clearly in later life and summed it up in this fashion:

> I was a great wanderer. I would wander all over town and of course, having come from America, I was a real *persona grata*. I was in everybody's house, having barmbrack and cake and lemonade. They were probably asking me a lot of questions about my family, questions which I was only too ready to answer, but equally I was seeing the intimate side of their lives – all the rows, the love affairs, the jealousies and whatever.

Though she was not aware of it, Mary Lavin was gathering material for her stories. It was not until she began to write that she realized the power of the Athenry experience and how much she could extract from her thoughts by writing. For years afterwards, she would find herself casting a character in the mould of one of the people there.

In several interviews in the early 1970s, she commented that perhaps a violent change of continent awakens an awareness. 'I think there was a shock at leaving East Walpole at such an early age and only a few days later waking up in a small town in the west of Ireland.' It opened your eyes to everything around you and, she believed, you tended to look where most people no longer bothered to look.

Mary's gypsy-like existence ended when pressure was applied by her uncles. Her mother was told that, visitor or not, she was to be got off the streets of Athenry, out of the houses, and into school. Accordingly, she was enrolled in a convent school in Athenry. 'I loved it there,' she wrote later. 'It was so different, so strange.'

In 'Lemonade', and in the character Maudie, Mary Lavin described the experiences of a little girl on her first day in a small-town, convent school. Maudie recognised one of the town children: the daughter of the town madwoman. The little girl was sitting by herself at the back of the classroom. When Maudie told the nun who was seating her that she would like to sit by that child, the nun said that the child wouldn't want Maudie to sit there. 'Sadie isn't very friend-ly . . . [She] hasn't learned yet that we have to behave in a certain way if we want people to like us, and be friends with us.' To this Maudie replied, 'I don't mind how people behave, if *I* like *them*!' And she 'smiled straight into Sadie's eyes.' After a minute Sadie smiled back and the two girls became friends.

That the fictional Maudie's experiences at the convent school were Mary's own is borne out by comments she made many years later in a radio interview. In both she described the schoolroom as heated by a stove and, in order to keep the fire going, town children had to bring a penny. The country children, who did not have a penny, were told to bring a sod of turf. Apparently the distinction gave the town children a reason to look down on the country children. Mary found the whole situation difficult to understand and to accept. As she said, 'I must have had a very early sense of justice. Children do have a great sense of justice, I believe.'

The Athenry period in Mary Lavin's life lasted only eight months. Nora, urged on by her brothers, had at last bought a house in Dublin: 48 Adelaide Road, not far from the Leeson Street bridge, then one of the more desirable parts of the city. The house, on a terrace, was quite small and when, shortly after they settled in, Tom joined them, he was disappointed and sure that she could have done better with the money he gave her.

It seems that Tom's returning to Ireland was not simply a reflection of his wife's desires. He had always hoped to return to Ireland some day. Mary remembered that he once suggested to his wife that they buy a house in County Roscommon and return to 'God's country'. That suggestion was greeted, typically, with the contemptuous reply that in

Roscommon she would not be able to find 'a soul to speak to from day-up to day-down'. A desire to return to the homeland would not have been unusual. There is an old Irish wish – *Bás in Éirinn* ('Death in Ireland [to you]'). The old folks prayed that their children could make enough money in the States to end their days in Ireland.

For years Tom had invested his money wisely and regularly, with a return to Ireland in mind. His investments had paid off handsomely and his savings had mounted. He returned to Ireland with a car young Mary thought enormous. He must have been quite a sight, driving on Dublin's narrow streets and even narrower roads in the surrounding countryside. As she wrote in 'Tom', 'Sitting up at the wheel of that car in a big coat with an astrakhan collar was a far cry from running barefoot across country in County Roscommon, where he had been born.'

Her father's arrival in Dublin completed Mary's happiness, for she had already fallen in love with the city. It was her first taste of city life and she wandered downtown, explored the Liberties – old Dublin – and walked as far as the Bull Wall, a good distance. It was an area she never tired of exploring.

An added reason for joy was the presence in Dublin of a member of the Athenry family. One of her mother's sisters, Nan, had – with her husband and children – lived there for some years. Mary thought Nan one of the most beautiful of the Mahon sisters. Nan had married against her mother's wishes and had been left out of her mother's will. Mary saw her grandmother's action as unjust and had been moved by Nan's acceptance of the action and her 'wholehearted forgiveness'. As she said of Nan in an interview years later, 'She had the strength to make her own moral decisions.' When Mary had come to Athenry as a child, she had seen members of her mother's family 'content to take their spirituality from the Church, to live out their lives on a quite material level and draw from their religion all they felt they needed of spirtuality.' Her aunt Nan, however, 'seemed to have her own depth of spirituality *in herself*'.

In some of Mary's stories, she uses her aunt Nan as one of her characters, calling her Lally. Lally appears predominantly in 'The Will', which Mary would say later was undoubtedly her favourite story. There Lally is drawn as a remarkable human being who rose above poverty and who understood true love. In the story too the mother had been bitter because Lally had married against her wishes and had left her out of her will. Because she had died without forgiving her, Lally feared for her mother's soul. Against all obstacles, she managed to have Masses said for her mother with money from her own meagre income. Only by having those masses said, she believed, could she save her mother from Purgatory.

'The Will' was one of Mary's early stories and she was sure that the character based on her aunt would be recognized. 'I could see myself fleeing the land,' she once said. But no one seemed to recognize Nan in the character of Lally. Talking with Eileen O'Toole after many years had passed, Mary could not resist asking if Eileen had recognized her mother in the character of Lally. She had not and was astonished. She said later, however, that she had been assured by Mary that all her characters were composites. Mary herself has said that it was her belief that she did not write 'with anything like fidelity' about a person she had known. Eileen, however, had thought Lally was drawn as 'a very beautiful person'. It was the way she had seen her mother as well, she said. Lally appears also in 'A Bevy of Aunts.' There she is described as needing to support her family and having neither time nor money to think about her appearance or to take proper care of her house. Only her garden was never neglected. As Mary described it, it was a narrow strip between the gardens on either side. Winter and summer, in contrast to the neighbouring gardens, hers was as beautiful as the gardens at St Stephen's Green.

In winter a profusion of evergreen billowed over her fences, and formed dark grooves where early snowdrops came out with the thrilling suddenness of the first stars of evening. And in summer flowering climbers entwined in this greenery, burgeoned into blossom. In that sooty city soil she could coax any plant, however tender, to grow and luxuriate. You'd be tempted to think she could have reaped a harvest of emeralds and sapphires, if she had had a few clippings to use for seed.

According to Eileen O'Toole, that description is accurate. Their garden was a thing of beauty. But except for the part about the garden, Eileen O'Toole has said, the facts about her family are fictional. She grew up in a happy home and with a mother who was, in the eyes of her two daughters, a 'great lady'. She sacrificed a great deal for her two children uncomplainingly. Her father was a gentle and kind man who kept the house painted and took pride in the garden as well.

The accounts do not necessarily conflict. The O'Tooles apparently had a fine, loving marriage and Mary Lavin must have been very happy visiting with her aunt Nan. In that household, she was seeing the kind of love between a husband and wife she surely did not see in her own home. She got to know her Aunt Nan well in those Dublin days and, of all the aunts, she was the one that Mary admired and loved the most. Nan, Eileen O'Toole said, felt the same way about Mary and took great pride in her accomplishments.

Shortly after the move to Dublin, Mary was enrolled as a day pupil at the Loreto College Convent School on St Stephen's Green. It was not her mother's first choice. She had wanted to enrol Mary in the school nearest their home, which was Sacred Heart in Leeson Street. She was quite ready to pay the rather high fee but was told that the school took only the daughters of professional men. Later Mary mentioned to a friend that it did not seem to be a distinction that a convent school should be making.

As far as Mary was concerned, Loreto was a good choice. The school was a pleasant walk from her home and she was happy there. In a brochure issued by the college in 1988, there is a short biographical sketch written by Mary Lavin in which she says, among other things, 'I revelled in the company of my classmates and so I managed to have the time of my life as well as get through my exams with reasonably good marks. I was, I suppose, a good all-rounder.' All accounts indicate that Mary Jo, as they all called her, was popular with her classmates and was certainly an all-rounder. Her father had told her that as a youth in Roscommon he had been 'a champion athlete'. Always eager to emulate him, Mary participated in as many sports as possible and received medals for running and jumping. Tom made a point of being on hand to watch her whenever possible. When she was on the hockey team, Tom, himself a good athlete, had come to watch her play on one occasion, and then gone on to Liverpool on business. From there he wrote:

Dear Litte Daughter, This is a Pound for Pin Money and I hope you will win. I was very much disopinted how you Plead. you seem to wait till the Ball Came to you that is Rong you should Keep Moving and Not to stay in the one Place. Good Luck, Dadey.

In the Senior School, there wasn't time for much except work. Mary thrived on it. The teaching staff at Loreto was excellent and extremely knowledgeable in their various fields, and they filled for her a void left empty by a home atmosphere lacking in intellectual stimulation. Those dedicated nuns gave her 'the most precious gift a teacher can give, a love of work for work's sake,' she said. She studied hard, formed good working habits, and, as a consequence, won the Bishop's Medal for Christian Doctrine and got a first in English. During those years at Loreto the love of literature that had begun to develop in the States grew stronger.

Years later Mary was asked if there was a point at which childhood ended for her or had she just gradually drifted into adolescence and then into adulthood? She replied that she believed that it was through reading that she made the transition. 'I slipped out of the solitude and beauty of childhood into the books which touched on what I felt and thought,' she replied, 'and through those books I progressed to adulthood.'

> One day I read *Adam Bede* by chance and that was the end of the school stories that I had been reading. I loved the Russian writers and later when I was at college I grew to love French literature, particularly Racine, not so much for the content as for the technique. I became tremendously interested in technique, in the music and architecture of words.

As he always had been, Mary's father was a key figure in her life from the time he returned to Ireland to stay. He had no compunction about calling at Loreto and taking her out of class for trips to the Leopardstown race track, to Aintree for a few days, or to the seaside. Mary always thought that one of their trips to the seaside might have been responsible for her deep-seated preoccupation with death. It was at the seaside that she saw him in contrast to other fathers and realized that he was older. 'It gave me a terrible fright. That fright could have led to having a special love for him; on the other hand, it could have led to the obsession with death which people say runs through my work.'

It was a miracle that she was a good student, she once said, because her father would come to the school and say, 'Reverend Mother, I want to take Mary out. I don't see why she should be cooped up here.' Whenever he saw her studying, he would say, 'Put that book away. What do you

mean studying on a day like this. Go out in the sunshine.'
And in 1936, when Mary was writing her MA thesis at
University College Dublin (UCD), Tom interrupted her
work to take her with him on one of his business trips to
the States. To hell with the MA, Tom had said. She could
put on a little extra push later on. Mary never questioned
the advisability of any of this. It appears that she never
questioned any of her father's ideas or attitudes. In his
daughter's eyes, Tom Lavin was quite perfect and, as she
once wrote, 'a genius'.

Mary's love for her father was matched by his for her.
But his devotion to and his preoccupation with his daughter
– his need to spend time with her – may have been, in part,
a substitute for what was missing in his marriage to a woman
who considered herself far superior to him and who never
hesitated to express her discontent with her lot. Their
marriage was far from happy. Had it not been for religion
and the temper of the times, it is more than likely that they
would have divorced.

CHAPTER 2

In 1926, a whole new life opened up for Tom Lavin. Early in his association with the Birds, Tom had become a friend as well as an employee of Charles Sumner Bird and an indispensable part of the Bird household. It was quite natural, then, that when Charlie Bird Jr visited Dublin in 1926 he would search out Tom. Like most people, he enjoyed Tom's company, and they spent a great deal of time together touring the countryside. One day, in their ramblings, they passed Bective House, in Bective, County Meath. It was part of an estate of some three hundred acres, the greater part of which was woodlands. If Mr Bird would buy it, Tom said, he would manage it for him. It wasn't too difficult for Tom to persuade Mr Bird. The purchase was made and that year Tom Lavin became an estate manager.

In 1978, in the *Irish Press*, James Stern, a writer and the son of the previous owner of the Bective estate, wrote details of that time. He had been seventeen and he and his family were returning to England to live. 'A Mr Lavin had arrived to take care of the place while the new owner was preparing to move in,' James Stern wrote. 'Did it really happen, or did I dream that on the day we drove away I dared to look back, and there, framed in the front doorway, stood a girl of maybe ten?' Undoubtedly, that was Mary. It was 1926 and she would have been fourteen.

Mr Bird had not made a mistake. Bective, on the banks of the Boyne, was a place of haunting beauty. In 'A Likely Story', Mary Lavin describes it.

> Like a bird in the nest, it presses close to the soft green mound of the river bank, its handful of houses no more significant by day than the sheep that dot the far fields. But at night, when all its little lamps

38

are lit, house by house, it is marked out on the hillside as clearly as the Great Bear is marked out in the sky. And on a still night it throws its shape in glitter on the water.

Tom's new position served a double purpose: it gave him the kind of work at which he excelled and also gave him a chance to live separately from his wife without the inevitable gossip. Nothing was ever spelled out for Mary on the subject but instinctively she knew that her parents were not happy together. As she put it, 'Certainly they managed not to be in the same house very often.'

Her father's position had a lasting effect upon Mary's life as well. She lived with her mother and attended school during the week but her weekends were spent with Tom in Bective House. What she saw and experienced there would be reflected in her own style of living as an adult.

Charlie Bird Jr was a Harvard graduate and his wife, the former Julia Appleton, appears to have been a gracious hostess and her home something of a showplace. A privately-printed publication titled *A New Englander* serves as a source of information about life in Bective House, as well as Tom's part in it. It makes it clear that the management of the household depended heavily upon him. In the autumn of 1937, the author of the publication spent a month at Bective House. There were hearths in every room, she wrote, and glowing coal fires. She never forgot the roses at Bective. In her bedroom there were usually at least a half dozen of them: beautiful varieties, their fragrance permeating the room. From that room and just below her windows, she could see a wide, gravelled terrace, bordered with velvety green turf stretching a short distance to the Boyne. On the other side of the river, she could see grassy meadows dotted with lofty trees. 'Under Lavin's care and Mrs Bird's beautiful hospitality that autumn, "Bective" presented a picture of perfect country life,' the author wrote.

The publication indicates that Mrs Bird had the usual prejudices of her class. She was violently critical of the Roman Catholic Church. One Saturday afternoon the author, taking a walk, noticed priests bicycling past her with empty baskets. She saw a gardener piling water lilies into one of the baskets, and soon she saw the priests returning, their baskets filled with flowers. She thought it a beautiful picture: 'the reverent gardener gathering the choicest lilies for his beloved priest'. Julia Bird was furious when she was told about it. She did not want 'their churches' decorated with Bective's flowers. She had to be convinced that, since Bective was a Roman Catholic stronghold, 'all its produce would flow naturally into the priest's hands'. It is impossible to determine how aware Mary, a Catholic and a convent student, was of Mrs Bird's prejudices.

No liquor was served at Bective House and Mrs Bird often discoursed on its evils. The author prevailed on her, however, to serve liquor at one of the race meet parties. Finally Mrs Bird said: 'Well, go ahead. I see you think it very important. Tell Tom Lavin to get a sufficient supply of the best.'

How exactly the young Mary Lavin interacted with the members of the Bird family during the weekends she spent with her father at Bective House is not known but in a collection of Mary Lavin's short stories called *The Patriot Son and Other Stories*, there is one called 'Scylla and Charybdis' that is seldom mentioned and does not appear in any of her later collections. The collection was published in 1956 but Mary may have written the story a great deal earlier. It centres around Pidgie, a fourteen-year-old girl described as 'a small bundle of fat, with black hair and black eyes, who perpetually stood with her hands behind her back and her small stomach poked out in front'. Pidgie is the only child of Cotter, the house steward. She is a 'bright and lively' child, well liked by the other servants. Pidgie 'had no time' for them, however. Her father urges her to take walks with them, but instead she hangs about in the corridor that separates the servants' quarters from the front of the house or lurks in the bushes and watches 'The Young Ladies of the House' as they stroll about.

Pidgie is an extremely bright child who, according to what her schoolteacher tells Cotter, is remarkable. 'It isn't altogether a matter of brains — there's something about her.' From time to time the master or the mistress enquires about Pidgie's age and her abilities. Cotter interprets that to mean that, when Pidgie leaves school, there will be a place for her among the servants. But he is puzzled by her attitude and, when he asks her what she wants to be when she grows up, Pidgie answers: 'I want to be a lady.'

From time to time, to Pidgie's great delight, one of the young ladies, seeing Pidgie standing about, asks her to accompany her to town to mind the dog while she shops. Late one day, after such an excursion with Miss Gloria, they return to the house where, since it is too late for dinner, a cold supper has been left on the buffet for the young lady. She fills her dish and fills one for Pidgie as well. It is the realization of Pidgie's dreams. She will sit down to eat with one of her idols. Only when Miss Gloria goes over and opens the door to the corridor and tells Pidgie to be careful carrying the dish to the servants' quarters — 'it's a Worcester plate, you know' — does Pidgie realize that she is not to eat with her.

Mary Lavin concludes the story in this fashion: 'Did she cry?' It really doesn't matter. What mattered is what happens the next day. 'It was a small thing: just like not going for a walk with the maids. But just as she had evaded that Scylla so now she was preparing to defy Charybdis.' She is lurking in the shrubbery as usual when the young ladies come out on the terrace, but there is a difference this time. 'Pidgie's little pink tongue was stuck out at them as far as it would go.'

The scholar Zack Bowen, in his critical study of Mary

Lavin's work, saw that rebellious act as a possible reflection of Mary's own feelings. The parallel is there. As Bowen wrote: 'Mary's father was a steward, and her description of Pidgie sounds much like what I imagine the writer to have been.'

Tom ran the farm well and, as he had proved in the States, he knew horses. The people in the area still remember the days of the famous 'Heartbreak Hill', a mare Tom bought for forty pounds. She had never been known to win anything but went on, to the joy and delight of Bective, to win the Galway Plate, the Grand Sefton at Aintree, and to become a favourite in the Grand National at Aintree. According to Mary, Tom also bought a horse named 'Workman' who won the Grand National.

It seems that Tom had found a niche worthy of his talents. He reported how he felt about his position in an item in *Bird's Neponsett Review*, published monthly by the employees of Bird and Son, Inc. Mills in East Walpole. The heading read: 'Tom Lavin, Old Timer, Sends Us Greetings from the Old Country', and there is a small, not very clear picture captioned, 'Tom Lavin and part of his crew'. Tom is in the centre and, obviously befitting his station, is wearing a straw hat and three-piece suit, while his crew are in shirt-sleeves and wearing caps.

The first paragraph states that Tom had been an employee of Bird and Son for thirty years. A letter from Tom to a Mr Wyman is then quoted in part:

I must say that I am very happy and I hope you can come over and pay me a visit some day. I can show you all kinds of livestock, horses, cattle and sheep. These make the industry of Ireland. I send my best wishes to all my old friends at the mill and office and I hope to see them all some day. Tell them that I have a cottage all ready for any of them when they want to come. I wish that some of the Old Timers might come over. A visit would add ten years to the life of some of them. I wish them all a happy New Year.

Thanks to her father's position, Mary now had what was for her the best of both worlds: the city and the country. Both Bective and Dublin became equally dear to her, though perhaps the scales tipped slightly in favour of Bective.

In the autumn of 1930 Mary entered University College Dublin, then located in the heart of the city, at Earlsfort Terrace just off St Stephen's Green. The morning she enrolled, her father, eager to share in the experience, went with her. Tom, although uneducated, had a great respect for learning. He often mentioned with pride an ancestor who had been a hedge schoolmaster, keeping learning alive in the countryside.

To see his daughter as a college student was for Tom the fulfilment of a dream and he was, as he had been when she was winning prizes at Loreto, proud of her achievement. He did not, however, hesitate to make comparisons between her and her mother, of whose beauty and patrician demeanour he had always been proud. 'You have not got your mother's looks, but you have her ways,' he once said to Mary. His remark to a young and sensitive girl who had already been made well aware of the contrast was unkind and tactless. Mary said later that she understood, but there were many indications subsequently that the hurt was there and that she never forgot. It was true that Mary had not inherited her mother's kind of beauty: the fragile, delicate prettiness. But she had, by college age, become an attractive young woman with the vitality and personality that made her difficult to overlook or to forget.

Financially, Tom had no difficulty putting Mary through college and supporting the Dublin establishment as well. Free State Ireland in 1930 had not yet begun to feel the effects of the Depression. As Professor Terence Brown, in his *Ireland: A Social and Cultural History*, put it, 'the country continued to export its livestock products at relatively stable prices, whilst the price of imports dropped sharply'. But even later, when conditions worsened in Ireland, Tom was able to protect his family from economic insecurity. His position with the Bird family was solid and, as he had proved in the States, he was a practical man and well able to manage finances. After his return to Ireland, it was not unusual for his wife's Athenry family to turn to him for advice on financial matters.

Mary soon found that life at UCD bore very little resemblance to life at Loreto College. For one thing, after years of education in single-sex institutions, UCD, where she attended classes with men, was a new and pleasant experience. In an interview with the historian Bonnie Kime Scott, carried in the Autumn 1979 issue of the *Irish University Review*, Mary admitted that right from the start she had preferred male companionship. With them, she talked about writers, past and present, about Paris and American writers who had settled there, and about books she was reading. The time she spent with her men friends at UCD contributed materially to the deepening of her pleasure in and her understanding of good literature. She thought at that time, she told Professor Scott, that the men 'seemed to have better minds than the girls, who seemed only interested in the men'. She was very young, of course, when she held that belief. She changed her opinion later when she saw in her daughters – as well as in some of her women friends – a certain pliability and a lack of rigidity of mind that she did not find in males. She came to believe that the female mind was, especially in matters concerned with the emotions, more flexible. 'Contact with the minds of my daughters . . . gave me more sheer pleasure than contact with any other mind, male or female,' she stated.

Mary managed quickly to establish a wide and varied circle at the college. There were among her fellow students a fairly large number of both men and women who went on to notable careers in various fields. Roger McHugh, Carmel Humphries and Lorna Reynolds earned fine reputations in academia. Donagh MacDonagh became a District Justice and was a poet and playwright as well. Denis Devlin, doing postgraduate work then, became Irish Ambassador to Italy, and Brian O'Nolan (better known as Flann O'Brien) became famous as a novelist, a humorist, and a journalist, with a column in *The Irish Times* for some twenty-five years. While at UCD, he had become well known while campaigning for the presidency of the Student Representative Council. And Cyril Cusack, already clear about the road he was to take, was the idol of the drama society.

Many of the friendships Mary made during those early years at UCD were lasting ones. Cyril Cusack, known worldwide later for his acting ability, was one of those with whom she established a life-long relationship. When he married the actress Maureen Kealey, the Cusacks and their five children became close friends with Mary, her husband, and their children.

That was the period of a growing awareness among college students of social issues. There are, however, few facts available as to Mary's views. Some mention has been made by family members of a period when she refused to wear animal furs and flirted with vegetarianism but there is no concrete proof.

During her undergraduate years, there were two men who were of special importance to Mary and not, it appears, solely for their stimulating conversation. One was Michael MacDonald Scott, a young and handsome Australian seminarian, whose field was mathematics. Two years older than Mary, Michael Scott had entered the Jesuit order at seventeen and, after completing his studies at the Preparatory School for St Ignatius College at Riverview, had been sent to Dublin and to UCD to further his education. Mary noticed the young Jesuit student shortly after he had arrived from Australia and years later she wrote a friend that she had fallen in love with the back of his head in a lecture theatre.

Thanks to her father's financial situation, Mary was a somewhat privileged student. She dressed well, took occasional trips to the States with her father when he went there on business for the Bird family, and drove a sports car. For a student to have a car – and a sports car at that – in those days was a rarity. Tom Lavin was doing his best to see that no one looked down on his daughter.

Mary was also, as not too many students were, a member of the Royal Dublin Society and, as a member, was entitled to use the Society's library. Michael Scott took advantage of that membership to establish a friendship with Mary. One day he told her he was having difficulty finding a certain book and asked her if she would try to obtain it from the Royal Dublin Society library for him. He arranged to meet her in the main hall of the Society to get it. They met but, when she handed him the book, he just tossed it aside. 'To hell with the book,' he said, 'I only wanted to meet you.'

The other young man was William Walsh, a student in the law school and an aspiring writer. His interest in literature and his desire to become a writer were what formed a bond between them. As she once said, she felt sure that he would fulfil his ambition and she found the idea of being a writer's wife attractive. But she considered Michael Scott, even though he was a seminarian, to be very much in the running. One of her fellow students, Professor Lorna Reynolds, has fond memories of those UCD days. She was majoring in history and Mary in French but they managed to spend a great deal of time together. They took long walks around St Stephen's Green, with Mary talking at length about her feeling for both young men and her inability to decide between them.

In Mary Lavin's opinion, she was only an average student as an undergraduate at UCD. Once, when she was asked how she rated, she replied that she had had a great time there but 'pupils who have a great time don't usually do too well academically but they don't do too badly either'. Obviously she was a better than average student, because her BA was granted in 1934 with first honours in English and second honours in French. Her grasp of the French language was poor, she knew, and consequently she kept to the back of the class in order not to call attention to herself. When, however, she submitted her undergraduate paper, her professor was amazed at her discriminating knowledge of French literature. Had she known her French grammar better, he told her, he would have been able to give her first honours; had he realized it was so poor, he added, he might have failed her. She had been wise to keep out of his way, he said.

She apparently accepted without question that she would follow an academic career and, consequently, went on to do graduate work. For the subject of her master's degree thesis, she chose the novel and Jane Austen. Her thesis showed, her professor said, 'a great love of literature', and it won her first honours. While working for her advanced degrees, she continued to live at home and to spend her weekends at Bective. She also accepted a position to teach French at Loreto College. She found it amusing that the nuns had assigned her to teach her weakest subject. She would have been willing to teach any subject, however, since she had taken the position primarily to earn money. Her father was both astonished and pleased when he learned what her salary would be. He would put an equal amount in the bank for her each payday, he said. It was a typical Tom gesture.

For her PhD thesis she decided to write on Virginia Woolf, for whose work she had a great deal of admiration. As she once said, 'Virginia Woolf had a great impact on me. *Jacob's Room* was the first thing I read by her. It was like a painting, seen at one glance, tremendously new.' Her thesis was coming along nicely when, one day while awaiting her turn in the bank, she began to talk to an elderly woman. In the course of the conversation, she told the woman that she was working for her PhD and was writing her thesis on Virginia Woolf. The woman was struck by the coincidence. Just the other day, she said, she had had tea with Virginia. Mary couldn't believe it. Virginia Woolf was alive? She had always assumed that all great writers were dead. Back at the college, she looked at the pages of her thesis and thought about her subject. Would Virginia Woolf be wasting her time this way? She very much doubted it. She turned over a page and began writing a story.

Mary invariably told that tale as if her reaction had been a fairly casual one rather than that of a budding writer. As she always maintained, she never intended to be a writer, regardless of what others thought. In a Preface to a 1959 collection of her stories she wrote: 'Before that first erratic impulse I had absolutely no yearning to write. Indeed I would never have presumed to think I could until I made a sudden sally at it. Once started, though, there was no question of ever reaching an end.'

It is true that she did not fit the stereotype of the creative writer who, practically from childhood, was writing stories. But it is also true that she displayed a talent for and an interest in writing much earlier than she herself believed or was willing to acknowledge. When she was fourteen and at the Loreto College convent school, she was always proud of the essays she wrote, received 'high marks' for them, and 'neglected other subjects'. In addition, she wrote a 'school story' but, she insisted it had only been 'for fun. I was a bit of a show-off at the time.' That story, however, came to the attention of an American critic, who felt strongly that she had an instinct for writing. To her that seemed quite ridiculous because she had also illustrated the story and 'had no more wish to be an artist than I had to be a writer'.

In an introduction to her first collection of short stories, she offered one explanation for why she did not for a long time seem to be willing to accept the fact that she was – and

48

wanted to be – a writer. 'Looking back I think it may have been vanity that held me back from attempting something at which I feared I might not succeed.'

Lorna Reynolds, Mary Lavin's confidante, was not at all surprised by Mary's decision. She felt that Mary was not a scholar by nature. She knew, she said, that Mary could have completed her thesis and obtained her PhD without any great difficulty if she had so desired, but it would have been pointless. It seemed obvious to her that what Mary Lavin wanted was to write.

Teaching French at Loreto was not onerous and undoubtedly Mary did it well, but her writing was absorbing her completely. On the walks with her friend, Lorna Reynolds, she talked of nothing else. Her friend enjoyed those conversations and was undoubtedly helping Mary by showing interest and by bringing her own keen mind to the discussions. She delighted in Mary's vivacity, her outgoing personality and, too, in the fact that she had chosen writing as her career. After all, as she said, everyone was teaching. It was neither glamorous nor unusual.

Mary called her first short story, the one she started on the back of a thesis page, 'Miss Holland'. For a time it suffered the fate of many first efforts: rejection. Finally, Seamus O'Sullivan, editor of *The Dublin Magazine*, accepted it and it appeared in the April–June 1939 issue. The magazine, then a quarterly, was publishing the work of writers of the calibre of Liam O'Flaherty and Frank O'Connor and of poets such as Padraic Colum and Patrick Kavanagh. Mary Lavin was delighted to be added to the magazine's distinguished list, and she was always grateful to Seamus O'Sullivan for giving her her first break.

There was an added reason for her gratitude, and a very important one. For some time Mrs Bird had taken an interest in Mary and her development as a writer and she had read Mary's story in the *Dublin Magazine*. She had been so impressed that she had called it to the attention of her friend, the philosopher, playwright and short story writer Lord Dunsany. In mid-August 1939 Mary received a letter from him in which he said that he wanted to 'welcome a new writer.' He asked how long she had been writing and how many other stories she had on hand, and he urged her to go on with her work. He added that, if she liked and if she felt she needed such help, he would be glad to bring her stories to the attention of editors. He assured her, however, that since the standard of the *Dublin Magazine* was so high and her story 'well worthy of that standard', she was well on her way. He would follow her reputation's development with the greatest of interest.

Mary lost no time. Within less than two weeks she had sent Lord Dunsany three additional stories and he had indicated that he would like to see more. He was also pleased to learn that she had written poems and urged her to send them along as well. Before the end of 1939 and to Lord Dunsany's great delight, Seamus O'Sullivan, himself a poet, had published two of her poems in his magazine.

For part of each year, Lord and Lady Dunsany resided in his ancestral home, Dunsany Castle, in Bective, County Meath, not too far from Bective House where Tom Lavin was employed. The fondness the Dunsanys and Mary Lavin shared for that region helped to cement their friendship: a friendship that lasted until Lord Dunsany's death and continued long after that with Lady Dunsany.

Early on, Lord Dunsany invited Mary to come to tea with Lady Dunsany and himself and she soon became a regular visitor to the Castle. Edward Plunkett, Lord Dunsany's grandson, remembered meeting her there in the late 1940s, when he was about seven. She had seemed to him radiant, youthful, interesting and captivating. He had been struck, he remembered, by her penetrating eyes and heavy, dark, straight eyebrows. His memory of her in those early days was vague, since he had been at school for much of the time which followed his first meeting with her. Years later, however, he had occasion to meet her from time to time when she was well established as a writer. He recalled encountering her by chance at the Gramercy Park hotel on Lexington Avenue on one of her visits to New York City. She liked hotels, he said. When he had asked her where she liked best to write, she had replied 'in hotel lobbies'.

Edward's grandfather had often spoken about Mary and his affection for her. He especially enjoyed her sly, oblique sense of humour and her quick wit. Edward has always marvelled at the fact that his grandfather, himself an ambitious professional writer, was so completely without jealousy or envy in his attitude towards other writers. For Mary, he had only admiration and a desire to help further her career.

Literature was also a primary interest with Lady Dunsany, and she too looked forward to Mary's visits. Those visits must have been exciting for this fledgling writer, then only in her twenties. Not only was Lord Dunsany a brilliant conversationalist and Lady Dunsany an accomplished pianist and gracious hostess, but the castle, with its beauty and its history, could not have failed to please and impress her.

According to Edward, the drawing room was where Mary was entertained and he said he can still picture her sitting in one corner of a graceful, brocaded sofa there. It was a warm, welcoming room, decorated in the style of the 1780s. Occasionally they would go to the library, like the drawing room very impressive, with its Gothic bookcases and deep red brocade damask on the walls. A much more formal room, it was little used, and it was in the drawing room that Lord Dunsany would sit at his desk, facing the well-tended lawns while writing.

On one of Mary's visits, she was surprised to see the signature of D. H. Lawrence in the Dunsany guest book. When she asked Lord Dunsany to tell her about Lawrence's visit, he said that all he could remember was that the 'fella' had to borrow ten shillings to get back to Dublin. The definite impression remained that D. H. Lawrence was not one of Lord Dunsany's favourite writers: no doubt he was a bit too *avant garde*.

The Dunsany letters to Mary Lavin indicate that, although he believed she was 'well started' on her career, he did everything possible to smooth her path. He thought she might be wise to use an agent and urged her to send some of her stories to a Miss Pearn in London, and he enclosed a note to be sent along with them. In his opinion, he wrote, Mary would 'one day have a considerable name'. Perhaps Miss Pearn might like to approach editors on her behalf. Miss Pearn, it appears, was not as enamoured of Mary's work as he was, for he wrote Mary later that he expected some day Miss Pearn's opinion of Lavin's work would equal his. He suggested another agent but was also promoting her on his own. Among Mary's papers, a letter to Lord Dunsany from Sean O'Faolain, dated 27 November 1939, on behalf of the Irish Academy of Letters, indicated that the Council of the Academy was 'very interested' in Lord Dunsany's promise to introduce a new Irish writer to them. 'Would you,' he wrote, 'be so good as to let us know a little more about your discovery, and perhaps you would give the Council an opportunity to appreciate the work of this writer? If your discovery is all you feel about her/him (?) we should have great pleasure in organising the dinner to introduce your protege, through you, to the public. The writer must be of Irish birth or descent.'

In December Lord Dunsany had sent the letter on to Mary. He explained that his enthusiasm for her work had led him to suggest the dinner, but that he realized later that such a dinner would be premature. Consequently, he had written the Council to that effect. As he explained to Mary:

The effect of such a dinner, if the Press were present & if their glasses were refilled as they should be, would be to drive the literate citizens of Dublin, except those of them who had got a book already, to go to the bookshops & ask for your work. The booksellers would then say, 'How do you spell it?' which is rather a blasting thing to have said of your name; & when they added, 'Nothing in stock', you might as well be dead as far as Dublin is concerned.

He hoped she did not feel that he had cheated her out of a dinner. Surely it would be better to wait until her first book came out.

Lord Dunsany's faith in Mary's ability seems to have been exactly the kind of reassurance that she needed. At one point, unhappy with some of her earlier stories, she told him that she was considering burning them. He cautioned against any such action and assured her that some day she would agree with his estimate of her ability. When she was depressed by both the outbreak of World War II and the number of rejections she was getting, he wrote that war was, of course, a profound calamity but 'one has to rise above its power to oppress one'. As for the rejections by editors, it was no true measure of the quality of her work. 'Some work is below the editors' standards, some is above them, and some is just what they want. So, on the face of it, it is 2 to 1 against getting a story accepted.' Rejections, he continued, were not going to change his opinion that the country had been blessed with a fresh talent.

One of the stories Mary sent Lord Dunsany early on was 'A Story with a Pattern', and it is one of her few 'pattern' stories. Even at such an early stage in her career, she seemed to realize that it was a form where she was not at her best. The story was written before 1939, but it did not appear until 1945, when it was carried in *Tomorrow*. *The Bell* carried it again in 1946, it was in the *A Single Lady and Other Stories* collection in 1951, and in *In a Café*, a 1995 collection.

In 'A Story with a Pattern', there is a lengthy dialogue between a writer, surely herself, and an older man who has read some of her work. He feels that her stories are limited because of lack of plot and inconclusive endings. She argues that life, with its inconclusive endings, is like that. And as for plot, life has no plot – no pattern. 'Perhaps so,' he says, 'but readers want a diversion from the inevitabilities of life. It is their reason for turning to books.' His point was one Mary never was willing to accept. She was unconvinced and, as her stories proved, rightly so. She maintained throughout the years that a story did not have to have 'a beginning, middle, and end. I think of it more as an arrow in flight or a flash of lightning, lighting up the whole landscape all at once, beginning, middle, and end.' When, many years later, Radio Telefís Éireann (RTÉ, Irish television) produced a documentary on Mary Lavin, it was entitled, very appropriately, *An Arrow in Flight*.

Pleased and grateful for Lord Dunsany's friendship and his confidence in her ability, Mary sought his advice eagerly, but advice was not something he felt she needed. He was fearful that it might divert her in some way from what she was already doing. He wouldn't want to either 'spoil or vulgarize' her stories. And yet, he wrote to her, he did agree with the fictional critic in 'A Story with a Pattern' to a certain extent. He couldn't, it seems, resist saying that perhaps she ought to have a little more plot. He suggested that she might look at O. Henry, hastening to add that his suggestion was a bit like 'introducing a goldsmith to a blacksmith'. At least he was not making the mistake of suggesting that the goldsmith should use the blacksmith's hammer on his brooches, he wrote, and he did admit that even those millions who read O. Henry avidly began to find his pattern too artificial.

Lord Dunsany had sometimes thought, he told Mary, that she should do an autobiography. 'Possibly your finest story will be the idea you got from me, though its admirable plot was written in only one word, autobiography.' Had he lived longer, it might have become clear to him that Mary was doing just that to a certain extent in her fiction.

An early story called 'Watching the Clock' particularly intrigued Lord Dunsany and caused him to warn her not to change her style or take seriously his advice or anyone else's. He forwarded it and 'The Nun's Mother', which she had sent him earlier, to W. Heinemann Ltd as possibilities for a collection. He was right about 'Watching the Clock'. A letter from C. S. Evans at Heinemann informed him that *Good Housekeeping* had taken the story immediately and were offering sixteen guineas for the British serial rights. Lord Dunsany had accepted for her since, he added, Mr Evans had said that *Good Housekeeping* had only paid Michael Arlen fifteen guineas for *his* first story.

'Watching the Clock' appeared in *Good Housekeeping* in May 1940. 'You might write and thank [Mr Evans] to keep him in a good humour when we send him your stories to publish in a book,' Lord Dunsany advised Mary. When that happened, he promised, he would do a preface for the book if she wished. Heinemann did not publish her first collection, *Tales from Bective Bridge*, but it was brought out by Michael Joseph Ltd in 1943. The Dunsany correspondence indicated that the paper shortage during the war may have been the reason.

As promised, Lord Dunsany wrote a preface for the collection. His 'first impression' of Mary's work, he wrote, and he had never changed his mind, was that he had no advice to offer her about literature. He had only helped her, therefore, with her bad punctuation and with hyphens, 'about which she shares the complete ignorance that in the fourth decade of the twentieth century appears to afflict nearly everybody who writes'. Since he disliked classifying writers, he went on, he would let others classify Mary Lavin. But to him she seemed to resemble the Russians more than any other school. He went so far as to write that 'with the exception of the gigantic Tolstoy, her searching insight into the human heart and vivid appreciation of the beauty of the fields are worthy in my opinion to be mentioned beside their work'.

The conclusion of his preface is as high praise as any young author could ask for. He wrote of the stories in the collection:

> The bold plots and the startling events of the modern thriller are to these tales what a great factory is to the works of a gold watch. Those looking for great engines running at full blast might overlook the delicacy of the machinery of such a watch.

And he concluded:

> Years hence this preface of mine will seem quite unnecessary. It is only the unimportant circumstance that I was born in the last century, and she in this, and that after twenty or thirty years of writing I have a few readers, whereas she at present has none, which accounts for my writing a preface for her instead of asking her to do the same for me. I do not write it because I think there is anything whatever that I can teach her about literature. I merely stand, as it were, at the portals of this book to point within to what you may find for yourselves, and to recommend you to look for it.

Comparing Lavin to the Russian writers, as Lord Dunsany had, was not unusual. Richard F. Peterson, in his critical study of Mary Lavin's work, wrote that 'the form of her fiction is indebted to sources more Russian, English, and American than Irish', though her 'subject matter is as Irish as the town of Athenry'.

The short-story writer and literary critic, V. S. Pritchett, in his introduction to Lavin's *Collected Stories*, wrote that many of her stories 'describe country deaths and widowhood, the jealousies of young girls, the disappointments of courtship, the terrible aspects of lonely lives, the sly consolation of elderly love'; and Pritchett asked, 'Where else have we read stories of this kind? Not in English or American literature. The obvious suggestion is in the Russian of, say, Leskov, Alsakov or Shehedrin; not of Turgenev or Tolstoy.' Pritchett thought also that Mary's work resembled that of Russians of the nineteenth century in that women play a particularly important role in her stories, and they are often lonely women. In Ireland, as in Russia, Pritchett wrote, 'the women became lonely and powerful because the manhood of their men was destroyed by political tyranny'. He hastened to add that he did not mean that Mary Lavin was writing propaganda. 'Far from it. Her stories are not the quick glances we get in other writers, they are long gazes into the hearts of her people.'

It was Mary's own opinion that, although she had read Chekhov and Turgenev, Flaubert and Joyce and the shorter works of D. H. Lawrence, Tolstoy and Henry James, it was perhaps Edith Wharton, the pastoral works of George Sand, and especially Sarah Orne Jewett to whom she owed the greatest debt.

By 1940 the friendship between Lord and Lady Dunsany and Mary Lavin had reached the stage where letters to her were headed 'My dear Mary' rather than 'Dear Miss Lavin'. Lord Dunsany's praise of her continued to be tempered by criticism of her grammar and spelling, and also by correction of errors in fact. He often took the historical approach, an area in which Mary Lavin was not very comfortable. In her 'Brother Boniface', one of the stories in the *Bective Bridge* collection, she mentioned Brother Boniface riding a bicycle. Lord Dunsany, worried that the critics might pounce on that error, told her that the bicycle had not yet been invented in her time frame. Call it a velocipede or a cabriolet, he suggested. Reading the story today, it would seem that she did not heed his advice, but at least he tried.

It is not difficult to understand why Seamus O'Sullivan saw promise in this young writer and Lord Dunsany saw a superior talent. In 'Miss Holland' she showed a keen understanding of the divergent strata of society, an understanding of her characters, and a remarkable ability to bring them to life for her readers.

Miss Holland, middle-aged and unmarried, has been brought up in a manner suitable to an earlier era. She has been a constant companion for many years to a father recently deceased. As the story opens, she is moving into a boarding house and into a world completely foreign to her. In just a few sentences, Mary Lavin succeeds in giving the reader an insight into the world of Miss Holland and her father and a picture of the character herself: shy, self-effacing, sensitive, and always the lady, as she has been taught to be. She has come with her three trunks by taxi to her new home and is worried about the size of the tip she should give the taxi driver. 'Her dear father despised over-tipping.' Whenever they travelled, even when he was ill, he took care of all the details. 'She had always stood aside while these awkward negotiations were going on, averting her head, but never failing, when they were concluded, to turn and smile at the porter or the waiter or the taxi-driver . . . and thank the man, in English, of course, hoping he understood the language.'

At Miss Holland's first meeting with her fellow-lodgers, she notices that one of the women is wearing a 'machine-knit' jumper. 'Could [she] not see how much more tasteful handknit woollens were?' But she chastises herself. She blames herself for her inability to enter their conversation and for noticing their bad manners and, in the case of the women, the poor quality of their clothing. She tries desperately to be accepted. Only when one of the boarders is cruel to a neighbour's cat that Miss Holland has seen as graceful and lovely does she allow herself to see them as they are: self-centred, crude, insensitive and ill-mannered. 'I must take one good, hard look at them, she thought, so I'll never forget how awful they are, and so I can try to protect myself from people like them, in the future.' No longer does she need to make allowances for them, no longer does she need to try to fit in. At last she can see that they are unable to appreciate the beauty around them as she does. They live in two different worlds and it is no one's fault. Miss Holland is an unforgettable character and the story is ample proof of Mary Lavin's ability as a writer. She was undeniably on her way.

'Miss Holland' won the James Tait Black Memorial Book Prize for the best work of fiction published during 1943. A letter from the Secretary to the University of Edinburgh, W. A. Fleming, informed her that 'the Professor of Rhetoric and English Literature' at that university had recommended her for the prize. The cash award for 1943 was £185 and, if she was willing to accept, they would send her a cheque at once. There was no obligation involved in the acceptance but 'if you care to give a lecture or address in the University Department of English Literature, you will be most welcome'.

One of the stories she had told Lord Dunsany she would like to burn was 'The Nun's Mother'. He had thought it exceptional and had told her that if she thought it wasn't good then she didn't know what a good story was. As a matter of fact, he liked it so much that he sent it to the editor of the *Atlantic Monthly*, a friend of his, as a form of introduction to Lavin's work. The editor, Dunsany later informed Mary, agreed with him about the quality of her work and promised to get in touch with her. He kept his promise.

The first Lavin story that appeared in the *Atlantic Monthly* was 'The Green Grave and the Black Grave'. A month after it appeared, Mary received a letter from Seamus O'Sullivan. He was happy to see the story in the *Atlantic Monthly*, he wrote, not only because he enjoyed it but also 'to satisfy the very natural desire of an editor to see the features of a contributor whose work he greatly admires'. She had submitted another story to him – 'A Fable' – and he planned to use it in the October-December 1940 issue. Was she at all inclined to publish a collection of her stories in the States, he asked. He had received a request from his friend Diarmuid Russell – the son of George Russell (Æ) – asking to see manuscripts from Irish writers, and Mary's work had occurred to him. He suggested she write to Diarmuid Russell at Russell and Volkening Literary Agents, and to say that she was writing at his suggestion. A letter of 4 February 1959 from Diarmuid Russell indicated that Mary must have followed his suggestion and not only communicated with Diarmuid Russell but at one point used him as an agent. As he wrote to 'Dear Mary', he would 'be the last person in the world to persuade anybody that they ought to have an agent. But if you find that it becomes tiresome or too much of a problem, I'll always be here and would be glad to have you back.' A 1991 letter from Mary to a friend shows that Mary did indeed return to the firm of Russell and Volkening and as late as that year they were still acting as her agents.

When Lord Dunsany first read 'The Green Grave and The Black Grave', he had thought of it as imitation Synge. Later, he tempered his criticism of the story when he heard it read on radio. He decided it was undeniably very good; as he wrote Mary, 'after all, Synge never bought the Aran islands' and, though she was writing of Synge's territory, her story was perfectly original. 'Moreover, where your tale comes nearest to him, at the apex of his *Riders to the Sea*, he himself was not original, but borrowed from Kipling.'

In Mary's opinion, as she told a group of students later, the plot was distinctly original. The dialogue may have seemed to readers to resemble Synge but what she had been attempting to do was to make it repetitive 'in the way that the sound of the waves on the shore is repetitive'.

The story was carried, as was 'Miss Holland', in Mary's first collection of short stories, *Tales from Bective Bridge*. 'The Nun's Mother', however, was not published until 1944 in her second collection: *The Long Ago and Other Stories*. It is an exceptionally strong story and stands as one of her early attempts to deal with her thoughts on religion. She had not been satisfied with the original version, as she had told Lord Dunsany, and she did do some polishing before and after its first appearance. She did not agree with Sean O'Faolain who once said that rewriting stories years after they appeared was a kind of forgery.

Mary Lavin's portrayal of relationships between husbands and wives and between mothers and daughters in 'The Nun's Mother' is thought-provoking and insightful. The story is told through the musings of Mrs Latimer, the nun's mother, who has just witnessed her daughter taking her vows. She dwells on aspects of her daughter's choice of a vocation and what it will mean for herself as well as for her daughter. Has her daughter realized what she is renouncing? She will not experience a sex life, which her mother has found a source of great joy, unlike, she thinks, many women of her circle. She can see that from her conversations with them. 'Women had a curious streak of chastity in them no matter how long they were married or how ardently they had loved.' She is sorry for her daughter but what about what she, her mother, is renouncing? And here Mary Lavin shows a keen appreciation of the feelings of any mother whose daughter has grown away from her. The nun's mother will have 'no more fun out shopping, no more flippancies, no more visits to the Small Women shops . . . no more need to lay aside linen, no more need to be on the lookout for bargains in silver spoons and forks (even when they were going for a song)'. No need, in short, to remain young. And is she supposed to be grateful for the fact that, as she grows old, she will have a daughter who is a nun? She can just hear her friends. 'Well for you, Mrs Latimer: well for you with a daughter a nun to pray for you.' To depend on her daughter's prayers – a daughter 'who up to her last day at home always sat so immodestly with her bare thighs showing' – is a ridiculous thought. She can 'frankly discount' that.

61

Mary Lavin is often at her most satirical and wittiest when she is writing about aspects of the religious life. The nun's mother speculates on whether there really is anything at all in the idea of a 'Personal Call, a Divine Choice'. It is difficult to accept. Yet here is her daughter – so beautiful, so normal in every way – seized by 'this sudden fanaticism'. What else can you call it? How can you explain it? 'How had those nuns succeeded in talking the girl into taking such a step? But need one ask? She herself had only to think of their try-outs with her when she was Angela's age! The Church had the trump card when it came to talking about love. The fulfilling of the law. Greater love hath no man! All that bosh.'

As Mrs Latimer thinks of the role to which her daughter has assigned her, it is enough to make her shudder. She has acquired a title: a Nun's Mother. 'How people would fasten on it.' She can just hear them. 'May I introduce Mrs Latimer, who has a daughter a nun. Have you met Mrs Latimer? Mrs Latimer has a daughter in the convent.' From now on she is going to be 'a sort of exhibit'. She will have to change the way she dressed. Maybe give up smoking in public. And, awful thought, hang holy pictures even in her parlour. 'And what else? Oh yes, punctuate her conversation with pious little tags like *God willing*, *Thanks be to God*, and *God between us and all harm.*'

The story ends with the nun's parents arriving home. The housekeeper greets them with a wonderful gentleness, saying that she saw the taxi arriving. 'I put on the kettle. I'll make you a nice cup of tea . . . Sit down, Mrs Latimer, ma'am.' The fire is lit, the silver gleams, and both her slippers and her husband's are warming by the fire. The whole atmosphere seems unfamiliar. And then the realization comes. It is inevitable. From now on everyone is going to treat her with respect. Mary Lavin understood and had the ability to portray accurately the attitude of the average Irishwoman of that period towards a mother whose daughter had become a nun or whose son had become a priest.

With the advent of the 1940s, Mary's reputation as a writer of short stories was growing in the States and, in Ireland, her name was becoming well known among members of the Dublin literary scene. As the novelist, short story writer and critic Benedict Kiely said, already 'she was well recognized as a writer and a considerable person. It was an honour to spend an enthusiastic evening with her. She was very quiet but very decided in her speech. There was always thought behind what she said.'

Mary's career was getting under way at an inauspicious time, however. In 1930s Ireland, conservatism was deeply ingrained. Tradition was the byword. There was opposition to any modern trends in literature and film, and even sharp criticism of the hanging of nude pictures in the National Gallery. Ireland's largely rural population was church-dominated and rigid in its thinking and the Censorship Board was doing a fine job of what it saw as its responsibility: protecting the citizenry. Books and periodicals were being banned at a great rate: 1,200 books and 140 periodicals between 1930 and 1939.

According to the novelist and playwright Mervyn Wall, the Censorship Board made its decisions as to which books should be banned on the strength of letters from members of the Catholic Truth Society, who pointed out what pages in a particular book should be examined. The situation was so repressive that, as he recalled, in 1925 the church hierarchy were thinking seriously of excommunicating anyone who went into a dance hall.

Writers were suffering excessively from the prevailing mood. Frank O'Connor, Liam O'Flaherty and Sean O'Faolain were having their books banned with regularity. O'Faolain had hoped and indeed believed that conditions would be better under the de Valera government that replaced Cumann na nGaedheal in 1932, but, if anything, conservatism had become even more deeply rooted and the general lack of interest in things cultural had deepened. The magazines that might have been a market for Mary Lavin's short stories were finding it difficult to stay in business.

The writers were fighting back, however. They showed in their novels and short stories Irish life as they felt it truly was. As Terence Brown pointed out, in the work of Frank O'Connor, Sean O'Faolain, and Mary Lavin, 'we see an Irish provincial world, in Cork, in the small towns, in the countryside, where inhibition is disguised as economic prudence, land hunger and stolid conservatism as patriotic duty, subservience to Church authority as piety'. Short story writers during that period – the 1930s and 1940s – were portraying in Ireland 'a mediocre, dishevelled, often neurotic and depressed petit-bourgeois society that atrophied for want of a liberating idea,' Terence Brown wrote.

One of the small monthly magazines that played an important part in changing the conservative climate was *The Bell*. In 1940 Sean O'Faolain became its editor and continued in that capacity until 1946. Mary Lavin's stories were carried twice during his editorship: 'A Story with a Pattern' in August 1946, and in November 1947 'A Glimpse of Katey'. The magazine's influence was being felt outside Ireland as well and its list of contributors was impressive: Conor Cruise O'Brien, his career just getting under way as a critic and a man of letters, the politician Erskine Childers, and the writers Elizabeth Bowen, Honor Tracy and Patrick Kavanagh, to name only a few.

After World War II, other literary periodicals began to appear in addition to *The Bell*. One of those was *Irish Writing*, edited by David Marcus. It too proved to be a good market for the new young writers such as Benedict Kiely, James Plunkett, Thomas Kinsella and Mary Lavin. In June 1947 the publication carried her 'Posy', 'The Small Bequest' in February 1949, 'A Gentle Soul' in March 1951, 'Limbo' in June 1954, and 'Frail Vessel' in March 1955.

The scholar Declan Kiberd, in his *Inventing Ireland*,

published in 1996, saw censorship forcing the artist to emigrate. He noted that the banning of so much good literature seemed to have the effect of turning the Irish reader into a reader of American westerns. Apparently, he wrote:

> the recurring legend of a seeming rebel who turns out on inspection to be a pillar of society seemed to sort well with the national condition after 1921. The underlying paradox was that by censoring modernism the Irish authorities maintained it at the level of an heroic opposition, long after it had begun to lose that status in other countries and especially in the wake of World War Two.

There appears to be nothing to indicate that Mary Lavin fought openly against the repressive church and the Censorship Board's puritanism but it was all there in her work. And, despite obstacles, her writing career was progressing fairly rapidly. In 1941 'At Sallygap' appeared in the *Atlantic Monthly*, and 'Say Can That Lad Be I' in the *Dublin Magazine*. In 1942 'Love Is For Lovers' was published in *Harper's Bazaar*, and that same year *Tales from Bective Bridge* appeared, with its laudatory introduction by Lord Dunsany.

As Mary came to understand, there is a necessary time lag for the details in semi-autobiographical stories to work themselves out. Thus, in the early 1930s and 1940s, it was all coming together for her in her stories: the awareness in the mind of the nine-year-old Yank of the attitude towards Catholicism in Athenry as opposed to East Walpole; the lifestyle and the conversation of her Athenry family and the town's inhabitants; the nuns in the convent school; the difference between the town children and the country children; her many conversations with Michael Scott at UCD; her own mother's self-aggrandizement. She came to realize that 'in solving the problems I posed for my fictitious characters, I was in fact solving problems that had preoccupied me since I was very young'.

As Mary had assured her cousin, Eileen O'Toole, her characters were composites. But occasionally the borderline between fact and fiction was thin. This can be seen quite clearly in stories where the principal character resembled her father, such as 'Say Can That Lad Be I' and 'Tom'. And, of course, those characters who resembled Tom invariably had many admirable characteristics.

This was not true when someone like her mother was the principal character. However fictionalized the facts are in 'A Cup of Tea', written in the early 1940s, a picture of Nora Lavin, as her daughter must have seen her during college days, emerges. The similarity in the cast of characters is hard to miss. In the story there is a beautiful mother, proud of her university student daughter, jealous of the daughter's preference for her father's company, and mired in an unhappy marriage. There is a daughter painfully aware that she has not inherited her mother's beauty. At one point in the story the mother says to her daughter, home for a visit, 'Hold up your head. Don't stir. You're too thin. It doesn't suit you. It throws up your likeness to your father.' It is a resemblance, the mother goes on to say, that she has not seen when people have pointed it out to her, but now she sees it. 'I suppose it's natural you should resemble him in something,' she says. And at another point, the daughter looks at her mother as she is kneeling to stir the fire in the grate.

> For a moment she envied the fine structure of bone that made the face so clear and attractive in spite of age, and she looked at the grey hair that was still so full of life that it sprang into curling tendrils whenever it escaped from the combs that held it. She thought of her own large pale face and straight hair that gave her a resemblance to her father.

That is the fictional daughter deploring her looks, but at four o'clock one morning in 1991, Mary Lavin, possibly with her memoirs in mind, jotted down these thoughts:

> I don't remember confession, but I had good reason to remember communion – the awful portrait. I don't remember when I became aware that I was not pretty, but I think it was on the day of my first communion – after which I must have been duly taken to the photographer in Boston who not only, etc., etc. The picture bothered me, even at that age I could see that in it I was very plain indeed.

As the story goes in 'A Cup of Tea', the mother has everything beautifully arranged for her daughter's visit. The tea tray is set out and waiting. But she knows in her heart that when her daughter comes home she will run upstairs directly to visit with her father, an entomologist working on a book. And it transpires just as she has envisaged it. She shows her jealousy, her lack of understanding, and there are harsh words and bitter feelings. The pretentiousness of Mary Lavin's mother, and her stress of the title 'Miss Imperious', comes through in the fictional mother's attitude towards a servant. She has the maid scrubbing and polishing all day without even a pretence of compassion. Think of Nora Lavin's attitude towards the wives of Tom Lavin's friends in East Walpole who would have been housemaids in Athenry. The resemblance is there too in Mary Lavin's description of the jealousy the mother feels as she realizes that her daughter much prefers the companionship of her father.

The mother has told her daughter over and over of the wonderful times she and her sisters had when they were young: the dances, the young men flocking around them, the beautiful clothes they wore. 'And she [the daughter] tried to feel sorry for her mother, all alone now, sitting here in the evenings filled with bitterness of those unfulfilled and foolish dreams'.

Mary Lavin shows extraordinary insightfulness in 'A Cup of Tea'. She could, even then, see her mother's unhappiness in her marriage, her loneliness. It took a long time but later on Mary would be able to see quite clearly that her mother must have been hoping that in her daughter she would find the companionship she had not found in her marriage, and been cruelly disappointed. Mary saw, too, her own inability to tolerate what she would later refer to as her mother's silliness, and she felt guilty. That feeling of guilt intensified with the years.

Was Nora Lavin proud of her daughter's ability as a writer? Still searching 'A Cup of Tea' for clues, it would seem that she was aware of it without understanding it. That was probably true of the whole family. Eileen O'Toole, Mary's cousin, said that the family simply took her success for granted and didn't think about it much. And Mary Lavin herself once wrote that if she ever stopped writing entirely 'it would be months, even years, before anyone in my household would notice that this had happened– if they ever did!' It didn't matter. Mary Lavin *had* to write.

It is difficult to trace how Nora Lavin felt, but certainly Mary's father was a proud man as his daughter's successes mounted. Mary was not only receiving recognition as a writer, but was mingling with aristocracy. She was not going to be subjected to the condescension to which his wife had subjected him and his friends. As usual, he managed to find some way to be part of his daughter's life. He bought her a typewriter.

II
SUMMER

CHAPTER 3

Those who knew Mary well knew her habit of examining a situation from all angles, of discussing it endlessly, and of often finding it impossible to come to a satisfactory conclusion. But the Michael Scott versus William Walsh quandary, so often discussed with Lorna Reynolds, had not, after all, required resolution. Michael Scott had left Dublin and continued his studies for the priesthood while William Walsh obtained his law degree and remained in Dublin. After they both graduated, he and Mary began to spend a great deal of time together and, in the early 1940s, they announced their engagement.

William Walsh was a fine looking man: tall, thin, with a sensitive, rather ascetic face. Although he and Mary were the same age, he seemed older. Some of their friends thought it a curious union, given what appeared to be their disparate personalities, but it was right for both of them. Willam was genuinely interested in people but his manner was somewhat reserved. Mary – vivacious, loquacious, warm – filled a need for him and helped him both socially and professionally. His methodical nature, too, was exactly what Mary, not very disciplined except in her writing, needed. However, though outwardly their temperaments seemed so different, there was a strong similarity. Fundamentally, William was shy and so was Mary. There is no indication that she gave others that impression but basically she lacked self-confidence. To see her the centre of attraction at social gatherings and later to witness her poise on a platform would contradict that assessment, yet Mary realized it was true. She and William needed each other.

The greatest difference between them was in their backgrounds. William, next to the youngest of four children, grew up in the sheltered atmosphere of Ashwood House, the family home located in Donadea, County Kildare. His father, a prosperous farmer, came from County Wicklow, as did his mother, Florence O'Grady, a member of a proud, old family in Killamoat. The Killamoat O'Gradys point with pride to St Mary's Church in Killamoat, Rathdangan, west Wicklow, where there is a memorial window to their family done by the famous stained glass artist, Harry Clarke. None of this had much effect on William: a man completely without affectation. For example, the family name is Walshe – spelled with an 'e'. William dropped the 'e'. It was, he maintained, pretentious.

At the age of five, William was enrolled in a Dublin convent school at Mount Sackville, joining his two brothers and his sister already in attendance there. There was a very good reason why they had all been sent to boarding school so young. William could have been no older than three or four when his father died and to his mother, left with four small children, boarding school seemed the best solution for the children.

Later William wrote an account, published in *Commonweal*, 26 April 1957, of his convent school days. He had never forgotten the drive to the convent on that first day. He and his mother rode through Phoenix Park in a horse-drawn cab with his trunks piled high on its roof: proof – as he saw it – that he would be away from home for a long time. He recalled 'the choking loneliness' which ever afterwards he associated with going away to school. But he had been eager to go, and he had to accept that loneliness as the price to be paid for the privilege of being a student.

The convent was situated in a wooded, secluded area adjacent to Phoenix Park, and as they approached the area they saw a sign that read, 'Young Ladies and Little Boys'. The boys' section of the school was small: simply several large rooms, separated from the girls' section, and with, at that time, only about twenty boys in attendance. Mass was celebrated each morning in the chapel, located in the girls' school, and boys and girls attended together. The girls, in their little white lace veils, apparently made very little impression upon the boys, except for one romantic figure among the older girls. She had the distinction of a sister said to be engaged to Michael Collins, already famous as a leader of the Irish revolutionary movement.

Each September, shortly after the beginning of the school year, an annual retreat was held. As William wrote in his article:

> The echoing of a preacher's voice still brings back memories of those thin days of shortening evenings, when the Convent grounds became bedded with red beech and yellow chestnut leaves, and the only consolation was playing 'Champions' with the great mahogany coloured chestnuts.

The lectures at the retreat dwelled on the dangers of the outside world. 'No doubt compared to the secluded life inside the Convent walls, there were many temptations outside,' William wrote, 'but I must say I have never found the passageways of life lined with such tempting sins as were hinted at in those lectures.'

William's upbringing had proceeded on solid, conventional lines and he seems to have been a tractable, unquestioning little boy, well suited to the school's rigid regime. According to him, he and his brothers were 'in no way wild, but very sensible'. He wrote with obvious admiration that 'inside those walls was an organization strong enough to imprint on one's mind forever, correct ideas of moral and physical well-being'. And of one of the nuns in charge of their health and 'moral instincts', William wrote: 'I do not think in my whole life I ever came across a person of greater character.'

Certainly it was a sheltered life William was leading. During the influenza epidemic raging in 1920, even those letters which came from family would not be given to the boys but would be read to them after they had been disinfected. And during those early 1920s, when outside the convent walls there was shooting and destruction and in Phoenix Park the boys were seeing signs of military activity, the nuns did not discuss the conflict but merely urged the boys to pray for Ireland. The whole atmosphere in the convent was non-political but William remembered that, before the visit of some clergymen, the boys were prompted to enquire about Archbishop Mannix, about whom William knew nothing at the time but learned later that he had 'raised his voice for Ireland'. On the other hand, when one of the parents, a major in the British Army who had served with distinction in 1914 to 1918, came to call on his son, he was entertained respectfully with no hint of prejudice. At any rate, the nearest the boys came to the conflict was when, one morning after the attack on the Lord Lieutenant's entourage at Ashtown, two Black and Tan soldiers took up a position on the convent walls. They spoke to the boys but all they seemed to want to know was where the big girls were.

A fellow-student at the UCD law school, Patrick (Paddy) Shanley, who after law school was one of William Walsh's close friends, provided a full account of their association. William was well liked and held in high regard by his friends and associates at the college, Paddy wrote, and it would have been difficult to find anyone who spoke harshly of him. He was:

> a person of extremely strong character and very sweet in his manner. He exercised influence easily over others including myself as he was a natural leader. I never heard him speak harshly and he always poured oil on troubled waters . . . In many respects he was much more mature than most of us.

William became an important figure in the law school, won the coveted position of Honorary Auditor of the Law Students Debating Society, and was awarded a series of medals for his oratory. One was granted by the Solicitors' Apprentices Debating Society; another by the Incorporated Law Society. Mary wore those medals for many years. In 1933 he delivered the inaugural address before the Solicitors' Apprentices Debating Society: the address was titled 'International Goodwill', and stressed the interdependence of nations.

After completing his law course, William obtained a position in the legal department of one of Dublin's banks and somewhat later he and Paddy Shanley entered into partnership. They rented an office on Grafton Street, one of Dublin's main thoroughfares: 'quite commodious,' Paddy wrote, 'and life was quite pleasant'. The bank in whose legal division William had been employed referred clients to them, and that helped to get them started. The young men rented a cottage at Rathcoole, about fourteen miles from Dublin, and William bought a small car in which they commuted to Dublin daily. Paddy wrote and talked about that period nostalgically.

With the outbreak of World War II, both young men joined the Local Defence Force. Invasion was expected hourly and they were trained in bomb throwing and shooting at a nearby range at Baldonnel. According to Paddy:

> It could be quite nerve-wracking at times as our companions were rather tough country boys who thought nothing of hurling bombs at one another to catch like a cricket ball. You could never be sure whether the pin had been pulled out because they did not know much about bombs.

William Walsh was an idealist and he and his partner played an active role in settling German-Jewish refugees in Ireland.

At one time a refugee, George Lis, was billeted in their cottage. William's idealism had been proved much earlier, however. In 1938 he had been nominated by the League of Nations Society of Ireland to attend the second World Youth Congress to be held August 16–23 at Vassar College in Poughkeepsie, New York. An unidentified clipping, headed 'Youth of World Meets in Quest for Peace by William Walsh', shows that he attended with two other delegates from Ireland – J. Harold Douglas and Seamus Ua h-Eigeartaigh (O'Hegarty) – and that he reported on the conference upon his return home.

During the war, the Shanley and Walsh practice dropped off precipitously and the partnership was dissolved. The firm of Shanley and Walsh was later re-established but, although the name remained the same, Paddy was replaced by one of his friends, James Kent. Paddy's friendship with William Walsh continued, however.

Many years later, Paddy volunteered the information that he had never been fond of either Mary or her work. When pressed for a reason, he said that it was always his feeling that William Walsh was second best with Mary. As for her work, he admitted that he had not read a great many of her stories. Possibly Paddy had felt supplanted. His friendship with William had been long and deep and the advent of Mary introduced a new element. Whatever his feeling, he must have suppressed it for he attended their wedding and was godfather to William Walsh's second daughter, Elizabeth.

On Tuesday 29 September 1942 Mary Lavin and William Walsh were married at Robinstown. The ceremony was performed by the Very Reverend M. J. Flood of Dunderry, with the Rev. Fr Healy assisting. Mary wore a suit of dark brown velvet and carried a bouquet of roses from the gardens at Bective House. The reception following the ceremony was held there – 'courtesy of Mr and Mrs C. S. Bird' the newspaper account read – and among the guests were Lord and Lady Dunsany. Of the groom, it said: 'Mr Walsh, who is a solicitor by profession, has made a study of international affairs, and before the war visited the United States in connection with work for promoting better international relations.' Mary liked to talk later of her peach-coloured trousseau, purchased at Walpole's – then one of Dublin's finer shops.

Both families were pleased: the Lavins because William was a successful solicitor and a fine man of whom they were very fond, and the Walshes because Mary was a successful writer and because they had become genuinely fond of her, despite of, or possibly because of, her capriciousness.

Because she had had no brothers or sisters, Mary was happy to become part of the large Walshe family and, as Florence Walsh, William's niece, phrases it, 'Mary was family.' After William's death they were very important to her and often she turned to Gus, William's brother, for guidance. Undoubtedly she did not expect them to understand her fully, but she was gathering impressions which would be reflected in her stories. Those impressions can be clearly traced in 'The Becker Wives' and in her novel, *The House in Clewe Street*.

The newlyweds settled down in a house on Clyde Road, not too far from all the places Mary was in the habit of frequenting: the Green, the National Library and Grafton Street. The Green was delightful for walks in an atmosphere completely divorced from the city around it; the National Library manuscript room was a quiet place to work; and Grafton Street had shops and Bewley's café, a good place to meet friends and to drink Bewley's famous coffee.

The Walshes' first daughter was born in 1943 and named Mary Valentine. Known simply as Valentine, she later chose to call herself Valdi, a name which appeared to suit her well. Their second daughter, Elizabeth, was born in 1945. Both were born in Bective House. Despite the children and her busy schedule, the pattern of Mary's weekends did not change. She spent them in Bective with her father and

William grew to look forward to those weekends as well. He liked helping out on the farm and visiting with the locals.

Neither their courtship nor their marriage had interfered with Mary's writing or her productivity in any way, nor did the advent of the children. She was producing a fair number of short stories that were being carried in American publications such as the *Yale Review* and the *American Mercury*. William Walsh, himself an aspiring writer, understood her devotion to her work and was proud of her success and recognition.

In 1945 the British firm of Michael Joseph brought out Mary's first novel, *The House in Clewe Street*. Prior to its publication, it had been serialized consecutively in seven issues of the *Atlantic Monthly* under the title of 'Gabriel Galloway'. The novel was widely reviewed and for the most part favourably. *Book Week*, the *Boston Globe*, the *Christian Science Monitor*, and the *Nation* all carried early reviews. According to the scholar Janet Dunleavy in her piece on Mary Lavin in the *Dictionary of Literary Biography*, the number of reviews which appeared fell only a little short of one hundred. Orville Prescott, in the *Yale Review*, Autumn 1945, wrote: 'There is a great vigour and shrewd understanding here.' And John Hampson in the *Spectator*, 30 November 1945, wrote: 'Miss Lavin has made herself an excellent reputation as a writer of short stories', and in her novel, 'She depicts a way of life that has vanished. She does it with richness and warmth but entirely without sentimentality.' With those critics of her novel who considered it overly long and somewhat disjointed, Mary agreed. In this novel, as in so many of her short stories, Mary, through the words of the narrator, drew a vivid picture of the conservative Catholic middle class, with its materialism, its narrowness and its snobbery. She showed the social chasm that existed between the city and country people.

The House in Clewe Street is a family saga and the story spans several generations. The locale is an area called

Castlerampart and its principal property owner is Theodore Coniffe. He is definitely middle-class, neither part of the Anglo-Irish aristocracy nor one of the poverty-stricken people who survived the Great Famine. Mary set the novel up in three sections, with each section bearing the name of one of the principal characters, and it relied heavily on what she had observed during those early days in Athenry when she had spent her time visiting its inhabitants and when she was exposed to the values of the Mahons. The position of the Coniffe family in the town might be compared to that of the Mahon family in Athenry. In addition, by the time she wrote this novel, she had been able to study William's family closely.

It was not until five years later that Mary wrote another novel and *Mary O'Grady* was her last attempt at that form. Novels, she felt, were not her métier, and the writing of them ran contrary to both her temperament and the amount of time she had, as a wife and mother, to devote to them. It was necessary to write with great intensity and the novel, in her opinion, was not an intense medium. The short story, on the other hand, was 'a powerful medium in which anything, anything, anything that is to be said can be said'. It was in that form, as she saw it, 'that a writer distills the essence of his thought. I believe this because the short story . . . is determined by the writer's own character. Both are one. Short-story writing – for me – is only looking closer than normal into the human heart.'

Mary O'Grady is written in the third person and its characters are Mary, the strong mother, her husband Tom, and their five children. The depiction of the love Tom and Mary feel for each other is masterful: subtle and moving. The time is the early 1900s and the place is Dublin, Tom's home-town. Mary O'Grady grew up in the country and her love of country life has never waned during all her years of living in Dublin. Mary Lavin portrays that nostalgia early in the story and in doing so she conveys her own love of nature. Each day Mary O'Grady takes her husband's lunch to the car-barn where he works and each day on the way home she stops at a spot on the bank of the Grand Canal where a little grass is still growing. She looks forward to the summer. Here, she thought,

> the children could have no better place to play and get the sun. Then the bleached old sward was lanced with a million shafts of young green grass, and lo! in the middle of the city there was the full splendour of a country meadow, as rich as any in the Midlands; a meadow tossing with myriad grasses, rye and timothy, cocksfoot, fescue, and the delicate tremble-grass; a meadow glowing bronze upon its surface, but lit in flashes everywhere by big white daisies. And when the wind swayed, it revealed an underworld of baby-faced blossoms hiding their heads in the cooler depths, out of reach of the burning, golden sun that, in those days, seemed ever to sail the high blue heavens.

Mary O'Grady is depicted as extremely happily married and delighted at the birth of each child but tragedy follows upon tragedy in this novel. As the story and Mary O'Grady's life end, she faces death, happy to be reunited with those members of her loving family who have gone before her.

It is Richard Peterson's belief that the 'sudden importance' of religion to the O'Gradys 'places a further strain on the credibility of the novel'. But the stress on the importance of religion is in actuality not that sudden. Mary O'Grady is drawn as a deeply religious woman and religion sustains her throughout. Her Catholicism would have helped her to weather all the tragedies which befell her, since she believed she would be getting her reward in the hereafter. As Augustine Martin, Professor of English at UCD, wrote in an 'Afterword' to the Virago Modern Classics edition of *Mary O'Grady*, Mary O'Grady's 'visions of an eternal reward' are 'implicit in her character and actions throughout her life'.

In his overall appraisal of the novel, Peterson says further that 'Mary Lavin allows the narrative voice to fall into a subjective role in the novel.' Professor Martin thought that to say that 'misses the narrative technique of the book as a whole by confusing the writer with the character'. He continued:

> Those who identify Mary Lavin with Mary O'Grady would do well to remember that the characters called 'Jane' in Jane Austen's fiction are those least like the author herself. This is not to say that there is a schematic sense of distance between the author's view of things and that of the heroine; Mary Lavin is far too instinctual a story-teller for that. But a sensitive reading of the novel will reveal that many of Mary O'Grady's responses and attitudes – her innocence, stubbornness, sentimentality – are almost as much a mystery to the writer as they are to the reader.

'I even wish that I could break up the two long novels I have published into the few short stories they ought to have been in the first place,' Mary once wrote. Martin believed she 'underrates her skill with structure', but he did agree that some sections could be taken out and used as short stories almost without editing. That is exactly what she did with one section of *Mary O'Grady*. 'A House to Let', which appeared first in 1970, is taken from the novel. A young couple who have recently decided that they will marry are taking a stroll when they see a house to let. (The man is called Bart in both the novel and the story but Ellie is changed to Ella.) To see a house to let is rare. Mostly the houses are for sale. After some discussion as to whether or not they will go inside, Bart inspects the house alone. Though it is depressing and in disrepair, he does not seem to notice it. 'He was suddenly as excited as if they were about to enter into some mysterious cavern where ecstasy and rapture awaited them.' Somehow his desire to be married, and soon, is strengthened: possibly because he becomes uncomfortably conscious of the passing of time.

Whole paragraphs in 'A House to Let' are taken from the novel with only the change of a word or two. It is a fairly slight story but Mary made one important point, which she understood so well and which she believed completely. She has both Ellie in *Mary O'Grady* and Ella in 'A House to Let' say 'How strange it all was. How little part one seemed to play in determining the course of one's life.' That line is taken from the novel verbatim.

Martin, while admitting that possibly parts of *Mary O'Grady* might be 'greater than the whole', remained 'partial to its haunting and ineradicable wholeness – which is the personality of its heroine, one of the most memorable characterisations in contemporary fiction'.

When, in 1995, Martin commented on Mary Lavin's work, he said that reading her in a way required skill – one had to be very learned, very sensitive, he believed. It took him, as he looked back, a very long time to discover how good she was.

Certainly Mary had no reason to apologize for *Mary O'Grady* so far as Jack B. Yeats, the artist and brother of W. B. Yeats, was concerned. Correspondence indicates that in 1950 she sent him a copy of the novel. In November he wrote to compliment her. He found her characters always brave and her ability to 'put them in scenes which have walls and floors and ceilings' quite remarkable.

When Mary was pregnant with her second child in 1945, Tom Lavin, then in his seventies, developed colon cancer. She tended him all during the summer of his terminal illness and it was then that she wrote *Mary O'Grady*. The story proved easy to write and she wrote it quickly: in a month except for the ending. She had known a woman whose experiences resembled those described in her novel and, because she felt she understood the woman, she was eager to tell her story. 'I wrote it while I watched my father dying,' she said during an interview in the 1980s, and added: 'Summer and death dominate the story.'

Eager to have a grandchild named after him, Tom was hoping that Mary's child would be a boy and was already referring to 'young Tom'. But fate did not allow him to learn that his second grandchild was a girl, nor did it give him time to get to know Elizabeth, born after his death. Tom Lavin died late in September 1945 and a report of his death in the 4 October 1945 issue of the *Irish Independent*, after noting that he was the father of writer Mary Lavin, read: 'A well known figure in sporting circles, he purchased the famous 'chaser, Heartbreak Hill.' He was, Mary believed, seventy-six when he died but, as noted earlier, there was no way of knowing with any certainty Tom's exact age.

Lord Dunsany wrote Mary very percipiently that he suspected the death was no worse for her than the long period when she was anticipating it. He told her, in expressing his and Lady Dunsany's regrets, that he had always been fond of Tom and, like many others, would miss him. Tom often rowed him out on the Boyne for duck-hunting, he wrote. As Lord Dunsany pointed out, those months when Tom was dying must have been torture for Mary and, without a doubt, working on *Mary O'Grady* helped her to live through the days.

Her father's death dealt Mary, then thirty-three, a crushing blow and she was a long time becoming reconciled to it. More than a month passed before she was able to write to the Bird family, then in the States, about his death. It would have been her father's wish that she write to them immediately, she wrote, but she had been unable to do so. Yet she knew that her father would have understood better than anyone 'the weight of the sadness that overwhelmed me and kept my hands idle'. She had been able to answer formal letters of sympathy – that had come easily to her and she had devoted considerable time to it – but writing to those who knew the depth of her sorrow 'was so hard as to be almost impossible'.

Years passed before Mary was able to write about her father as fully as she did in 'Tom', which appeared in the *New Yorker* in 1973. Even then, her longing for her father persisted. He had always brought such joy into her life and his pride in whatever she achieved had spurred her on to win laurels in athletics, in education, and in her writing. In a diary which she kept very late in her life this note was found. 'I should not have burned on the night of my wedding the diaries of my youth and my early adulthood because if I had kept them now I would be better able to find myself in touch with my dear father.'

She had often heard her mother talk of all the women in East Walpole who had pursued Tom before they were married and at one time Mary had teased him about it. She remembered happily that he had said that none of them would have given him a daughter like her. That consoled her somewhat after his death, as did the fact that he had lived long enough to see her happily married, a mother, and firmly established in a writing career.

There is a character in Mary Lavin's 'Happiness', published in 1968, who, in trying to explain to her daughters that 'even illness and pain could coexist with happiness', says: 'Take my own father! You know what he said in his last moments? On his deathbed he defied me to name a man who had enjoyed a better life. In spite of dreadful pain, his face *radiated* happiness.' That is undoubtedly the way Mary saw Tom Lavin's death and the way Tom Lavin saw his life.

CHAPTER 4

Tom Lavin's will, which William Walsh had drawn up, named Mary as his sole heir and William as his executor. Tom had defied custom and left his daughter in charge of her mother instead of the other way around. This cart-before-the-horse arrangement did not surprise Mary. It was, she believed, simply another example of the troubled relationship between her parents. And yet, in Mary's letter to Mr and Mrs Bird after Tom's death, she had written:

> My mother is writing to you soon too but she was very worn by the almost incredible care and attention with which she watched over him, night and day, it mattered not, throughout the whole of his illness. We all three of us gave him every moment that was possible of our time but she, with less other cares, was with him almost continually.

Assuming the responsibility for her mother was not an easy assignment. Nora was almost impossible to please. But Mary's task was made easier by William, whose relationship with Nora had always been a good one. He appeared to be charmed by her slightly girlish manner, her gentility, and her propriety. He would take her to tea at Mitchell's Restaurant – one of Dublin's finest at the time – and seemed to enjoy her company.

Directly after his father-in-law's death, William as executor had begun corresponding with the Birds and, as Mary wrote to them, she was grateful for it. 'His wisdom and love have done a lot to uphold me, & my father knew that this would be so.' She was pleased that William had taken over so thoroughly for she realized that, apart from their grief about Tom's death, the Bird family must have been concerned about the fate of Bective. As Mary wrote, 'I think it is a very valuable thing for all of us that through him there is a continuity in Bective affairs, and not a break until such time as you can come over.' It gave them all time to gather their affairs together and to make plans that were not hurried or ill-considered.

It was a source of regret for both Mary and William that the Birds had never met him – had never had an opportunity to get to know him – but Mary hastened to assure them that she was keeping up with all the correspondence between them and that all decisions were made jointly. Apparently the arrangement had all worked out remarkably well. A letter from William to Mrs Bird in response to one of hers mentioned the relationship that had arisen between them through correspondence. 'What you said touched me very much, perhaps more than you intended or more than your letter on its face would call for.'

When Tom became ill and William had needed to intervene, he had realized that he had 'come upon something very special and rare in his loyalty and devotion to you and your family,' he wrote to Mrs Bird. He had, for that reason, done his best to carry on in a similar fashion. 'I felt from the start much of the special attachment that went with his work. It makes me very happy that you have written to me so warmly and justifies anything I have done for you at Bective.' He knew that there was a possibility that, while he was acting for them at Bective, his work would be open to criticism at times, 'but loyalty and affection towards you is and will be a tradition in our little family'.

With the money that Mary inherited – about five thousand pounds, a considerable sum in those days – the Walshes decided to buy land in the proximity of Bective House and, with the royalties from *Tales from Bective Bridge*, to build a house. Meanwhile, they were occupying the nursery wing which they had furnished attractively with their own furniture. As William explained to Mrs Bird, because the unit was not self-contained, they were using the main kitchen. 'I think your suggestion of making the unit self-contained is very interesting, and if it were we would not be so pressed about getting out in case anyone came to stay.' Mary had suggested that the storeroom off the kitchen could be converted into a kitchen and he was calling in an architect to study the situation.

By 1947, their house was ready for occupancy. The land they had purchased was on the banks of the Boyne, near the remains of Bective Abbey, a Cistercian foundation which dated back to 1147. Because of its closeness, they named their new home the Abbey Farm. In the late 1950s, Mary wrote a story called 'In the Middle of the Fields', and that title describes quite accurately the way the house was situated.

During her father's life, Mary's happiest times had been at Bective House and settling nearby and in the country was right for her, for William, and for the children. The house – in a modified ranch style – was modern and compact. The exterior was whitewashed stucco with a roof of dark red shingles. It appeared to be small but the interior was roomy. The sunken living room had a large picture window that covered almost the whole south wall and framed the lush green fields and the ruins of the Abbey. A tall bookcase extended along the north wall and there was a fireplace on the left side of the room. Three steps up from the living room was the dining room and friends and family, long after the Abbey Farm was sold, still talked of Mary's dinners and the wonderful soups she served there, often made from vegetables she had grown.

Mary's gardening talents had full play at the Abbey Farm but her writing career was not being neglected either, even though she now had her mother and two small children to look after. In 1944 a second collection of her stories, *The Long Ago and Other Stories*, had been published. The themes of the twelve stories in the collection are wide-ranging. In one of them, 'The Cemetery in the Demesne' her preoccupation with loneliness and death and the effect of both on her characters is apparent, as it is in a great many of her stories. It was a preoccupation which critics mentioned often over the years.

Another story in that collection, 'A Wet Day', illustrates well Mary's considerable wit. The narrator is a young Dublin university student visiting her aunt in the country. The parish priest – an old, ailing, self-centred man – has come to call and incidentally to cadge vegetables. The conversation between the gardener and the priest never varies from visit to visit. The priest: 'We must keep the old machine going, Mike. Isn't that right?' The reply: 'That's right, Father. Mind your health. It's the only thing that will stand to you at the finish.' When the priest, an experienced cadger, brings up the subject of preserving lettuce, he is told by the gardener that he can always get fresh lettuce from them, and the aunt echoes his sentiments. Says the priest: 'You're working for a kind woman, Mike. There aren't many like her going the way nowadays. She spoils us all. She spoils us all. I suppose it isn't right for me to let her spoil me like that. Eh, Mike?' To which the gardener replies, 'Ah! Why wouldn't you let her spoil you, Father? She loves giving you the few poor vegetables!' The priest agrees. 'She does indeed. She does. I know that, Mike . . . Isn't it a grand thing the way the Irish women are so good to the clergy?' And, with great certainty, the gardener replies, 'Why wouldn't they be, Father? Where would we be only for the priests?'

Before the parish priest leaves, his car loaded down with fresh lettuce, he tells a story which he finds most amusing. His niece, a nurse, brought her fiancé from Dublin to meet him. The man was burning up with fever and she suggested it might be wise to stay the night. The priest, not wanting his home and his routine disrupted, said she had better take him right back to Dublin and to a hospital. After all, he said, 'there's only one hot jar . . . There's no one but the one woman to do everything and she with her hands full looking after me.' The niece protested but then agreed to take her fiancé's temperature and, if it was normal, to take him back to Dublin. She asked for a thermometer and was told there was not one in the house. Shocked at such a lack, she bundled the man up and departed for Dublin, calling back as she went that she would send a thermometer.

At this point the narrator's aunt comments that his niece was right to be shocked at the lack of a thermometer in the house. The priest replies, 'and his face was criss-crossed with lines of aged cunning', that he has three thermometers but 'I wasn't going to let on to her that I had.' He had the presbytery fumigated, he goes on, because the young man had double pneumonia and was dead by the next evening.

Much later Mary Lavin wrote: 'I have never to my knowledge written an anticlerical story, although I have written about priests and nuns who were weak and human.' Her priest, in this story at least, proved her contention. In her opinion, he was not a mean, insensitive man because he was a priest. He was simply a self-centred human being.

The publication of *The Long Ago and Other Stories* was followed rapidly by the publication of two more collections of her short stories: *The Becker Wives and Other Stories* in 1946 and *At Sallygap and Other Stories* in 1947. *The Becker Wives* collection differed from the two collections which preceded it in two respects: it contained only four stories and two of them – 'The Becker Wives' and 'A Happy Death' – were novellas. After the publication of *The Becker Wives*, Jack B. Yeats again wrote to tell her how much he had enjoyed it. A third collection of her stories, *A Single Lady and Other Stories*, was published in 1951.

'At Sallygap', the title story in *At Sallygap and Other Stories*, appeared first in the *Atlantic Monthly* in 1941. The critic Clifton Fadiman, in his review of the story in the 30 May 1942 issue of the *New Yorker*, wrote: 'I think any sensitive reader who chanced upon it should have recognized in Miss Lavin a modest oasis in the dreary waste of the contemporary short story.'

'At Sallygap' appeared again in her *Tales from Bective Bridge*, *At Sallygap and Other Stories*, *Collected Stories*, and *The Stories of Mary Lavin II*. Favourable reviews of the *At Sallygap* collection were carried in the *New York Herald Tribune Weekly Book Review*, and C. M. Brown in the *Saturday Review of Literature* wrote: 'Miss Lavin writes with a lovely lilt. She deals reverently with fundamentals.' It was one of the first Lavin stories to be carried in the United States.

There were two good reasons why Mary could handle everything so successfully: Mr and Mrs Rahill. The Rahills had been with the family for many years. Mary had told her daughters that they were employed when she was quite young: in her very early twenties. The couple were from County Cavan, in those years a poverty-stricken area. The story of their employment, as Mary related it, was that one day Tom Lavin was walking along the road near Bective House when he met a weary-looking young couple. The young girl was obviously very far along in her pregnancy. Tom stopped to talk with them and discovered that they were homeless and penniless. He took them in, the child was born shortly afterwards, and Mary and Paddy Rahill had worked for the family from that time forward. Mary Rahill was like a sister to Mary Lavin and Mary's daughters cannot remember a time when Mrs Rahill was not there to take care of them, to listen to their triumphs and failures, and to mother them.

The years after the Walshes settled into Abbey Farm were idyllic. The children, Valdi and Elizabeth, were thriving in the country and were proving a delight for their parents. As Mary had once said of East Walpole, for them the Abbey Farm was a fine place to grow up. They roamed in and out among the ruins of the Abbey, quite oblivious of the fact that it was one of the best-preserved historical sites in all of Ireland. Mary was doing a great deal of gardening, which always made her happy, writing was continuing to go well, and her reputation was growing steadily. Thanks to Mary and William's connections in literary, academic, and political fields, they were enjoying an interesting social life as well. Mary felt fulfilled.

The early Abbey Farm years were productive for William Walsh as well as for Mary. His law practice was thriving and, like Mary, he seemed to find time for everything. He was busy in his Dublin law firm and, in addition, he set up an office in Blessington, County Wicklow. It had always been his ambition to help the small farmer and one of his first trials involved the flooding of a farmer's land in order to construct the Blessington reservoir. The farmer was seeking compensation and William saw to it that he got it. In addition to his law practice, he was continuing to supervise the management of the farm and even doing a certain amount of the farm work and the gardening himself. He was especially proud of his roses, grown in a garden at the back of the lawn.

Even in college, he had been interested in politics and his nephew, Michael Walshe, recalled that Liam Cosgrave, who became Taoiseach, was William's friend and that William had at one time acted as Cosgrave's 'agent'. That friendship may serve as an indication of William's political leanings, for Liam Cosgrave was conservative in his politics and a believer in maintaining the status quo. With William's predilection for the political scene, it was not surprising, therefore, that he should enter into County Meath politics, and stand for councillor. Nor was it surprising that he was elected.

In 1953 the Walshes' third daughter, Caroline, was born. They were both delighted but in that year William Walsh's heart began to trouble him. Mary, with her thoughts so often on death, worried constantly. William was, however, working as hard as usual. Happy in his role as a politician, he stood for the Dáil in the 1954 elections. There is every indication that he would have won handily but, several months after

91

he declared, he suffered a severe heart attack.

While her husband was in the hospital – St Vincent's nursing home in Lower Leeson Street – Mary took a room in a small hotel across the street so that she might be able to spend as much time with him as possible. Although she had a feeling of impending doom, she refused to believe that William was terminally ill. The truth seems to have been brought home to her cruelly. Mary drew on that period in her story 'Happiness' and family members believe that the story closely approximates the actual occurrence. One day when the wife is bringing an armload of flowers to the hospital, she is met in the corridor by one of the nurses – a nun. The flowers will do a dying man no good, the nun tells her. 'Your prayers are all you can give him now!'

Early in May of 1954, William Walsh died. As befitted his importance, his death was celebrated with a Requiem High Mass. In a lengthy tribute in the *Meath Chronicle* it was noted that he had been the first president of Macra na Feirme in Meath, and had acted as election agent for Liam Cosgrave in his Dáil candidature in Dublin. Before settling in Meath, the account read, he had 'engaged in literary work and had many short stories and essays published in various periodicals'. It went on to record that, when Tom Lavin died, William Walsh had been appointed manager of the Bective Estate Company and in addition had farmed some 120 acres of his own there. He was 'a stout champion of his political party, but he had the gift of cool self-restraint, which kept him completely aloof from personalities'. The tribute was headed 'A Gracious Personality Passes'. Michael Walshe Jr always considered that heading a fitting one.

As far back as Mary could remember, there had been someone in her life to protect her: someone for whom her welfare was all-important. There had been her father and, when he was gone, there was William Walsh. Now she had to stand alone, with three small children and her mother to care for.

Edward Weeks, literary editor of the *Atlantic Monthly*,

visited Mary during what was obviously William Walsh's terminal illness. Seeing how burdened she was with all she had to cope with and with her sorrow, he found it difficult to believe that she would have either the time or the energy to write after her husband's death. Certainly she did not have either now, but the difficulty went deeper than that. She had lost faith in her ability to write.

Mary's older daughters report that their mother seemed to be 'almost fatalistic' in her acceptance of her husband's death, 'at least outwardly'. But 'outwardly' was the key word. For a time she found it almost impossible to face its consequences. Her marriage had given her and the children the comfort, the security, and the shelter they needed, and the prospect of life without William was unbearable. Mary expressed well what he had meant to her and the children in 'Happiness'. She had one of the daughters in the story comment:

> Our father, while he lived, had cast a magic over everything for us as well as for her. He held his love up over us like an umbrella and kept off the troubles that afterwards came down on us, pouring cats and dogs!

Everyone was free with advice as to what steps Mary should take to rearrange her life. Put the older girls in a boarding school, she was told, sell the farm, and get comfortably on with your writing. There were even offers of marriage. Three elderly local farmers – bachelors – were interested enough to invite her and the children to come for Sunday lunch. Mary paid no attention to either the advice or the bachelors.

Her major and immediate concern was the welfare of the children. Caroline would be all right with her but something had to be done about the care and education of eleven-year-old Valdi and nine-year-old Elizabeth. Therefore, one of the first steps she took was to send them to Kylemore Abbey, where they would be looked after and where their education could be continued. Elizabeth later referred to it as 'a kind of orphanage'. With the two children safely in Kylemore, Mary gave up. She succumbed to depression and exhaustion. For a time she was in a psychiatric hospital and upon her release was warned by the doctors, manifestly unsure as to how well she could handle life, to seek psychiatric help immediately should there be a recurrence of her depression.

Within little more than a year and with the strength she would display throughout her widowhood, Mary Lavin was back on her feet and ready to fight. During the period of her hospitalization, she had leased the Abbey Farm with the thought of selling later. Her tenants had left the farm in poor condition and there was a great deal of work to be done there. But, as soon as she felt able, she brought Valdi and Elizabeth home from Kylemore Abbey. They loved the farm as she did and they never tired of wandering about the fields. Their favourite spot was at the back of the lawn where their father had built a rock garden shortly before he died.

As Elizabeth looked back on that period, she did not believe that she suffered any of the setbacks one would expect at the death of a father. She thought this was attributable to her being a 'sheltered middle child', between a caring older sister and a baby sister with whom to play. She remembered well, however, that she suffered for her mother.

As good as life in the country was for the children, the question of education for the two older children had to be settled. That meant housing would have to be found in Dublin, at least during the week. Mary settled that problem temporarily by taking advantage of the generosity of friends: the family stayed in hotels. Her daughters' favourite haunts were Fox's Hotel, run by Florrie Fox, a friend of Mary's, where they were allowed to eat in the family dining room rather than in the dining room with the guests; and Buswell's Hotel on Molesworth Street, where they stayed for an extended period. Mrs Duff, who with her husband had established the hotel in the 1920s, was a kind woman with strong intellectual leanings and a soft spot in her heart for writers and artists. She took Mary and the children in, gave them a large room on the third floor – later partitioned off into several small rooms – and, for what was apparently a very modest sum, gave them their meals in the hotel dining room. Noel Duff, the son of the hotel's founders, remembered the children dashing about at mealtimes to the delight of some of the guests and the consternation of others. The children found the sweet trolley particularly attractive.

Very soon the older girls were enrolled in Loreto – the Green, as they called it – as day pupils, and it wasn't too long before Mary was able to find a school for Caroline as well. It took a great deal of persuading but Mary succeeded in getting Caroline into a Montessori school near home before she was four years old. At first the school refused even to consider her because of her age, but Mary persisted. Would they just give the child whatever tests they felt would show whether or not she was qualified? Finally they consented and Caroline passed and was admitted.

Later, when Mary looked back over that period in her life and speculated on how she managed to keep going, she thought Bewley's café on Grafton Street should be listed as one of the reasons for her survival. As she said, she had had awards, Guggenheim fellowships and a *New Yorker* contract, but she felt Bewley's should be listed right up there with the others. Often Mary drove down from Bective in the morning, worked at the National Library until noon, and then went to Bewley's to meet the girls for a late lunch. She would arrive first and take a table, and then the older girls would come in, and finally Caroline. As they arrived, they would be ushered to her table 'like royalty'. The help graciously ignored the pre-empting for hours of a table in the busy restaurant. Mary didn't realize how well known she was at Bewley's until one day when, driving along the road to Madrid with her girls, she stopped to give an English girl and an Irish girl a lift. 'Oh, I know you,' the Irish girl said. 'You were always in Bewley's.'

Unquestionably, the worries engendered by the care of the children, the management of the farm, and the responsibility for her mother's welfare helped Mary to become hardened to a life where she had no one to depend upon but herself. The recognition she was being accorded both at home and abroad helped as well, and it was fortunate that she was already firmly established in her career before William's death. Finally, having survived disaster, she had learned how strong the pull was to write, and had settled down to it. It was in her work that she found her own identity.

Two years after William died, Mary put together another collection: *The Patriot Son and Other Stories*. It was there that 'Scylla and Charybdis', described earlier, made its only appearance. One of the stories in the collection, 'A Tragedy', was always a favourite of Mary's. It is a strong and effective story which deals with the discord between a husband and wife, Tom and Mary. The tragedy from which the story takes its title is a plane crash reported in the local papers. Tom is interested in the technical aspects of the plane crash but impatient with those who dwell on the personal details. Mary tries to view the tragedy as he does but knows that 'left to herself she would have wallowed in the gruesome details'.

One of the sources of contention is Mary's sister, who lives with them. Mary Lavin uses an argument between the sisters effectively to make two telling points. First, through her sister's eyes, Mary can see that she has changed her personality to conform to her husband's standards. She accepts the accusation with this reply: 'That I can't change. Not twice, not back again. For good or bad, I've made myself over into Tom's ways now.' The second point is made when Mary's sister, the victim of an unhappy marriage, indicates in oblique fashion that she would be better off if she had been a victim of the plane crash. When Mary tells her husband that her sister has indirectly indicated that she wishes she were dead, he says bitterly: 'Ask her to tell it to the dead'. . . and see what they will say to her.' And the fictional Mary knows that he is right. 'Not one of them . . . but would fling back, if he could, his mantle of snow and come back to it all: the misunderstandings, the worry, the tension and cross-purposes.' Mary Lavin seemed once again to feel that life was worth living.

In 1957 Lord Dunsany died. Lady Dunsany wrote Mary a brief note. She said only that his heart had stopped after an operation and added, 'You know how much he liked and believed in you.' Earlier that year, after reading the manuscript of 'My Molly', a story which would not appear until 1961, Lord Dunsany had written her to tell her it was 'far above your average and at least as good as your very best'. He liked it so much that he was moved to write a critique of it, though that was seldom done before a story was in print. He had called his critique 'Two Great Writers' and had compared Mary to Evelyn Waugh. As he saw it, Waugh could make a credible story from an impossible plot, while Lavin could make one out of no plot at all. His death was a crushing blow to Mary. It had apparently been quite sudden and had followed too closely upon the heels of her husband's death.

To Mary's great delight, in 1958 the *New Yorker* accepted a short story called 'The Living'. The publication of that story initiated a lengthy and very profitable relationship with the *New Yorker*. In the next ten years, that magazine published eleven of her stories and added considerably to her reputation outside Ireland.

Mary chose 'The Living' again for her 1961 collection, *The Great Wave and Other Stories*, for *Collected Stories* in 1971, and for *The Stories of Mary Lavin, Vol. II*, published in 1974. It is one of several stories concerned with the reactions of children – in this story their reaction to facets of death – and is a fine example of how well she understood their point of view. As a matter of fact, two of her book-length stories are concerned with the world of children: 'A Likely Story' (1957) and 'The Second Best Children in the World' (1972). Of 'A Likely Story', A. A. Kelly, in her critical study of Mary Lavin, states that it is a story that can be enjoyed by adults 'who can still recall the luminous strength of their own childish imagination'. In both stories, as well as in 'Scylla and Charybdis' and many others, Mary proves conclusively her ability to see aspects of life through the eyes of a child.

In the late 1950s Mary felt able financially to rent quarters in Dublin. It would no longer be necessary to rely on the kindness of friends or to commute during the week when the girls were attending school. They settled into the Mespil Flats, near Leeson Street bridge and not too far from Loreto. Mary rented a place there for her mother as well, where she lived until shortly before her death.

Mary's flat was modern, with low ceilings, built-in radiators, and a fireplace: very much like an American flat in the 1940s. Elizabeth has often wondered how much influence the first years of her mother's life, those in the States, had upon her. It seemed significant to her that Mary took one of the Mespil Flats with its American tone. It was not a place, as she said, where you had to put money in the meter. Significantly, the American Embassy often recommended the Mespil Flats to Americans applying to them for suitable places to live.

Elizabeth, near fifteen then, enjoys looking back on that period. She was always delegated to do the shopping in nearby Feeney's Market while her mother was busy writing. She had only to say 'charge it' and then buy whatever food appealed to her at the moment. Even earlier, and certainly later, Mary trusted and relied upon her girls.

Through it all, as her stories and her family testify, Mary's sense of humour never failed her. In 1956, the *Atlantic Monthly* published 'My Vocation'. It is Mary Lavin in a rollicking mood and is Irish to the core. The setting is a lower-class neighbourhood and the narrator a thirteen-year-old girl who has decided she would like to be a nun. She likes the smell of them. When she has to analyse what she means by that, she says it is the 'no-smell' she likes. 'There were so many smells fighting for place in Dorset Street, fried onions, and garbage, and the smell of old rags, that a person with no smell stood out a mile.' Mary captures the dialect to perfection. The young girl is one who enjoys dancing and boys, and the family have a fine time teasing her about her chosen vocation. As her brother says: 'We'll be all right if it isn't the Order of Mary Magdalen that she joins.' He adds that she is 'mad for boys'. What if she does 'feel a bit sparky now and then,' she thinks. 'Wasn't that the kind that always became nuns?' When she learns that she might be sent to work among the lepers, she decides that perhaps she doesn't want to be a nun after all. 'I may as well admit straight out that I wasn't having anything to do with any lepers . . . Did you ever get the feeling that when a thing was mentioned that you *had* it? Well, that was the way I felt.' As the story concludes, she concedes that she still has 'a great regard for nuns even to this day, . . . They're grand women! I'm going to make a point of sending all my kids to school with the nuns anyway, when I have them.'

Mary Lavin's ability to portray humorous situations is apparent in other stories but not in as broad a fashion as in 'My Vocation'. Analysing her humour, the American critic Robert Caswell called 'My Vocation' broadly comic, 'The Small Bequest' and 'My Molly' humorously ironic, and 'Bridal Sheets' grimly humorous. Mary must have been fond of 'My Vocation', because she chose it for her 1956, 1959, 1964 and 1971 collections. It also appeared in *Short Story International* in 1964.

In 1959 Macmillan brought out another collection, called simply *Selected Stories*. By then, Mary's confidence in her ability was fully restored and she felt ready to apply to the Guggenheim Foundation for a fellowship. She was granted a Guggenheim for the year 1959–60 and it was subsequently renewed for the year 1960–61. In an interview years later with Professor Zack Bowen, she talked about what that grant had meant to her and what grants in general could mean to the recipients. With the first grant, she said, she got the lift – the confidence – that one gets from knowing that someone in authority thought your work worthwhile. On the second one, as she remembered it, she had written the whole of 'The Great Wave' – in ten days – and just about the whole of 'In the Middle of the Fields'. Of *Selected Stories* and of Lavin, American literary critic Granville Hicks, in his column in the *Saturday Review of Literature* (13 June 1959), wrote:

> She is close to the simple people about whom she writes. She accepts the meagreness of their lives, respects their pride, feels their triumphs and their tragedies. Grimness and compassion are her character-istic notes. She looks straight down into the depths of human suffering.

Mary's stories continued to be published with great regularity. In 1962 'The Lucky Pair' appeared in the *New Yorker*, and 'The New Gardener' in *Cosmopolitan*. In 1963 'The Tempt-ation' was published in *Country Beautiful*. In 1964 the *New Yorker* carried 'Heart of Gold' and 'The Cuckoo Spit'. They were two excellent choices.

In 'Heart of Gold', Lucy is a middle-aged spinster, jilted years earlier by the only man she really wanted to marry even though, since she was a beautiful young girl, she had many chances. 'She was forever shooing men away like wasps.' The man in question, Sam, married someone else, but he returns to her just as soon as his wife dies. He persuades her to marry him and to go to Dublin to live. On the train going to her new home, Sam talks incessantly of his dead wife. At the thought of how the first wife is going to dominate her life from then on, Lucy is at first frantic and desperate to find a way out of her situation. She longs to 'undo her folly'. But then she grasps from his conversation that his poor first wife, Mona, had just as surely had to live with anecdotes about her. 'Ah, yes, Lucy, your name was a household word with us in the early days of our marriage,' Sam says. She becomes reconciled to her destiny. And, as the story ends, she is more than simply accepting, for she realizes that Sam has been gazing at her and thinking of 'the swains . . . whom in the end he had bested. Little did he ever think he'd do it, he who had nothing to recommend him but his heart of gold.'

'Heart of Gold' is a subtle story in which the narrative takes place both in Lucy's mind and in conversations. Through the inner dialogue Lucy resolves her conflicts and comes to understand Sam. As usual, and despite the ironic tone of the narrative, Mary manages to make the character of Sam sympathetic.

'The Cuckoo Spit' is undoubtedly one of Mary Lavin's best stories. The setting is identical with that of 'In the Middle of the Fields' and the leading character, Vera Traske, a widow for some four years, is clearly drawn from Mary's own life. In 'The Cuckoo Spit', William Walsh's personality, as perceived by Mary Lavin, is drawn more fully than in some of her other widow stories. In one powerful paragraph, Mary Lavin wrote of her fear that, after his death, 'the past would become altered in my mind', and that her husband would emerge as something that he had not been. She suffered when she had to listen to people talking about him – mainly his family, but others as well – because they were 'getting him out of focus' for her. As she saw him:

> he was nearly perfect, guileless. He knew only candour – the kind of person who'd make you doubt the doctrine of original sin! But to listen to his family you'd think he was a man of marble. They diminished him . . . I used to think, immediately, that that was

the way they would speak of him whatever he'd been; the dead are always whitewashed. And he didn't need it.

In several of her stories Mary indicated that her family and friends believed she was attached to the Abbey Farm because of the past. In 'The Cuckoo Spit' she offered a different and, for her, a much more logical explanation. The farm gave her the feeling of security – of stability – she badly needed. Through the dialogue in this story, Mary Lavin gave a good picture too of the stage she had reached in establishing a new life.

The story traces the relationship between the middle-aged Vera Traske and Fergus, a young nephew of a neighbour. When Fergus meets Vera, she is walking about in the darkened fields outside her house. 'This is the first time since my husband died that I've set foot outside the house after dark alone. Except in the car, of course,' she tells him. It is a beautiful night, just such a night as those on which Vera often walked about the fields with her husband. 'You must miss him very much,' Fergus says. 'I suppose the more beautiful it [the night] is, the more lonely it must be for you.' She 'got over the worst of it long ago' she replies; and continues:

> There is, after all, a kind of peace at last when you face up to life's defeats. It's not a question of getting stronger, as people think, or being better able to bear things; it's that you get weaker and stop trying. I think I couldn't bear anything now – even happiness.

As she dwells on that thought later that evening, Vera wonders if the way she feels is because she is getting old. In a good example of one of the moments when such a realization strikes, Mary Lavin wrote: Fergus called her *Mrs* Traske and she experienced 'a ridiculous ache' when he used her surname. She goes over their conversation in her mind. She wonders if she has lost the knack of small talk and thinks that what she said to him about happiness and not being able to bear it is ridiculous. 'Surely he understood that she meant a certain kind of happiness, possible only to the young.' Perhaps, she thinks, when there is no longer any hope of that kind of happiness 'the heart was emptied and ready for the simpler relationships – those without tie, without pain'. She pursues that thought further. 'Would there not always be something purposeless in such attachments?'

The central theme of the story is the possibility of a romance between people of widely divergent ages. Mary Lavin views the conflict from two points of view: one that of Fergus, the other that of Vera. In their discussion of their ages, Vera says that, at least since her husband's death, she is attracted to people younger than herself. 'I was beginning to think,' she says, 'that my heart was like a clock that had stopped at the age he was when he died.' It is as though she is starting her life anew, as though she is trying to get back to the person she was before she married. Fergus grasps at that idea. 'It would explain what I said – that from the first you seemed so young to me. It was because you were making a new beginning.'

It is Vera's contention – contrary to that of Fergus – that a relationship between them is impossible, even if the physical were ruled out and it was only a friendship. 'Friendship is so exacting,' she tells Fergus. It and love can never exist side by side nor can they be substituted for each other. The story ends when, after the separation of a year, they meet again and Fergus acknowledges that she was right. And she says: 'Don't blame me for being right. But isn't it strange that a love that was unrealized should have . . . ' She doesn't finish the sentence but Fergus says, 'Given such joy?' She agrees but, when he leaves, she says quietly, 'And such pain.' It is the right, unsentimental ending.

There was much speculation in literary circles in Ireland

after the appearance of 'The Cuckoo Spit' as to the extent of the autobiographical nature of the story. The general consensus was that it was highly autobiographical. And then the speculation moved on to the identity of the hero. There appear to have been a fair number of candidates.

The twin plagues in Mary Lavin's life as a widow early on were loneliness and fear. The title story in her *In the Middle of the Fields* collection centred around both. As in 'The Cuckoo Spit' and 'Happiness', Mary called her heroine Vera, and the Vera heroines are her most strongly autobiographical characters. It is hard to miss Mary's own reaction to that period shortly after William's death as she describes the reactions of Vera in 'In the Middle of the Fields'.

Vera, a widow, is attempting to keep up the farm where she and her family live. There she misses her husband the least and she is annoyed at the inability of friends and family to understand that. They are sure that every moment she is in the country she is thinking of him and reliving their days together, and apparently they believe that by imposing their own memories upon her they can form some sort of bond. 'What did they know about memory? What was it but another name for dry love and barren longing.' They say dolefully that every time they look out at the fields, they imagine they can see him coming through the trees. And Vera thinks, 'Oh, for God's sake!' The truth of the matter is that every time *she* looks out over the fields she can see that the grass will have to be mowed. She worries about how much it will cost. And then, for just a moment, she manages to forget him and the pain eases. 'Anxieties by day, and cares, and at night vague nameless fears, those were the stones across the mouth of the tomb.'

When night falls, Vera locks herself in her upstairs bedroom, which connects with the room in which her children sleep. She prays that nothing will necessitate her going downstairs. A neighbour is arranging for someone to come and plough the fields and she tells him that the farmer he engages must come before dark. He is well aware of her fear and, as a form of therapy, tells her the story of the man who will be coming to plough for her. The man's first wife died in a tragic accident shortly after having a child. He married his second wife partly because he needed her to take care of his son but their marriage is a happy one. Now the man has been able to forget his first wife completely. Mary will be the same, her neighbour tells her. 'Take my word for it. Everything passes in time and is forgotten . . . When the tree falls, how can the shadow stand?'

The man who is to plough comes before dark, as arranged. While they are standing in the darkened hallway talking, he attempts to kiss her and then is filled with tearful remorse. The widow manages to console him by saying that he should not blame himself. He was not really responsible because as he looked at her – a younger woman – he was remembering his first wife whom he has never been able to forget. In consoling him, she convinces herself that she is right. The memories of her dead husband will haunt her always. There will always be 'the dry love and barren longing'.

The desperation of widowhood is captured to perfection in many of Mary Lavin's stories. 'In a Café', 'In the Middle of the Fields' and 'The Cuckoo Spit' are prime examples. The main character in 'In a Café', named Mary, is a widow who has come up to Dublin from her farm in County Meath to meet a friend, recently widowed. The café where they are to meet is one she frequented often: chosen, she realizes, because it is one where she has never been with her husband. She is striving desperately to recapture at least to some degree 'the identity she lost willingly in marriage, but lost doubly, and unwillingly, in widowhood'. In just a few lines, Mary Lavin sums up with accuracy and wit the reactions of the bereaved to expressions of sympathy. She lists replies the widow would dearly have loved to make.

Them: Time is a great healer.

Her: Thief would be more like: taking away even my memory of him.

Them: God's ways are wonderful. Some day you'll see His plan in all this.

Her: Do you mean some day I'll be glad he's dead?

As the fictional Mary waits for her friend, she is so filled with dislike for being coupled with someone else in this state of widowhood that she wishes she had never come. She begins, almost resentfully, to try to imagine all the ways in which their situations are dissimilar. Her friend was married only a year – such a short time. She has only one child and that child is being taken care of by her parents. She is as free as a girl. And when, finally, her friend arrives, Mary notes other disparities: her youth, her beauty, her almost 'virginal' quality.

While she is waiting, she becomes aware of the presence of the only other patron in the café. A brief conversation with him reveals that he is a foreigner, an artist, and lonely: a loneliness that they share. He talks of his work and invites her to come to his flat. After she and her friend part, she makes an attempt to visit him, telling herself that it is because of her interest in art, all the while knowing that she is going because she wants his companionship. When, upon reaching the door of his flat, she turns away, she is faced with the realisation that it is her husband she is trying to recapture. She is at last able to come to terms with her situation. She is lonely, she will continue to long for her dead husband, she will make her own life, and she must manage it as others have had to do and have done. And, of course, as the non-fictional Mary did. She was now well into the widowhood period of her life – a period which would turn out to be her most profitable and, in many ways, her strongest and perhaps her happiest.

The authenticity of detail in 'In a Café' and its auto-biographical nature are bolstered by Elizabeth Walsh Peavoy's preamble to a 1995 collection of Mary's stories called *In a Café*. The actual café was in South King Street in Dublin and was called the Clog, she wrote. She had the impression that it did not remain in business for very long. The area in which the Clog was situated was the Greenwich Village – the *rive gauche* – of Dublin. As she described the area, it was one 'where delicatessens existed side by side with a drayhorse van, delivering laundry or pigeon manure. The view is one of small backstreet cafés, the canal-side wharf, of houses and huckster shops where destruction abounds, so as to make it a hive of energy or pain.' And she added: 'Mary's inventive description of bohemian Dublin is new and exciting, coming from the pen of a convent-educated inhabitant of the Leeson Street complex.'

In the late 1950s Mary was invited to spend three months at Yaddo, the artists' colony in Saratoga Springs, New York. Invitations to Yaddo were eagerly sought and difficult to obtain. It was an excellent place for a writer to have free room and board in beautiful surroundings with enjoyable companions, and be given every opportunity to work in peace and quiet. But Mary turned it down. Her reason, she told the journalist Eleanor Gay, was that she was too tired to attempt any extended work at that time. 'For the past three years I've worked so hard that I feel the need to relax.' She was going to France and Germany to visit friends, she said. That trip to France and Germany, according to Gay, was to be made on her own. Plans were made for the care of the children and the farm and her itinerary carefully planned. At the last minute, all plans were changed and she took the children with her. As she proved time and time again, she did not want to be away from the children for any considerable length of time. Being with them was for her a source of delight, a source of healing.

Elizabeth and Valdi remember that trip well and Elizabeth talked of it with the journalist Patricia Deevy, as reported in the *Sunday Independent*, 28 May 1995:

We went on a crazy mad trip to France because somebody said we should go back to the same place where we had been with William the year before, to Saint Briac in Brittany – the same holiday, in the same house, except without him. Mother nearly lost her mind over there. The grief must have been appalling.

Elizabeth went on to say that Mary had been so distraught that she mislaid their passports and, as Elizabeth remembers it, could barely force herself to board the plane for the trip home. As a matter of fact, it was the last time that Mary ever flew.

Their mother had been a constant worry for Mary's girls after their father died and they would not have been surprised if she had been unable to survive. They hated to let her out of their sight and when at the farm, deeply troubled and seeking to forget, she went for long walks along the banks of the Boyne, they followed after her. In France, when she went walking on the cliffs they clung to her skirts to keep her from going too near the edge. She liked going to swim at night after the coast guard had gone and after the children were in bed. On those nights they would leave their beds and watch at the window as she ran down to the water and started to swim. If they lost sight of her for a moment, they were panic-stricken. Only when they saw her strike out for shore could they go back to bed and to sleep.

But, Elizabeth reported with pride, they were overly worried. Mary had managed to take care of her home responsibilities, to follow a career, and to fulfil 'the social and professional demands of being a leading light in the Irish literary community'. As she said, her mother endeavoured to stay on top. 'Not just intellectually – because that was a natural thing – but physically.' She cooked good meals and she dressed the children well.

All trips, and there were many after her husband's death, had to be taken with an eye to cost and were made whenever there was a windfall. From the time they were very young, Mary's daughters learned that when their mother got a cheque from a publisher or received grant money, they could start packing. The family often went on camping trips, and, in the *Evening Press* interview in 1963, Mary said they had camped in Italy, Germany, France, Greece, and Turkey. 'Actually Turkey was an accident,' she said. They were on their way to Greece but took a wrong turn. 'We only found out when we had gone 150 miles so we decided we might as well go on to Istanbul.'

In 1959, when Mary received the first payment on her Guggenheim grant, she felt wealthy enough to pack up, gather the children around her and head for Italy. She wanted them to see Florence where she and their father had had a glorious holiday. That trip to Florence gave her the inspiration for two more stories of early widowhood: 'Villa Violetta' and 'Trastevere'.

According to Elizabeth, 'Villa Violetta' describes that trip to Florence quite accurately, and since in 1959 Valdi was sixteen, Elizabeth fourteen, and Caroline six, the autobiographical nature of the story is quite obvious. The heroine, Vera, is a widow with three children, one of them very young, the other two teenagers. The mother is in Italy on a grant. She is attempting to recapture the beauty of an earlier trip with her husband.

More than half of 'Villa Violetta' is concerned with the trials and tribulations of a woman alone in a foreign country, with very little knowledge of the language, and an inability to cope in new surroundings. 'I made a mess of the trip,' Mary Lavin said in an interview much later. She had been insufficiently organized, no reservations made in advance, and no thought given to the need for schools for the children, she said. She did look at schools after they settled in at a small, expensive hotel. 'The little nuns would rush out and say "Oh, the darling children, we'll take them in."' But then Mary could not bear to leave them.

109

The Italian trip did much to cement the relationship between Mary and her daughters – her Three Graces, as she called them. It did much to further their maturity as well. It took no time at all for the children to pick up the language but Mary, though she had studied Italian for six months before leaving Dublin, was unsuccessful. Indeed, the children seemed to be able to manage better than their mother all the way along the line. Apparently their ability to cope had its effect upon them because, according to Mary, 'they raised hell in Italy'. She couldn't understand it. They were really very good at home, she maintained. As the mother in another Lavin story, 'Happiness', comments:

> You were really very good children in general. Other-wise I would never have put so much effort into rearing you, because I wasn't a bit maternal. You brought out the best in me. I put an unnatural effort into you, of course, because I was taking my standards from your father, forgetting that his might not have remained so inflexible if he had lived to middle age and was beset by life, like other parents.

For her three daughters, the Florence trip was far from 'a mess'. It was fun and excitement from the day they left home. They drove about in a broken-down sports car that lacked most of the necessary accessories. To signal a turning, Mary had to stick her hand out. There were no windshield wipers and in rainy weather Mary had to get out from time to time and wipe the windshield with her sleeve. The horn was temperamental and sometimes would refuse to sound at all. On those occasions Mary, if annoyed enough at another driver, would simply roll down the window and shout. The children found that enchanting.

Her mother, Elizabeth said, adored the words of the song they would yell as they drove around the *corniches* and rounded the gulf of Spezzia: 'Just what makes that silly old ant think he'll move a rubber tree plant.' She enjoyed the song most of all when the children would make up words to suit whatever predicament they were in at the moment. And the predicaments were many.

Rome, where they spent some time as well, proved to be as thrilling for the children as Florence. In Rome, Mary renewed her acquaintanceship with Desmond O'Grady, a poet and a professor of English at the American University there. O'Grady was one of a group called the Rome Poets: a group with which Mary Lavin could identify. Like her, they had no desire to be considered academics. Academia was simply a way of surviving. Of these and other frustrated expatriates, Terence Brown wrote:

> They scarcely found the attractions of an insecure, bohemian existence in the pubs of Dublin in the fifties adequate compensation for lack of public appreciation of their real artistic ambitions and of financial support . . . The only future that seemed open to the Irish writer in the late forties and early fifties was penury in his own country or an appeal to the wider public gallery through eccentricity, showmanship and bravado, that would distract both public and writer from the serious business of his art.

O'Grady was also editing the *Trans-Atlantic Review* (not to be confused with an earlier one edited by Ford Madox Ford). Printed in Italy and circulated in New York, the publication had contained some of Mary Lavin's stories. Mary and the girls were happy to take advantage of Desmond O'Grady's offer to squire them about in Rome. It was a tonic for Mary to have another writer on the scene to talk with and she and O'Grady enjoyed each other's company. Their friendship was resumed in the early 1960s when he spent a fair amount of time in Dublin.

Mary's daughters have often said that they got as much

out of their mother's grant money as she did. Disregarding her writing responsibilities, Mary took them through the Vatican Museum in Rome, into the catacombs, and out along the Via Appia Antica. Elizabeth and her mother especially liked walking across the Ponte Vecchio in Florence and hated to turn back to return to their hotel, even though they were exhausted. 'For me these were star-studded glorious times,' Elizabeth said.

The year in Italy ended with Mary Lavin having accomplished very little as far as her writing was concerned. By the end of the year and sure of a Guggenheim renewal, she knew that she would be able to work better in Bective and in Dublin and she was ready to work. She was also ready to go home. As Elizabeth said, 'Despite the richness of foreign travel our mother always seemed to favour that glimpse of the white cliffs of Dover.' But, although she may not have realized it, that year had contributed a great deal towards forming a scar over the wound caused by William Walsh's death.

CHAPTER 5

Mary's decision to return to Ireland to write during the period of her second Guggenheim had been wise. Her work went well both at the Abbey Farm and in Dublin. In 1961 Macmillan published *The Great Wave and Other Stories* in both London and New York, and Mary was awarded the Katherine Mansfield Prize for the title story. 'The Great Wave' had appeared first in the *New Yorker* in June 1959, and was carried again in *The Stories of Mary Lavin, Vol. I* and in her *Collected Stories*.

The story is reminiscent of Synge, as was 'The Green Grave and The Black Grave' written so many years earlier. As the story goes, a bishop is making one of his routine but rare visits – every four years – to the island where he grew up. As the boat heads for the island, the bishop reflects on his life there as a young lad and the tragedy that befell the island. Those reflections become a story within a story. Mary Lavin never lived in an area such as the one in which the story is set but she conveys the island's dialect and depicts the simple life of the islanders in truly impressive fashion.

The *Great Wave* collection deserved all the attention it received, and the title story the award it won. Orville Prescott in the *New York Times* – 2 August 1961 – wrote: 'Even when she is most aware of the weaknesses and sinfulness of mankind, Miss Lavin always seems to accept and expect such human failings rather than to be angry with them.' Padraic Colum in the *Saturday Review* – 12 August 1961 – praised 'her sense of humour, her strong sense of locality, a just perception of character. She has something too that probably belongs to her femininity – a subtlety of discernment with regard to relationships.' Muriel Spark in the *Observer* – 17 December 1961 – called the collection 'Mary Lavin's lovely, and I think undervalued, collection of stories'.

And Mary McCrory in the *Washington Star* wrote: 'Not even Frank O'Connor has looked deeper into the Irish heart, at its balkiness at love, its acceptance of death.'

In the course of a question and answer session with a group of students at Merrimack College in Andover, Massachusetts, on 10 May 1967, Mary was asked about the genesis of 'The Great Wave', and also her own opinion of it. The story was based on a tale told to her by the Irish writer Michael McLaverty, she said. She did not like it as much as some of her other stories, even though it had been so well received and had won prizes. She found it difficult to say why this was so. Perhaps, she said, because there was 'a certain amount of invention in it', and also because she had written it so rapidly. Her usual pattern was to take several months to finish a story and she would work on three and four at the same time. With the 'Great Wave', however, she had concentrated on it almost exclusively: it took approximately twenty-four working hours over a period of four days. She would write until she couldn't write any more, go home, do whatever had to be done, and next day go right back to work on the story.

'When I read about the bishop with his regal robes,' one of the questioners said, 'he seemed very pompous.' But upon reflection, 'he seemed to become purely a human person'. She went on to say that she had been surprised that an Irish writer could take as modern a theological view as Mary Lavin had. Her comment intrigued Mary. She had indeed meant the bishop to be seen as truly human, kind and good, she told the student, and she assured her audience that in Ireland – and in other places as well – there were an increasing number of both clergy and laity who were sound, forward-looking theologians.

It had taken courage and a kind of inner dynamism for Mary to get a grip on life after William Walsh died. But, fortunately, she had not had to go it entirely alone. At the farm, neighbours did all they could to help out. As Caroline

114

Walsh, Mary's youngest, wrote in an *Irish Times* article in the 1970s, 'Thistles would be cut and no bill sent or maybe a bush stuck into a gap in the hedge where otherwise cattle would have got out.' When, upon occasion, Mary hired help, she knew that she would not have to worry about being overcharged. Her neighbours were not only kindly: they were an honest lot. Once Mary had found a ten-pound note on the floor of a village shop and had turned it over to the proprietor. He would put a note in the window, he said. Two weeks later the money was returned to Mary. No one had claimed it, she was told, and 'finders keepers'.

Above all else, however, there was one very strong helping hand: that of her college friend, Michael Scott. In 1934, when Michael had said goodbye to Mary, he had gone on with his studies for the priesthood at the Imperial University of Innsbruck, Austria. There, according to his diary, he had had 'three very happy years'. Before leaving Innsbruck, he had been told by the Rector that he had 'got through' his exams. 'Great,' he wrote. 'So Innsbruck is over. Home for the summer in Ireland, and then theology in Heythrop College, Oxford.'

It was that summer when, if family legend is accurate, Tom Lavin, who was fond of the young seminarian, went so far as to suggest to Michael that he take off that dog collar he was wearing and marry Mary. It appears that Michael Scott had seriously considered doing just that. As Mary told her daughters later, the night before he was to take his final vows he phoned her. 'I am going back home tomorrow to be "professed",' he is reported to have said. 'Or am I?' And Mary had replied: 'Why, of course you are. What else have you been working towards all these years.' Perhaps she was not clear as to what he was asking but she always maintained that she had felt that it was right for him to 'go forward' and for her to encourage him to do so. If that is so, it is understandable. She was, after all, a young convent-educated Irishwoman. The story may have been embellished somewhat over the years but Michael's love for Mary from their college days is beyond question.

In 1940, with his theological studies at Heythrop behind him, Michael was ordained and assumed his duties as a teacher at the Preparatory College for St Ignatius College in Sydney where in the late 1940s he was promoted to Headmaster. From Sydney he went on to Aquinas College, Adelaide, and during the 1950s he served as Vice-Rector there and, subsequently, Rector. The honours awarded him during his years at Aquinas College are impressive. He was Chairman of the University Union and Chairman of the South Australia Branch of the Australian College of Education, as well as a member of the Advisory Committee of Federal Government on Religious Broadcasting.

In late 1961 Michael became Rector of Newman College, University of Melbourne. Although his background was in mathematics, physics, philosophy and theology, he had always had an abiding interest in church architecture and before long had made a name for himself in the field of religious art. He was instrumental in the founding of the Blake Prize for Religious Art, a prize that represented 'the most significant attempt in Australia to bring modern art into contact with the Church'. According to an illustrated catalogue compiled by Christopher Marshall for the Newman College Collection of Art and issued by that college, he was 'responsible for the acquisition of the majority of the works of quality in the collection'. The catalogue described him as 'An engaging and urbane man, who has the ability to move with ease between different social groups . . . ' A background of eleven years of study in Europe had enabled Scott to develop a deep interest in the arts. He used this knowledge to interpret modern art to the Church and the Church to artists, a complex role which, at times, led him to what seemed like the no-man's land between the two worlds.

Reproduced in the catalogue is a portrait of Michael Scott, painted in 1967 by his friend, the artist Clifton Pugh.

In the 1970s the portrait was purchased from the artist by a friend and presented to Newman College where it hangs in the dining room to the immediate left of the High Table.

Not long after the death of William Walsh, Michael Scott and Mary resumed their friendship. It was the subject of conversation among family and friends, and they did not hesitate to take the matter up with Mary as well. 'A Jesuit priest – what do you want with him?' And then: 'Oh, he's your spiritual adviser.' The truth of the matter was that, even though Fr Scott was in Australia, Mary grew to depend upon him for a great deal more than spiritual comfort. He advised her on financial matters and even offered advice concerned with raising her family.

It was not only among Mary's family and friends in Ireland that the Lavin-Scott affair was being discussed. Lengthy conversations were transpiring in Australia between Michael Scott and his devoted friend, Dr Robert S. Gillen, a psychiatrist. When Robert Gillen was a student of psychoanalysis in the late 1950s, as part of his training he had to fly from Adelaide to Melbourne once a week for the supervision of his work. He would visit Michael Scott at Newman College, have dinner with him, and on occasion stay the night before flying home. Scottie, as Robert Gillen called him, would often greet him with 'Well, old boy, it's an ill wind that blows from the bogs today.' It was then that they would 'yarn and decipher the latest blast from the bogs', written in Mary's almost undecipherable handwriting, and attempt to ascertain what was upsetting her or 'why one of the young women of Bective had her knickers in a knot'. In 1958, when Robert Gillen was interning in London, Michael Scott gave him Mary's telephone number and suggested that he go over to Bective to meet and to visit with her. Years later he wrote to Mary about that visit:

> It wasn't until I was entertained until 3 am one morning by a storyteller, that I realised that what I

117

had thought was fiction was turning out to be fact. Dumb that I was, I hadn't realised that [Michael] had created a link between Mary and himself that would be tested and strained over the years and teach me some essentials about human nature, particularly about the glue that sticks human beings together – no matter how unlikely the match.

During the late 1950s, Fr Scott was awarded a Carnegie Corporation Travel Grant which enabled him to spend three months in the United States, Mexico, and Canada, and four months in Europe. There is every indication that during those periods his path and Mary's crossed occasionally: 'one meeting in America, and the odd dinner in Ireland'. One of those meetings must have been when she took the family to Florence and Rome on her Guggenheim fellowship. In an 1995 interview, Elizabeth said that her mother never mentioned before they left Ireland that there would be such a meeting. 'Mary never actually told us where he appeared from.' But Eliabeth recalled that he had met them when they arrived there – 'a Jesuit priest in full Jesuit armour' – and had taken them to their hotel.

For fifteen years, through letters from Australia and those occasional visits, Fr Scott tried his best to keep Mary's affairs and those of the whole family proceeding smoothly. It was a role as enjoyable for him as it was valuable and a source of stability for them. A scrupulously honest man, he always financed his trips with his scholarship money. That, he said, did not belong to the church. He toed the mark in other respects as well. It seems that when he and Mary went out to dinner they invariably took Valdi along.

From the time Mary and her mother had moved to Dublin from Athenry, the city had always delighted her. In one of her stories, she described spring there. 'Where was it more intoxicating than in the city, the cheeky birds filling the air with song, and green buds breaking out on branches so black with grime it was as if iron bars had sprouted.' Her beat, as the girls called it, was the same as it had been in her youth: Leeson Street, Fitzwilliam Square, and along the canal. It was all easily accessible from the Mespil Flats.

Not very long after William Walsh died, a circle of young, aspiring writers had begun to gather around Mary in her Mespil Flats apartment. Elizabeth remembered the scene. 'They were all sitting about,' she said, 'discussing literature and drinking wine. I thought they were a bit daft. It was like the Dead Poets Society.' Towards the end of the 1950s, it was turning into something of a salon and Mary, tired of apartment living, decided to look for a house.

Crossing a short bridge from the Mespil Flats and running off Leeson Street to the right was a lane which ran down to the canal: Lad Lane. At that time it consisted of a few pieces of derelict property and a few small businesses. During the day it was noisy with the sound of welding and in one courtyard a merchant was dealing in scrap iron. In the evening, however, the lane, with its high walls, was quiet enough to hear the birds in the trees behind the houses.

Lad Lane was where Mary Lavin decided she would like to settle and No. 11, a property which at one time had been attached to a medical centre, seemed promising to her. With a bank loan, she bought it for three hundred pounds. William Walsh's nephew, Michael Walshe Jr, recalled the evening when his father – Mary's brother-in-law – read the news in the paper. 'Do you know what that Mary's done now?' he shouted to his wife. 'She's moved herself and Willie's children into stables.' It wasn't exactly stables, however. Number 11 was a coachhouse with rooms overhead for the coachmen to live in and space downstairs for five or six horses and a carriage.

Mary had taken a courageous step: one of many she took after William Walsh's death. It was certainly one that delighted her daughters. There were lengthy conferences about the renovation: could they have one horse stall apiece to sleep in, they wondered? 'It was very atmospheric,' one of the girls said later.

Not too far from Lad Lane, Sam Stephenson, a young architect, in his early twenties at the time and newly married, had purchased a house on what was essentially an alleyway for one thousand pounds. (In 1996 he estimated that the house would sell for £250,000.) His plan was to convert it into his home. He had difficulty in obtaining a permit to do so, since these places were considered unfit for human habitation. It was probably about 1957 when work on the house started, Sam Stephenson said, and it had been vacant so long that he found a 1932 newspaper on the second floor. (In Mary's place, she found a broken-down wicker cart – apparently one that would be harnessed to a pony – that had just been left there for junk.)

Stephenson's house was the first mews house in Dublin and upon its completion it received a great deal of publicity in the papers. Mary, who had seen the possibilities for 11 Lad Lane at once, knew she needed a good architect, and knew too that Sam Stephenson was the one she wanted. As he tells the story, the first time he saw Mary was when she came around with a friend and knocked on the door of his mews house. She had bought a coachhouse on Lad Lane, she said, wanted to make it habitable, and was impressed with what he had done. He liked her immediately. She knew pretty much what she wanted done and, he said, like every great artist appreciated artistic work. He accepted the assignment and they got along well together.

Mary had striven to maintain the character of the place and she had succeeded. Finally, the floors were put down over the cobbles and the family was ready to move in. The whole effect, when completed, was charming inside and out. The lines were clean and uncluttered. A wooden gate led into a courtyard and the entrance to the house was through a brick archway and a wooden door. On the right of the entrance was a combination dressing room and bathroom. On the left was the kitchen, and beyond that a dining area and sitting room that led to an open patio and the garden. The walls were painted a pristine white. A spiral staircase led to the upper floor where there were two bedrooms. The one in the front contained three beds, the one in the rear – a room with a fireplace – was Mary's.

Two desks were made especially for the sitting room in their new home – called the Mews – and placed one on either side of a stove from which the heat rose to the bedrooms upstairs. Book shelves on one side of that room housed Mary's collection of books: Irish folk tales, her college texts, Jane Austen, and a large collection of critical works.

Sam Stephenson had been unhappy with the high ceiling and the bare beams in the sitting area and had installed a false, low ceiling. A hanging lamp, suspended from this false ceiling and a round table beneath it, formed a good conversation area and often Frank O'Connor, Tom Kilroy, Valdi, Mary and others could be seen grouped around that table deep in discussion.

The importance of beauty in furnishing both the Mews and the Abbey Farm reflected Mary's exposure to the Bird dwellings and Dunsany Castle, as well as an innate feeling for the beauty of nature. Her girls often mentioned that she and William Walsh had bought Jack Yeats paintings before they had four chairs to sit on. Marion Fitzgerald, a journalist interviewing Mary for the *Evening Press* a few years after the family had settled in, called it 'a delightful Mews, which had been converted from a stable into a warm, wood-panelled, welcoming home'. The back garden, she wrote, had been transformed into 'a pocket of cool green'. It was like being out of the city. And when, in 1977, the writer Bonnie Kime Scott visited the Mews, she was impressed by its charm. 'At the entrance, in order to keep a large dog out of the house, there was a space heater, a dog bed, and some sleds.' She was greeted by Mary, in a 'well-worn grey skirt and blouse', who gave her a tour of the house. She also, upon learning that her visitor had a cold, gave her advice on how to treat it.

Mary had carried out a black and white motif with black drapes that made an effective dark background for the greenery outside. She commented to her visitor that her selection of black probably confirmed some people's opinion that she was 'preoccupied with death'. That was not wholly a misconception. Among her papers is one of her poems which is dated 22 February 1941 and titled 'Death'. It is remarkable that it was written by one so young.

When I pass unto my place
In the gallery of the dead
And press my face against
The grey gape glass
To see the end of man's parade
Proudly marching past
No trace of a gap where I fell out
I will see my written work
Tougher and far more
persistent than bone.
Perhaps a lyric will make its way
In and out among the years
To line sanctuary of library space
Pressed between straightened shelves
The yellow pages lost to life

Other lines may serve as wrappings
For fish hawkers in the market
And a poem on hand made vellum
Be slit to tissue by the silver scales
But the bulk of my work will live
Under dust covering
In a second hand shop
until raised to life

And winging its way out from
Tolerance of times passed
Then these eyes behind gaping plate glass
Can forget to look out
And finally to glaze your mistletoe tears
With frost on the rigid fields of earth
When I who living watch the post
In fear of the rejection slip
And telegram Tara to announce
Each success, watch while they
Who turn out desks of the dead,
Keep the birth and the marriage cert.
Letters from abroad, the manuscript
But throw away things I valued most
The faded sash
A cracked acorn
A piece of taffeta.

On view in the portrait hall of the Royal Dublin Society is a bronze head of Mary Lavin, by the sculptor Marjorie Fitzgibbon. The sculptor had succeeded in portraying in the head both the sweetness and the strength in Mary's face. But what Mary saw was 'a shadow of death in that hunk of bronze'.

With the advent of the Mews, Mary now had the perfect setting for her ever-widening group of young artists: for her salon. Where, one of her daughters wondered, did her mother get the idea and develop the desire for such a salon? Possibly, she thought, on her trips to the States and to France, where she saw such groups, often part of an academic community. Because there were none such in Dublin, she had to create one. The salon was bohemian but the 'right' kind of bohemian, according to Mary's daughter Elizabeth. 'Artistic, but correct. The guests couldn't be run down at the heel. They had to be chic.' Years later and reminiscing, Elizabeth described 1960s bohemian chic: 'a sweep of hair, scarf, cloth, and those "good" shoes Mary always bought us'. Sure that they were carrying out well the order of the day, Valdi and Elizabeth wore 'imported blue jeans and the shirts from the US', sent to them by Mary's publishers. 'Nobody had yet invented this casual dress in Ireland,' Elizabeth said. 'They also sent us chewing gum, maple syrup, and on one occasion a case of Boston baked beans.'

It was open house at the Mews. No one needed an invitation to visit. They felt free to call and they were always welcome and generally fed. It was the only place they could gather and talk endlessly. If writing was only one facet of Mary's life, as she considered it, conversation with these young writers was another: and a very time-consuming one.

The Mews became the centre of the lives of young people such as Tom Kilroy, Tom MacIntyre, Desmond Hogan and Augustine (Gus) Martin, among others. In a 1995 radio interview, Elizabeth said that the writer John McGahern had come to the Mews as well, when, according to her, he had not yet written a line. An extremely shy young man, he had not stayed very long. Elizabeth joked about that. 'We're still waiting for him to come back,' she said. When the interrogator laughingly asked if she thought that perhaps young McGahern found the company too intimidating, Elizabeth replied: 'I think so. The literati. Perhaps he couldn't stand the pressure of the other young men.' But she knew that Mary would have been kind to McGahern, as she was to all the young people.

What drew these young intellectuals – aspiring writers and artists – was Mary's personality and her keen interest in others. It was this genuine interest in the person with whom she was in conversation that made her irresistible. She made people feel that it was their work that was of the utmost importance, not hers. She gave the impression that, for her, writing was something to fit in between talk, fun, friendship, and the children. Undoubtedly, part of the interest Mary displayed in what her guests were doing and thinking was a writer's curiosity. Consciously or unconsciously she was always gathering material for her stories.

Another not inconsiderable attraction for those in her circle was the possibility that they might meet older, successful writers who would be not only interesting but helpful in furthering their careers as well. It might be Frank O'Connor, Sean O'Faolain, or Padraic Colum. On one occasion the poet and novelist Patrick Kavanagh, then in his sixties and not well, came to dinner. Elizabeth recalls that 'Paddy fell asleep on one of Mary's *avant garde* tweed entwined sofas.' They never knew who would be there. As a matter of fact, Frank O'Connor was a frequent visitor. He lived just around the corner from the Mews and was Mary's good friend, and she was fond of his American wife Harriet as well. Mary relied upon him for his opinion of her work and even for his help in the raising of her girls.

Tom Kilroy and Tom MacIntyre had joined Mary's circle in the late 1950s: before the days of the Mews and when both were in their early twenties. The first time Tom Kilroy had seen Mary was when she appeared before the English Society of UCD at Newman House to read from her works. He had been charmed by the appearance of this young widow, dressed in black, with her black hair pulled back in a bun, and with eyes 'bright as buttons'. He had been struck as well by her descriptive powers: by the freshness with which she described flowers. With the audacity of youth, he phoned her at the Abbey Farm, told her of his interest in writing, and asked if he might come to visit and perhaps bring his friend Tom MacIntyre. Of course Mary said yes. It was the beginning of a life-long friendship.

Very many years later, he told the story of his meeting with Mary and of her influence upon his life in the Foreword to a collection of her stories, *In a Café*. It was published in 1995 and was the last collection issued in Mary's lifetime. As he wrote, his friendship with her had given him 'an education in books'. He still had the copy she had given him of Tolstoy's *The Kreutzer Sonata*, 'still in its old yellow World's Classics wrappers, with its inscription: from Mary, May 1960. This, she had told me, was a story that had profoundly influenced her when she had first started to write.' She had also given him copies of Turgenev's books and of Flaubert's *Trois Contes*. Those, much to his regret, he no longer had: 'all lost in the migrations and the borrowings'. But he could remember 'how she talked about the death of poor Félicité in *"Un Coeur Simple"* and the great parrot in the half-open heavens above her head'.

Tom MacIntyre's first visit to the Abbey Farm may not have been with his friend Tom Kilroy. He recalled that as a young man, living in Cavan and just starting to write, he had asked to come to see her in Bective. She had invited him to call one summer evening. It was, he said, a 'charged' evening. 'She had style, she was giving, she was a writer.' He summed up what that evening and what Mary had meant to him this way. 'She pointed me to the magic abroad – and the magic at home.' And he added: 'You couldn't ask for more, could you?'

One young American writer who gravitated towards Mary in the early Mews days and on whom she made an indelible impression was Elizabeth Cullinan. She was just embarking upon her career as a short story writer and her introduction to Mary was by way of a note from the *New Yorker*. She had come to Dublin in 1960 and had remained until 1963. She hated to leave it then, she said, and undoubtedly one of the reasons for her reluctance was her association with Mary, her family, and her friends. 'I haunted the Mews in those days, and must have been a great nuisance.' Her visits were not limited to the Mews, however. On several occasions she spent time at the Abbey Farm and she visited with Nora Lavin in the Mespil Flats as well. She was impressed by Nora's ability as a story teller and also by Mary's attentiveness to her mother. To visit the Mews and the Abbey Farm was for her like going into a world teeming with life and with interesting people: outside and yet part of the modern world. She found Mary to be compassionate and with a keen understanding of human nature and a great love of people. She was impressed too by the bond between Mary and her children: children who were unusually generous and straightforward, she thought. She had never known a family quite like them.

Elizabeth Cullinan's memories of that period in her life are long-lasting and Mary's influence upon her work considerable. When, after Mary's death, she was asked by the *Irish Literary Supplement* to contribute some of her impressions to a tribute to Mary, she turned to a collection of her short stories, published in 1971, *The Time of Adam*. One of the stories in that collection, 'Maura's Friends', had been written after a visit to the Abbey Farm. Reading it over, she could see that it came as close to what it had been like to know Mary 'as anything I might hope to arrive at in retrospect'. The character Maura is, according to Cullinan, based on Mary, and the children on Valdi and Elizabeth.

To illustrate what she saw as Mary's 'attachment to and faith in the places of her life', especially the Abbey Farm, Cullinan quoted the character Maura: '"Come to the farm," she was always saying, offering it the way you'd offer a load of flowers or fruit, the way you'd ask someone to sit down to a wonderful meal.'

Cullinan had sensed a sadness at the heart of Mary's life then, along with the tactics she used against it. She had Maura say:

What it sometimes seemed she was trying to do was bring enough people and bring them often enough so that these rooms that had been planned with so much love would be what they were meant to be or, at least, might not to such a devastating degree be what no room was meant to be, wasted.

Tom Lavin in Boston, *c.* 1910

Two of the Mahon boys:
Mary Lavin's Uncle Leo
(left) and her Uncle
Vinnie

Mary Lavin
at eighteen months

(Standing) Grandpa Mahon holding little Mary and Kathleen Mahon; (seated) Grandma Mahon, Queenie and Nora, Mary Lavin's mother

Tom Lavin and Mary at Bective, *c.* 1926

Lord Dunsany at his desk in the drawing-room at Dunsany Castle

Tom Lavin, the proud grandfather, holding Valdi, 1944

Mary's girls in 1953: (from left) Elizabeth (8), Caroline (1) and Valdi (10)

She reached up with both hands to the waves at either side of her forehead – white wings that were a striking effect since the rest of her hair was still dark. But [her] really striking feature was her eyes, their expression, which was of someone passionately critical but passionately fair as well.

And Cullinan added in her tribute, 'Mary Lavin's face was, in fact, beautifully expressive of her whole nature, which was shrewd, generous, vigorous and fragile, querulous and kind and, above all, welcoming.'

'Maura's Friends' ended with what Cullinan believed was the conclusion Mary Lavin arrived at about those people she gathered around her. As she had Maura say, 'there was no one in the room she'd have wanted not to be there, no one she didn't feel warmly towards and wasn't ready and willing to take trouble over'.

There is another paragraph in the story which must be noted as well. Of Maura, Cullinan wrote: 'People who can bring their skill and talent to bear on life itself become a focus for other people, and those with great skill and great talent run the risk (unless they accept their own and the others' limitations) of also becoming the victim of their gifts.'

It was not just in Cullinan's 'Maura's Friends' that Mary Lavin appeared. In her novel *A Change of Scene* Mary Lavin is portrayed as the novelist Oona Ross. When the heroine tells Oona that she is twenty-six, Oona says: 'Twenty-six is when you begin not to know how young you are.' And when Oona speaks, 'the effect was of someone choosing at random among any number of interesting and suitable ideas'. As Cullinan describes her, 'She always made you feel that whatever was wrong wasn't a catastrophe – certainly nothing that couldn't be improved by a cup of tea, a long walk, and a conversation.'

Cullinan has a good description of the Mews in *A Change of Scene*. 'The carriage house had aspects of both cave and castle – walls whitewashed brick, furniture antique, chairs upholstered in Irish tweed.' And further: 'Of the three bedrooms, the largest was like a dormitory with trios of beds, desks and wardrobes. Oona's room was small but it had a fireplace and the embers of a perpetual turf fire gave the air there its sweet, burnt smell.'

In that novel also, she has what would appear to be an astute characterization of Mary's mother and her attitude towards her daughter. She has Oona's mother saying to a visitor: 'Oona's gone off to the shop for biscuits. Here we were about to have tea, and not a biscuit in the house. I can't think what's taken her so long. She's gone twenty minutes when she shouldn't have been two.' And later: 'When James died, Oona could have taught at university but of course she wouldn't. I've always thought she'd be far better off teaching than the way she is now, but no one can tell Oona anything. She always acted as she pleased, though I don't know what good it's ever done her.' When she is offered a plate of chocolate biscuits, she says: 'You didn't get any plain ones, did you, Oona? The chocolate always sticks to the roof of my mouth. I don't suppose you remembered.' And about her grandchildren: 'Where are the girls? Ah well, I don't suppose they can be expected to wait and see their grandmother.' As Cullinan has Oona Ross say at one time, 'My father once told me, look after your mother but look out for her too.'

Cullinan describes her first impression of the Abbey Farm in Oona's words:

As I stepped across the threshold I knew I'd never seen anything like that house and probably never would again. It was small but on a grand scale, and everything had been arranged with a thorough understanding of both delight and comfort. Remembering it now, I see the pleasing play of light and shadow which looked, and in a way was, built in − the house was cleverly windowed.

Her description of the drawing room reads: 'The rear windows framed fields where there were sheep and cattle, on the far left a small woods, and straight ahead in the near distance the ruined spread of a monastery.' She suddenly knew, she writes, the meaning of the word 'bucolic'.

Cullinan's contribution to 'A Bouquet for Mary', the *Irish Literary Supplement*'s tribute to Mary, ends: 'These many years later I can still scarcely believe the good fortune that landed me in that room with her.' Mary Lavin valued her friendship with Elizabeth Cullinan, which was life-long.

Another American whom Mary spent a great deal of time with during those days in the Mews was Anne Francis Cavanaugh. She also wrote movingly about the early days of their friendship in 'A Bouquet for Mary'. As she recounts, at the time of their meeting, in the autumn of 1965, Anne Francis was a nun in the Sisters of Mercy Order, working for her PhD in Anglo-Irish literature at UCD. One day, wearing the Mercy habit and working at her desk in the National Library, she noticed Mary Lavin, already well known in those days, sitting near her. 'I do not wish to meet her, by her stories I know she is anticlerical,' she thought.

It was Mary who spoke to her first. She came over to the nun and said that she believed they had a friend in common: Fr Frank Phelan, an American priest on leave in Dublin from Notre Dame to write his dissertation on Yeats. From then on, the conversation continued at such a great rate that the librarian had to intervene. Mary made her usual suggestion: 'Let's go for a coffee.' After that, when Mary was tired of writing and the nun tired of working on her thesis, they took long walks: to the Mews, to Sister Anne's lodgings, or to Bewley's for tea.

The day Mary finished writing 'Happiness', she came to Sister Anne's desk and asked her to go for tea so that she might read the story to her. 'It was Mary's own story,' Anne Francis wrote.

I knew her three beautiful daughters and their growing up struggles; I knew her mother, 'Miss Imperious', and Mary's every evening, no matter what, visit to say goodnight. I understood her life-long love and friendship for Fr Michael Scott and her ongoing conflict about resolution. But I was unprepared for the theme of happiness and death.

Anne Francis quoted from the story. 'Happiness drives out pain, as fire burns out fire. Isn't it more important than ever to be happy when you're dying,' Mary had written.

One day when they were walking from the Shelbourne Hotel along the iron fence which blocked off St Stephen's Green from the street, they noticed 'the fresh young faces of seminarian cyclists moving two by two away from the University to their religious houses'. When they got to the corner of Leeson Street, Anne Francis wrote, they met a friend of hers, Fr Ciaran Ryan. She was delighted to introduce her two friends. They chatted and, as Fr Ryan left them, 'her eyes wistful, Mary said vehemently, "Holy Mother the Church gets the best of the litter; the runts breed."'

One of the topics they discussed on their strolls was money or rather, as Anne Francis wrote, the lack of it. Mary was concerned with keeping her contract with the *New Yorker* alive, getting into other American magazines, and pushing Houghton Mifflin to bring out her collections. One day she was discussing the possibility of going to the States to earn some money by giving readings. Since she would not fly, she was afraid she could not afford the first-class ship fare. Anne Francis suggested that she might consider the Holland-American lines, since they had two classes and she could travel tourist. 'Impossible,' Mary said. 'What if Elizabeth Bowen is on that boat first class!'

One of Anne Francis's memories of those days concerned Mary's clothes. Every day she wore her black Aran jumper, and always the antique silver with amethyst brooch Michael

Scott had given her. When the weather turned cold, Mary had 'dragged out' a well-worn Nellie Mulcahy tweed coat. As she was walking towards the National Library, she passed Nellie Mulcahy's salon. As Mary told her friend, 'Nellie popped out from the salon and cried, "For God's sake, Mary, get in here! I don't want you walking the street in that old rag."' And Mary had added, 'her eyes sparkling with mirth,' Anne Francis noted, "'I'm getting a new coat.'"

Late in 1967 Anne Francis left Dublin and returned to the States, where she resumed her academic career and later 'led her community, the Sisters of Mercy, through the turmoil of the post Vatican II Catholic Church'. She and Mary met from time to time: in Erie, Pennsylvania, or Boston or Washington DC or New York or Cape Cod. Many times they met in Bective or in Dublin. In her tribute, she recorded one further incident concerning Mary and the church. On one of their Dublin meetings, they were standing in front of the American Express office on Grafton Street, where they were joined by Fr Frank Phelan. They were discussing the current upheaval in the church. Mary had turned to him and said 'with passion, "You fellows will always be needed. Everyone needs someone to help them die."' In 1975 Anne Francis left the 'religious life' and married the former Fr Frank Phelan.

In the early 1960s a frequent visitor to the Mews was Nuala O'Faolain, who later became a columnist for *The Irish Times*. Nuala was a student at UCD and had not yet considered writing as a career. It appears that she was welcomed into Mary's circle because she was 'palling around', as she would later put it, with members of Mary's salon. She always looked forward to spending time in the Mews and with Mary. As she said, where else would she have been served spaghetti and red wine?

It was not only conversation, food and wine that Mary gave the young people who visited her. Nuala can be cited as a case in point. Without a loan from Mary, she maintained, she might not have been able to complete her college education. No doubt Mary helped others in the same way and to the best of her ability. In those days Nuala, about eighteen, was typical of many others of her age. As she said, they left home, returned when there was no place else to go, and then left home again. More than once, when Nuala needed her friendship, Mary invited her down to the farm for a holiday with the family. It was a long trip then, although it was a relatively short distance, but it was well worth the time and effort. Bective for her represented peace.

By all accounts of that period, Mary was enjoying her widowhood. Still in her forties, an attractive widow, and already a success, Mary charmed them all. She paid little attention to her appearance. Invariably, she dressed in black and wore her hair parted in the middle with a chignon at the back. As Nuala O'Faolain described her, 'She was always making jabs at her face with a powder puff and a lipstick. You couldn't call it putting on makeup because she never even glanced in a mirror.'

It appears that there was always some young man on hand who was eager to help Mary sort out her problems: the kind of person, according to one of Mary's friends, who would see that she got to a train on time, would go back to get her a magazine, and would take pleasure in every minute of doing it. In the late 1950s and early 1960s, Desmond O'Grady, the young poet with whom Mary and the girls had had such a fine time in Rome, was in Dublin gathering material on Samuel Beckett. He stayed at the Mews and also at the Abbey Farm with the family. At that time, he recalled, Tom Kilroy, Augustine Martin, and Patrick Kavanagh were constant visitors. If the visitors to the Mews were predominantly male, it was because most of the known writers as well as those who had aspirations were men.

It was often difficult to distinguish between the young men who were coming to see her daughters and those who were coming to see her. 'If there was a fight on for Desmond

O'Grady or someone else,' says Elizabeth, 'mother was strong in the running.'

Talk, gossip, the give-and-take of discussions were Mary's relaxation. She was always mindful of the need to be precise in her writing but in these conversations she had to admit that she was fairly unsuccessful. She would make a statement and, before there was time for a reply, she would say that it wasn't exactly right and change it. Tom Kilroy believed that it was the imaginative quality of her mind, plus the fact that it responded to stimulation of any kind, that caused her to move so rapidly from one thought to another. She talked non-stop. Her wit was sharp and often satirical but it was pompous people who were its target, never the weak or the flawed. The wit of others delighted her as well, and she laughed easily and often. An expert mimic, her stories came to life. They never bored anyone although, it has been reported, they sometimes seemed endless. One of her friends observed that, as she went on in a story, the reason for beginning it at all appeared to be lost. Michael Scott's patient 'Come to the point, Mary!' became famous later on.

Another of her great charms was her ability to make even a common occurrence into high drama. Nothing in life, she seemed to feel, was commonplace. One of her friends would meet her walking through St Stephen's Green on her way to the National Library and stop to tell her some fairly trivial incident. 'Good heavens,' Mary would say, 'you're not serious!' And then: 'Oh, God, I've got to go back and finish off another story. I'll see you at five o'clock for a cup of coffee in the Country Shop.' And off she would go. When, at five o'clock, she arrived at the Country Shop, it was as though she had simply gone off to do a bit of housework for she made no reference to the story she was working on. 'You see,' Nuala commented, 'she treated writing exactly the way another woman might treat doing the family wash.' She led you to believe that it was simply a chore that she had to make time for. 'She never referred to it as anything other than ordinary, down-to-earth life.'

This lack of pretension was one of Mary's outstanding qualities. There was nothing of the driven, creative writer about her. The importance to her of her career was never visible though it was certainly there. A perfect illustration is the story of Jack and Joan Cahill: a story Jack Cahill, now a doctor in Phoenix, Arizona, delights in telling. In the late 1950s, he was a student at Trinity College: an American taking pre-medical courses. He and his wife Joan (Jody) occupied one of the Mespil Flats on the floor above Mary. Jody was pregnant and Mary Walsh, as they knew her, befriended the couple and was right there with advice and comfort when they needed her. So far as they were concerned, Mary Walsh was simply a widow with three little girls: good company, and someone they could always turn to.

Five months after the Cahills met Mary, they were in a bookstore and saw a novel called *The House in Clewe Street*. On the cover was a picture of Mary Lavin. Lavin? He and his wife were stunned. As Jack tells the story many years later, he is surprised that at the time he did not wonder at the presence in Mary Walsh's flat of such people as Frank O'Connor and Cyril Cusack.

The Cahills will never forget Mary Lavin – their Mary Walsh.

In the summer between Cahill's first and second year at Trinity, the couple could not afford to go back to the States for the holiday. 'We talked with Mary,' Jack said, 'and somehow she said "Well, Jack, why don't you come to Bective and you can do something like paint walls."' And so they went to Bective and he painted walls. He remembered one night in particular. The children were ready for bed and a storm was brewing. They all sat down and Mary read them one of her stories: he couldn't remember the title. All of a sudden the lights went out and they had to light candles. The lightning was flashing. 'Jesus, Mary, and Joseph, it was scary,' Jack said. The calmest of them all was Mary. She just went on reading.

In 1961 Jack Cahill graduated and prepared to return to the States. It was not until 1978 that the Cahills saw Mary Lavin again. They were on holiday and were staying at the Tara Hotel in Dublin. 'I called her and she answered the phone. I said is this Mary Lavin and she screamed "Jack!" She remembered me after all those years.' Mary came to have lunch with them at the hotel and Jody still recalls being startled when Mary 'lifted up her soup plate and drank out of it'. But, since in her eyes Mary could do no wrong, she added: 'I assumed it was an acceptable Irish or European thing.'

On other occasions Mary took particular note of the amenities. Once, after having a solitary dinner at the Intercontinental Hotel during Michael's travels, she wrote to him that she had watched 'some of the young whiz kids of Irish industry at nearby tables. You've no idea what I saw – the men always took the menu & ordered their own meal – in minute detail – before throwing it on the table in front of their lady friends to struggle with their own order as best they could. (Their best of course was better than the best of the yobs.)'

Although Mary made no great show about her writing, it was beyond question the vital force in her life. But she was always conscious that she was raising a family single-handedly. There was no division between the time she spent on her stories and the time she gave to her children. Elizabeth recalled that, when Valdi was fourteen, her mother often took her along when she attended meetings, leaving Caroline in Elizabeth's care.

Theirs was a close and quite unusual relationship. But then, Mary was no ordinary Irish mother. She was a formidable person and the kind of parent by whom children might be intimidated. But Mary was somehow able to give them a strong sense of their own identity. The girls were treated as equals. In fact, they did not hesitate to advise or reprove her. They had, in an attempt to shelter her, developed something of a practical streak and they urged her, in the interest of time, to be more selective in her invitations to people to visit the Mews or the farm for short or long stays.

Mealtimes were, as Elizabeth said, 'a forum for endless discussions of literature, art, and even life itself'. They discussed and argued about everything: a film they had just seen, university education, camping, anything that came to mind. They never really argued. 'It wasn't that kind of a scene. We were not at odds with her nor she with us.' As Mary often said to them, 'We're all in the same boat.'

Work and family were as bound together as they could possibly be. Mary's girls were never excluded from either the table or her thoughts. She never closed herself away in a studio but wrote in their company. Dishes were pushed aside and she would sit writing at the kitchen table. She called herself a 'one-armed writer'. She was interrupted, she said, twenty times an hour, disorganized, and 'held together with safety-pins'. Often she was not sure whether the manuscript was in the kitchen or under the bed. Yet, so far as her writing was concerned, everything was well organized and every detail crystal-clear.

For Mary talking with her girls was a source of constant enjoyment: entertaining and relaxing at the end of a long day's work. Those conversations with her daughters were her main source of entertainment in later years and they went on even with the addition of sons-in-law and grand-children.

All three of her daughters saw their mother as a very down-to-earth person, very much in touch with the realities of everyday life. They tended to forget a good deal of the time that she was a writer and a famous one. They could never forget it completely, however. There were constant reminders: the arrival of publishers and the comments of friends. The girls looked back, as they grew older, on those days in Bective when writers, actors, publishers, and critics came calling. As Elizabeth wrote in a 1985 article in *Inside*

Tribune, 'There were days of floor-polishing, dusting, scuffling the paths, and attempting to tidy Mother's papers.' They believed that Mary expected a great deal of them at mealtimes when there were visitors and they did not want to disappoint her so they joined fearlessly into whatever topic arose. They still like to talk about the time when visitors were expected and the girls were in their school uniforms. Mary made them put their jumpers on backwards because the V-neck was too revealing.

In many areas Mary seemed more like a sister than a mother to her girls. This can be noted in her letters, especially those to Valdi. They are full of what might be called women talk and at times the subject of clothes seemed more important than the readings she was giving in Ireland and abroad. All would be lost if she didn't manage to get those shoes she was looking for. Mary placed a very high premium on 'good' clothes. 'She wears beautiful couture tweeds in a "put them on and forget them" manner,' one interviewer wrote in the *Sunday Press*. Valdi had had a 'year-long feud' with her mother about Mary's unwillingness to wear Dunnes Stores cashmere sweaters, which sold for twenty-seven pounds as against ninety elsewhere. Valdi 'cited the old cant, you can't tell the difference,' Mary told Elizabeth.

Although Mary was, by her own admission, not particularly musical, she took the girls to many first-night performances of the Dublin Grand Opera Society. To their great delight, Mary bought each of them an evening gown, and they sat in the front seats of the dress circle in their party dresses, viewing performances of Verdi and Puccini operas. Mary always preferred a tragic opera, Elizabeth said. She would book a table in the coffee room 'with its funny, old-fashioned little wicker chairs', and sit there with her family during the intervals in preference to meeting friends and admirers in the cocktail lounge.

Occasionally they attended the opera in London as well. Then there was always a visit to Fortnum and Mason's for lunch or tea. They might also go with her to the ladies' department to watch a fashion show. A high spot for them was when chocolate cake was served during the show.

It would not have been surprising if the girls had felt a distinction between themselves and their peers, but they believed that they did not. Looking back, however, Elizabeth could see that being a celebrity's daughter had given them a slight edge: a slightly better chance of getting ahead in life.

The lifestyle in the Mews in those very early 1960s was singular. 'It is difficult to recreate how quiet and cold and static a place Ireland was as we came out of the 1950s,' Nuala O'Faolain noted. Society was 'extremely authoritarian and ruled by old men and by the church. The world then was quite unlike what it is today in Ireland. The ordinary person was just ground down. It was a dark, poverty-stricken life in every way, including intellectually.' You could see it in the schools and you could see it glaringly in women's role in Irish society. The independent woman was indeed a rarity. Even the fact that Mary Lavin owned her own house was unusual. She could not have owned property if she had not been a widow.

Mary was 'dead lucky that by accident Lord Dunsany found a way out for her,' Nuala O'Faolain said. 'Otherwise she would have been pushed aside, as other women were at that time.' Her point is well taken, though somewhat magnified. Undoubtedly Lord Dunsany helped to convince Mary that she was someone whose life was a serious, dramatic business, with all its values, all its dreams, in the face of a whole society of women who were thought not to matter.

A shift towards the intellectual was, however, apparent in the climate in Ireland. For writers it was slow in coming but it was taking place. By 1965, according to Declan Kiberd, younger critics were appealing to writers to 'engage with a new, confident, inclusive Ireland of advance factories, material affluence, liberal education and a self-reforming church'. Unquestionably, progress was being made but still, as V. S. Pritchett reported in *Dublin: A Portrait*, published in 1967, John McGahern lost his teaching job in 1966 because his novel *The Dark* was not 'approved'. As Pritchett wrote, 'The peasant clerics of Ireland even now have great difficulty in disguising a dedicated dislike of art and literature.'

In 1967 Brian Lenihan, the Minister for Justice, introduced legislation which would take books off the banned list after twelve years. The result was that a great many Irish artists who had settled overseas came back to Ireland. In 1969, thanks to Charles Haughey, the Minister for Finance, legislation was passed exempting artists and writers from paying income taxes on their royalties. Understandably, this tax rebate also brought authors from England and the United States to settle in Ireland. Further measures to ease the financial burden on writers did not take place until the mid-1970s, however, but then the Arts Council began to grant bursaries. Those grants proved helpful, even though there was not a great deal of money available.

In 1977 the Arts Council inaugurated a programme which encouraged writers to visit schools in a few counties in the Republic and shortly thereafter they expanded the programme to include schools throughout Ireland. The writers were to read from their work and engage the students in discussion. Letters indicate that Mary Lavin participated in the programme.

All the changes, however, applied to a far greater extent to men than to women. It is fair to say that Mary Lavin in her lifestyle was a leader in that period of social reform. For one thing, she was earning her living for her family through writing: rare indeed for a woman at that juncture. Yet, even in 1968, a subheading on the *Sunday Press* article read: 'Mary Lavin is one of our most successful writers, yet only recently was she honoured at home.' It amazed Nuala O'Faolain that she had no idea of Mary Lavin's importance until she learned that the *New Yorker* was publishing her. She pointed out that Lavin was not listed in any academic syllabus or school syllabus so that the next generation after her didn't even know that she was there. Of course, Nuala O'Faolain was a young student. The academics in Mary's circle might not have drawn quite so gloomy a picture.

But Nuala was not too wide off the mark when she felt that no one in Ireland was promoting Lavin in those early 1960s. Mary was perhaps more talked of in England and in the States. Her family wondered at this and felt, understandably, a certain resentment. Why, one of her daughters asked, was she not honoured more 'not just by her peers but by the economic status she undoubtedly deserved'?

In Mary's case, there may have been an additional reason for the neglect. She was very modest about what she was achieving. She was not eager to talk about her work – to some she appeared to be writing just to earn money. It was an attitude she apparently maintained over the years. When, much later, she was interviewed for a documentary, she did not want to talk about her books. What she wanted to talk about was life, love, men, her children and their men, and the memories of her mother and her father.

Meanwhile, and as usual, Mary Lavin was busy writing wherever and whenever she could. An article in *The Irish Times*, titled 'A Moralist of the Heart' and written by one of the *Times* staff, described how this 'striking young widow could be seen enthroned in a deckchair on St Stephen's Green, scribbling in one of her large, green notebooks – *The Ink Paper Jotters* – her youngest daughter occupying herself in another deckchair beside her'. She also wrote regularly in the peace and quiet of the manuscript room in the National Library and often Caroline sat beside her doing her homework.

The novelist Carson McCullers once asked fellow author Hortense Calisher if she had wanted her children and if they interfered with her writing. Calisher replied that she had wanted them and that they did indeed interfere. But everything did. Everything also contributed. 'Writers know this instinctively,' she had added. Mary would have added a hearty Amen. Certainly her devotion to the girls and her trials and tribulations enriched her work rather than detracted from it, as witness the fact that so many of her stories are very little removed from autobiography. There was a real problem, Mary realized, when one attempted to separate fact from fiction. Her 'Happiness' is an excellent example and there are many others. In 1972 she told Zack Bowen, who was interviewing her for his critical study of her work, that she had wanted the story about her father, which she was writing at the time of the interview, to be entirely fictional. Yet when she began writing she found herself writing it factually. She discovered that she was 'writing a fraction of autobiography'.

Interviews were beginning to take up a great deal of Mary's time. In most of them, she consented to taping but disliked it heartily. The very fact of the taping caused her, at least in the beginning of an interview, to become tense and to search carefully for every word: an attitude contrary to her very nature. She was a delight to interview, however. She talked easily, needed no prompting, and often acted out her anecdotes. Interviewers invariably mentioned her charm and her hospitality. 'You'll stay and have a meal, of course.' Most of them did. It was the rare interviewer who could bear to tear himself or herself away. As the journalist Marion Fitzgerald wrote: 'Interviewing her, which started off as a job, became a pleasure. I stayed longer than I had intended and came away with a kitten into the bargain.'

Mary did her best to limit the number of interviews but, once they were granted, she gave each interviewer a great deal of time. With Bríd Mahon of the *Sunday Press*, for example, they lingered over coffee in the Shelbourne talking at random and then went to the Mews to talk some more. Mahon wrote that sometimes Mary seemed like a rather vague, motherly woman, with a sweet expression: 'in an absent-minded manner she poured the end of the milk into her coffee cup, which was now empty'. At other times she was the intellectual who talked well on many subjects: emancipation of women, ecumenism, Vietnam, moral responsibility. She was adamant on the subject of censorship, and her opinions were far from conventional. She was bored to death, she said, with all the talk of it in Ireland because it was so parochial. The worry should be about censorship on a worldwide scale and about whether the country was getting the truth about Vietnam and ecumenism.

It was to journalist Marion Fitzgerald that Mary mentioned she had vowed to do 'the impossible', something that others seemed not to have achieved: to put her work last 'and still make it good'. She had often read and heard that 'good writers' put their work before everything else. She could say truthfully that it did not apply to her. For her, writing came last, or so she believed. What was probably closer to the truth was that, though the actual writing may have come last, her work was never far from her mind. Outwardly, however, she succeeded quite well in achieving 'the impossible'. Fitzgerald was intrigued by life in the Mews. 'The talk and the laughter and the love of life is rich in the air,' she wrote. And Valdi and Elizabeth in their teens and Caroline not yet ten were deeply involved. It was certainly true that, for Mary, writing *per se* was definitely only one facet of a busy life and, as she said, she wouldn't 'have it any other way'.

CHAPTER 6

It seemed to Mary that, as far back as she could remember, she had always had to worry about finances. Obviously, this was not true since, before her marriage and while Tom was alive, she had not had to give money a thought. But certainly, since her widowhood, she had spent a great deal of time thinking about the problem. It was Elizabeth's feeling that this was a reflection of her basic insecurity about her ability to continue earning a living from her writing. That may very well be true, since Mary was always conscious of her responsibility for the family.

Nuala O'Faolain, who knew grinding poverty in those early 1960s, felt, that, in fact, much of the money worry was not actually justified. 'She hasn't a clue – even to this day [the 1990s] – how privileged she was in every way. She thought she was an ordinary Irish woman when she was anything but.' As Nuala O'Faolain saw it, Mary was convinced that she was 'just seconds away from the work-house' when, in fact, by Irish standards she was quite comfortably off. For Mary, she said, it was considered economy to bring the girls to tea in the Shelbourne: something that was a once-in-a-lifetime for many people. Wasn't it cheaper than going out and buying the tea, sugar and bread? Like all Mary's friends, Nuala smiled at the memory as she spoke of Mary's ideas, and there was a world of affection in her account. After William's death, people were quick to say that Mary could have sold the Abbey Farm but there was no question in the family's minds that that would have spelled defeat for her. As she told the journalist Marion Fitzgerald, as happy as they were in the Mews, their place in Bective – the Abbey Farm – was 'really the heart of us'.

If Mary's picture of her financial situation was a misconception, her daughters appeared to share it. According to one of them, Mary was 'on the breadline' most of her writing life. And yet, in retrospect, the girls always had the feeling of abundance – of plenty – even though they were told, and believed, that they were poorly off. Discussions of finances were a common occurrence and Mary had even suggested at one point that it might be wise to have a round table discussion every Friday night: like a committee. Elizabeth had no recollection of that plan materializing.

No financial matter was too small or no occasion too remote to be neglected and Mary availed herself of every opportunity to lecture her girls on the subject. When she was in the States doing a series of readings in the mid-1960s, she wrote to the 'dear, dear girls' about money they had lost through carelessness. After assuring them that she wasn't going to say anything more about the loss, she went on to say plenty. How many times, she asked, had she protested *violently* against the way they stuck money in their pockets or in their books. It was something she *never* did although they knew she was not a particularly careful person. She hoped they would learn from experience. And, just in passing, she also brought up the subject of their carelessness with needles. She summed up in her usual dramatic fashion: 'Believe me, these are not oddities of mine – they are the common wisdom of the ages.'

In a 1965 letter to Valdi, Mary wrote: 'We have only one problem – to survive financially.' They would all have to struggle, she wrote, because she could not manage alone. It was not because 'I am no longer willing but because I am no longer able'. She could, she believed, continue to support all of them – 'clothes apart' – if they would be careful of their expenditures.

Clothes were certainly an item. When, years later, Elizabeth and Valdi talked over those early days, one fact stood out. Their mother always bought them the best clothes. Was it to keep up appearances? Elizabeth thought not. Appearances were something, she said, that her mother did

146

not think about very much. She merely wanted to teach them the value and ultimately the practicality of buying good quality.

It was true that, like so many writers, Mary never was compensated well enough to have a feeling of security. Although her work was appearing in a wide variety of publications – the *Aylesford Review*, *Cosmopolitan*, *Country Beautiful*, *Kenyon Review*, *Southern Review* and *Threshold* – not many of them paid well. For the most part, they merely added to her prestige. The most lucrative source by far was the *New Yorker*.

In its December 1968 issue, the *New Yorker* carried 'Happiness', mentioned earlier, and subsequently it was the lead story in a collection brought out by Constable in 1969: *Happiness and Other Stories*. It ranks with her best. In that story, told through the eyes of the oldest of three daughters, Mary Lavin reconstructed with objectivity and insight her thoughts and feelings at the time of her husband's illness and death, the problems and the joys of her trips with her daughters, her feelings about her father – the 'redoubtable father, whose love blazed circles around her, making winter into summer and ice into fire' – and the problems associated with caring for her mother, as well as the guilt which that burden engendered.

There is a section in the story in which the middle daughter, whom Mary called Bea, speculates on the relationship between her mother and a priest Mary called Fr Hugh, who was family for them after the death of their father. There can be little doubt that the character is based on Michael Scott. 'I'm so glad he has Mother, as well as her having him, because it must be awful the way most women treat them [priests] . . . as if they were pariahs. Mother treats him like a human being – that's all!' And the oldest sister wonders: 'Bea, do you think he's in love with her?' Bea's reply is 'If so, he doesn't know it. It's her soul he's after! Maybe he wants to make sure of her in the next world!' The children's mother in 'Happiness' is called Vera, and Mary describes Vera's attempt to make up to her aged mother for what she feels was her neglect earlier: an almost impossible task. As Fr Hugh phrases it, 'God almighty couldn't make that woman happy.' One of the daughters in 'Happiness' speaks bitterly of the evenings after the mother comes home from the library where she works. The girls see her standing there, holding her car keys and trying to decide whether it would be worse to walk the short distance to her mother's flat or get the car out again.

Except for Elizabeth Cullinan, those of Mary's friends who remember Nora do not seem to have been aware of that side of her. They thought of her as a rather sweet old lady who told very amusing stories. There is, in 'Happiness', a description in the words of one of the daughters which may sum up how others saw Nora Lavin. 'Most people thought our grandmother was a gay creature, a small birdy being who even at a great age laughed like a girl, and – more remarkably – sang like one, as she went about her day.' And then the narrator goes on, 'But beak and claw were of steel. She'd think nothing of sending Mother back to a shop three times if her errands were not exactly right.' When the youngest of the girls in the story finally loses patience and accuses her of being 'mean' and of enjoying 'ordering people about', she takes it as a compliment. 'I always was hard to please,' she says proudly.

Her favourite phrase is 'if only'. When one of the children visits her, she says:

If only you'd come earlier, before I was worn out expecting you! Or if we were early, then if only it was later, after she'd had a rest and could enjoy us, be able for us . . . Our own father – her son-in-law – was the one person who had ever gone close to pleasing her.

But even here there is something to feel unhappy about. 'If only he was my real son!' And then she sighs.

Like her character Vera, Mary's feeling of responsibility for her mother weighed heavily upon her. After Tom died, she settled Nora comfortably in the Mespil Flats. It was proving very costly to keep her there and Tom Kilroy said many years later that it had been his impression that money was one of the causes of friction between Mary and her mother.

Unlike her mother, Mary knew that for her, even though she might not be able to define it clearly, happiness was something she possessed. She firmly believed that the secret was to live life to the full with all its joys and its sorrows. In 'Happiness', she attempted to define it. As she explains it in the story, it is not something that can be handed down or perhaps even understood by her children. They speculate about it and ask themselves, 'What was it, . . . that quality that she, we felt sure, misnamed? Was it courage? Was it strength, health, or high spirits? Something you could not give or take – a conundrum? A game of catch-as-catch-can?' In one section, Vera tries to explain it by telling her daughters that she possessed it even as a child. Then, 'as if by magic', she creates a picture for them of the child she was: 'a small girl with black hair and buttoned boots, who, though plain and pouting, burned bright, like a star'.

As Mary realized so clearly, through her stories she was attempting to resolve and to come to terms with her life. Consequently, there was a good reason why, during the mid-1960s, so many of them were concerned with the Church and the clergy. The family was becoming as dependent upon Fr Scott as he was upon them. But it was not only in the 1960s that Mary Lavin's stories stressed the prejudices generated by organized religion. She had begun to perceive what she considered flaws in her religion much earlier.

There is a story in Mary Lavin's *Tales from Bective Bridge* called 'Sarah', which gives a picture of how inhabitants of a small Irish town define a good woman. It is by her devotion to the church. Sarah is a cleaning-woman who has, as the townspeople put it, 'a bit of a bad name'. She has borne three children out of wedlock: each child with a different father. But she does not stay in bed of a Sunday morning. She keeps the commandments of the Church, she never fails to attend Mass, and she abstains on the days when it is required to be abstinent. And she often does the Stations of the Cross. 'If . . . some outsider showed disapproval of her, Sarah's neighbours were quicker than Sarah herself to take offence.' She is a good woman. But Mary Lavin does not fail to add a typical touch: 'All the same, charity was tempered with prudence, and women with grown sons, and women not long married took care not to hire her.'

In 1944 'Sunday Brings Sunday' appeared in her second collection, *The Long Ago and Other Stories*. The opening section is devoted to a Sunday morning service by the curate of a church in a town very much like Athenry. He is stressing his insistence upon prayer. 'I ask you to turn over in your mind whether it is better to get down on your knees for three minutes or to spend an eternity in the dark pit of damnation, lit only by the flames of hell,' he says.

In the 1950s she wrote 'Limbo', a story which shows the attitude of some Catholics towards Protestants and the lack of understanding between the religions. A new family has settled in a village. At the first glimpse of the young girl in the family, the schoolteacher tells someone that she knows the family is Protestant because they have 'a Protestant look'. The teacher is stunned when she is told by the young girl that they are not members of any church. In Africa as missionaries, they taught the Word of God, the Gospel. 'God had no church, when He was on earth,' the little girl tells the teacher. The family is non-sectarian. Because she is not a Catholic, the child is not allowed to attend the prayer sessions in the school with the other children. In the minds of those children, she obviously will not go to heaven when she dies – she is not a Catholic – but, since they know she is not bad, she will not go to hell either. They are puzzled and troubled. 'To the one or the other everyone in the town would one day be dispatched.' And then they remember Limbo and, though they do not understand exactly what that means, they are reassured. That is where she will go.

It was in the *Happiness* collection that Mary's stories dealing with aspects of Catholicism sharpened. There were three in that collection: 'Happiness', 'A Pure Accident' and 'The Lost Child'. 'The Lost Child', carried first in the *Southern Review* in January of 1969, was one of her favourites. In it she was quite explicit with regard to her feelings about Catholic dogma, about the attitude of both Catholics and Protestants towards intermarriage, about the need for a greater role for women in the Church, and – quite strongly – about the superior attitude of men towards women.

As the story opens, a Protestant woman, the mother of two children and married to a Catholic, is once again pregnant, and about to become a Catholic. Mary Lavin describes accurately the resistance that she, Renee, encountered in her family before her marriage took place. Was she going to be married in the sacristy? Submit to a 'hole and corner' ceremony? And, when her first child was baptised a Catholic, her mother 'nearly hit the ceiling'. 'But I promised,' Renee reminded her. Such a promise should never have been asked of her, her mother insisted. 'It was given under duress, emotional duress.'

On the day she becomes a Catholic, Renee, looking back, remembers a weekend trip to the seaside. Her sister had gone with Renee and her husband. Walking along the shore one evening, they saw gravestones almost completely buried in the grass. The guide book said that this was the Cemetery of the Children. Why were they not buried in the cemetery in the village, Renee's sister asked. Were they illegitimate? The answer given by Renee's husband, shocked at such an idea, was certainly not. It was merely because they had not yet been baptised. 'Oh, Renee,' her sister said, 'are you prepared to accept things like that?'

That incident occurred during Renee's instruction and before she made her final commitment. As she talked it over with the priest, here called Fr Hugh as in 'Happiness', he used her concern about the dogma as one more reason why she should not hurry about making her final decision. 'What's the hurry?' he asked. 'Your faith will be all the stronger if it comes as a result of living with a good Catholic like Mike.' Unable to resist, she asked, 'What if it's the other way round?' He laughed but Renee was sure that he could say what he did because 'like his Church, he believed too staunchly in the superiority of the male intellect, he couldn't imagine Mike being influenced by her in such a matter'. As the story goes on, Renee, very early in her pregnancy, has a miscarriage. In the hospital, she becomes deeply depressed and her husband is certain that she is brooding about the cemetery for unbaptised children they saw on their walk. He brings Fr Hugh to the hospital to reassure her. And Fr Hugh tries to do so. 'I hear you are worried about your little baby's soul, Renee. But you know God's love is infinite, don't you?' Would she be happier, he asks, if she learned that 'there was a growing body of opinion in the Church that the Vatican may be prepared to admit to error in teaching about Limbo?' It has, after all, never been dogma.

Father Hugh then asks Renee's husband if her doctor is a Catholic. 'Some doctors are very scrupulous and they have been known to give lay baptism to unborn babies.' By her obvious irritation at what he is saying, he realizes that he has misconstrued her need. He thought, he says, that she was worried about the baby's soul. She assures him that he was wrong and that she agrees with her sister, present at the bedside, who has said, 'I've heard about such baptisms and what I heard turned my stomach. What does the Church know any more than the medical world which is not prepared to be definitive about the issue?' And Renee adds: 'Whether the idea of Limbo is dogma or not, why were no women given a say about it?' Mary Lavin takes one of her strongest stands on the subject in this story.

In 'A Pure Accident' Mary Lavin uses satire to make her points. She draws an insensitive, miserly canon, who shows no sympathy for his weak-minded curate, placing him in a situation with which he is unable to cope. He discusses the curate with three of his parishioners who have come to plead with him to spend money on illumination in the church and in the chapel yard. In the course of the conversation, he says of his curate, 'It's hard to see what sends the likes of him into the Church at all . . . Pushed from behind, that's what they are. Oh, the mothers of Ireland have a lot to answer for.' When he was in Maynooth, he goes on,

> I used to see them on visiting days walking around the grounds with their poor weedy, pimply-faced sons, wrapping their own mufflers around the poor fellows' necks, and giving them their own gloves to put on their hands, instead of letting them stiffen into men of their own making. Ah, the right kind of mother is a rare creature. My own mother, God be good to her, would sooner have seen me a bank manager, but when I made my choice she put all her weight behind me. No wonder I have contempt for poor slobs like Fr Patton.

In her portrayal of Fr Patton in 'A Pure Accident', Mary Lavin touches on the tragedy of celibacy as well as other pressures of the Church, such as poverty. It is a powerful, bitter story, depicting the subservience of the parishioners – especially the women – to the clergy.

Mary Lavin was nothing if not fair and she understood that there was much about priests that she could admire. She balanced the insensitive canon against kindly clergy such as Fr Hugh in 'The Lost Child'. As she once wrote:

> I see priests and nuns as just the same as the rest of
> us, victims of curial despotism. Sometimes I have
> portrayed clergymen as less than they ought to be or
> as downright destructive, but that is not anti-clerical-
> ism. It only means that when a man acts according to
> his nature he sometimes behaves in a way that is
> contrary to the accepted purpose of his calling. I've
> written of similar failings in doctors and mothers.

The idea for 'The Lost Child' had been in her mind when
she was still quite young. She had given a great deal of
thought to Limbo and it seemed repellent to her. Only later,
she said, had she realized that her instinctive rejection of
that idea was only part of other things that she could not
accept in the doctrine of her church, while feeling at the
same time that she had every right to consider herself a
member of that church. She likened religion to a race – a
nationality. 'It's what you are and you can't throw it off. It's
like being Irish or American or white or black.' When people
told her that they had no religion, she would ask what their
father's religion was or had been. When they said he was an
atheist, she asked about the religion of the grandfather and
so on back until the reply was that he was Protestant or
Catholic or Jewish. As she saw it, one could not be nothing.
'You may not believe what Protestants believe, but you are
what Protestants are.'

In an article by Bríd Mahon in the *Sunday Press*, entitled
'The Quiet Authoress' and written at the time Mary received
a D. Litt. (Hon.) from UCD in 1968, she made her position
clear. 'I am a Catholic and it's important to me.' And much
later she wrote:

> Even as a child I was preoccupied with my right to
> exercise private conscience. From an early age I would

not accept that God would not have equipped me with the ability to tell right from wrong without interpretation. If my attitude is not acceptable to some, I still see no reason to consider myself anything other than a member of the Church in which I was baptised. Life presses too hard on most of us to allow time for searching out, finding and then testing another religion.

As she said in the Bríd Mahon interview, 'How can you say who is a committed Christian? For myself, I would try to sacrifice the material to the spiritual. I hope I would succeed.'

Late in the 1960s, speaking to a group of students, Mary said that she believed something rather strange was happening. She did not think that the Celt could have been such a dedicated person throughout the ages and end up as deplorably narrow a person as the Irish clergyman seemed to be now if something good was not working out. Perhaps we have always been slower to make changes, she said. Basically, she thought the Irish clergy were very idealistic. 'I think they were very much betrayed by the Vatican. But I think that when all the capers that are going on in the Church are over, they will go forward and that by being a little slower they will avoid some of the nonsensical changes.'

By the measure of Sarah's neighbours in 'Sarah', and by that of the curate in 'Sunday Brings Sunday', Mary Lavin might not have been considered a truly religious person. But perhaps, in the best sense of the word, she was.

Mary's opinions about religion did not seem to be foisted upon her children. As they recall, they were more or less allowed to accept it or not in their own way. The result appears to be that Elizabeth is more religious in the conventional sense than her sisters.

Mary's stance on the subject of religion – her rebellion, so to speak – was part of considerable debate on the subject among intellectuals in Ireland. With the growing urbanization of the country, its inhabitants were becoming more aware of changes in the attitude towards the strictures of the Catholic church outside Ireland, and even in the late 1950s a certain number of the more enlightened clergy were beginning to write of the need for modernization. Another sign of the times was the decline in the number of young men attracted to the priesthood. And, though not in large numbers, there was a growth in the number of priests applying for laicization.

Inevitably, the changes in thinking and lifestyle all along the line, especially among the young, would be reflected in Mary's family. At times it was a little too much for Mary. She was impatient, she said, with 'all the talk of sex and birth control. I think every moment of life creates its own moral decision, and each time a proper moral solution must be found.'

By 1965 Valdi was studying law and Elizabeth was enrolled at UCD. In her free time, she worked as a barmaid at the Coach and Horses in New Bond Street where, she recalled, her mother would come in, stand at the bar, and talk with the manager. She appeared to be proud of her daughter for working and for working there.

Elizabeth had wanted to major in French at UCD, but was assigned to the English Department because, she felt, she was Mary Lavin's daughter. That she undeniably was: she not only looked like her mother, but she had inherited her spirit and her love of life. Among Mary Lavin's papers was a photocopy of a page from E. M. Forster's *Howard's End*. Mary had marked a passage which described the heroine, Margaret Schlegel, and in the margin she had written 'Elizabeth'. The passage read:

Away she hurried, not beautiful, not supremely brilliant, but filled with something that took the place of both qualities – something best described as a profound vivacity, a continual and sincere response to all that she encountered in her path through life.

As Mary's girls grew up, her relationship with them continued to be a close one. And it was fine that they could think of themselves as all girls together. It did, however, mean that Mary did not always remember to take the ages of Valdi and Elizabeth and the changing times into consideration. She could not expect them to react to the various aspects of their lives like a woman in her middle years.

Valdi had grown into a striking beauty. Tall, lithe, fair-skinned, with perfect features and auburn hair, she had inherited the Mahon looks and something of Tom Lavin's outgoing personality. The girls were doing well in college and Valdi, then about twenty-two, was getting ready to take her final law exams when the first real rift took place between mother and daughter.

It was probably around 1965 that Mary attended a convocation at UCD and noticed a young, handsome solicitor who was one of the speakers. She found him quite attractive and, after talking with him a little, invited him to visit the Mews. He did and, when he saw Valdi, he could see no one else. Dermot Bouchier-Hayes was some years older than Valdi and already settled in his profession. He came from a highly respected Dublin family and was the son of a famous Dublin doctor. With his residence and offices around the corner from Lad Lane on Leeson Street, he became a regular visitor to the Mews.

It was inevitable that Dermot and Valdi would fall in love. He was an attractive man and he and Valdi, the young law student, had a great deal in common. Before very long, they were contemplating marriage. When Mary raised strong objections to the marriage, Valdi left Dublin before taking her law exams, went to England, found employment as a cashier at the Dog and Fox on High Street in Wimbledon, and moved into a room in Shields House at Egerton Gardens, a girls' hostel. Her job was a hard and responsible one and the hours were long, but Valdi persevered.

Mary's objection to their marriage plans was in part based

on her belief that Dermot was responsible for her decision to leave home before completing her law exams. She felt, too, that he had poisoned Valdi's mind against her and caused even her own love for Valdi to suffer. The whole situation can be reconstructed from a series of letters Mary wrote to Valdi while she, Valdi, was in England. It is worth examining them since they say a great deal about Mary and reveal very clearly her attitude at that time towards many of the issues vital to young people, especially in the 1960s. The letters indicate that, at one point in their courtship and despite the strong objections of her mother, Valdi had gone away with Dermot for a weekend. A letter from Mary to Valdi read:

> How could you defy me in that – how could you think that if you loved each other you could be alone without too great a strain. How could you risk total intimacy in the circumstances when you knew that you had a lot of misgivings about other things . . . and that a rift might come. Are you going to risk pregnancy – and if you were going to take measures against it were you prepared to take a moral step that millions of very great thinkers of all religions (and of none) are still uncertain about its validity even in marriage?

Valdi should, Mary went on, have paid attention to her mother's objections since she 'was probably more experienced on sex matters than almost anyone' having had a long and happy marriage. She went on to tell Valdi that 'only total sacrifice can bring the full beauty of total surrender. If you don't see that you have lost your *mental virginity* beside which that of the body is a mere nothing.' And, in a clear indication that the Lavin-Scott friendship was ripening into something more than that, she wrote that she had 'after a sad and lonely life of forced asceticism finally a chance of love, which again calls for incredible sacrifice in order to bring it – as is now almost certain – to bring it to a happy end'.

It is unclear what Valdi had said or written about her attitude towards Catholicism, but about that Mary was not particularly concerned, she told Valdi. What was important, she felt, was that Valdi be 'a serious person about matters of the spirit and the moral laws'.

Mary needed to be reassured that both young people were ready to undertake all the responsibilities involved in marriage and parenthood. She wanted to stress the point that marriage was, as she put it, for life. There were practical questions for which Mary felt Valdi needed to have definite answers. What exactly did her prospective husband have to offer her and the children? Was Valdi sure that Dermot was the one she wanted to marry? Could a definite date be set when her final decision had to be made?

Mary wrote further that there appeared to be a rumour circulating that she, Mary, had wanted Valdi to pursue a career as a lawyer in some way to compensate for her father's death in mid-career. The fact was, as Valdi knew, her mother had wanted her to pursue the arts but it was Valdi's desire to study law. Since she knew that, Mary asked, why had she not attempted to dispel the rumour?

There was a further exchange about the whole matter but finally Mary, rather reluctantly it appears, decided to abide by whatever decision Valdi made. She was no longer able to see her daughter suffer and to know that she was responsible for it. She was trying to pray for her, she added, which, she wrote, 'for me is hard', and whatever decision was finally reached, she would 'put a public face on her own feelings'.

That Mary was always conscious of the fact that, as the sole parent, she was doubly responsible for Valdi's future, may explain to a certain extent the violence of her reaction to the whole affair. But the reaction may also have had its roots in rivalry. Dermot was older than many of the Lavin entourage. He was also, from all indications, a charmer. Years later Elizabeth wrote to her mother that she might have 'had an eye for him myself if it wasn't for he had his heart set on Valdi'.

A period followed when the prospective marriage was off and then on again. It was finally decided that Valdi was to come home to work out all the final details. If a September 1965 letter from Mary to Valdi before she left England was intended to elicit guilt feelings, it was a masterpiece. She urged Valdi not to worry 'as I know you must about the bad example you gave your sisters. Things work out very strangely in family life and both of them are very chastened and docile at seeing the one in whom I placed most faith and held up to them as a model – act – even temporarily as you did. They will have gained by it all in the end and I cannot but think in a way I will too.' These sanctimonious sentiments were followed by her assurance that she would accept the marriage and would hope that Valdi would have 'the almost superhuman strength' to make it work. She concluded that letter by assuring Valdi once more that she would not put any obstacle in the way of the couple's plans if Valdi believed they could be happy and make the children 'that I hope God will give you' happy. Making the children happy was for Mary an extremely important part of marriage.

Mary's fear of flying was no secret to the family so surely Valdi was not surprised when the same letter begged her to write, before she got on the plane to return to Dublin, to assure her mother she understood that all along she, her mother, had acted 'in love and from a sense of duty and not . . . from any other motives'. She had visions, she wrote, of the plane crashing and she could hear people saying 'only for her mother, she'd be alive today, a happy, laughing bride'. Mary ended, with the irony so prevalent in her stories, 'For God's sake, I am too hard pressed for money not to want to get rid of you at all costs, except your happiness. Please take time to write me one kind word before you fly home knowing my silly fears.'

That Mary felt able to write to and discuss with her daughters as she did indicated that there was no lessening of the great love and dependency which existed on both sides. It is so often the correspondence between friends. 'Get Salinger's *Catcher in the Rye* for Caroline,' she wrote to Valdi, 'and get *The Bachelors* [Muriel Spark] for yourself. No sign of the jacket.' (The jacket was due in from the Weaver's Shed in Anne's Street, where they all purchased their handmade clothes.)

The novelist and short story writer Mervyn Wall gave a vivid example of Mary's attitude to her daughters as he witnessed it on one of his visits to the Abbey Farm. One of her daughters was driving back from Cork to Bective. 'Great Scot,' Mervyn Wall said, 'Mary sat at the phone for hours and rang twenty gas stations in between to ask if they had seen the car go by.'

The letters to Valdi, during this period and during a bad time for both of them, were proof of Mary Lavin's ability to concentrate on family concerns such as Valdi's love affair and on money problems, and at the same time engage in an active social and professional life: in 1965 she became president of Irish PEN, an office which must have been time-consuming.

With all that, she still did not neglect her writing. One of the letters was written in the peace and quiet of the manuscript room in the National Library. That morning she was 'full of such excitement of the kind out of which I can do *new* work, not just editing,' she wrote to Valdi. There is then a section concerned with all the day's doings but concluding with

> I am working very hard – I think I am very tired and aged and that it is nearly too much for me, but the *Saturday Evening Post* keep pressing for a story. I have waived all their rules re first rights and so I am trying to re-write 'The Becker Wives' and 'Magenta' as this

seems a better bet than trying to put 'The Mock Auction' right.

Requests for her to give readings of her stories both in and out of the country were increasing, and she enjoyed the appearances. She read well, and liked the audience reaction and the question periods which followed. In addition, these trips were a fine way to augment her income. Apparently receiving good-sized remunerations, she boasted that she was really a good money-maker when she got herself organized. She seldom missed an opportunity, furthermore, to attend conferences. They gave her a respite from her problems and she found trips rejuvenating. In 1966, she sent glowing notes home from the Hotel Cosmopolitan and Royal in Brussels. It was terribly expensive, she wrote, but she was getting 'marvellous meals from writers and painters' and there were the banquets. Her room was so filled with 'cursed orchids that seem so alive compared to other flowers' that she would have to find a home for them before leaving. This letter was written while she was sitting in the sun, drinking beer and speculating on her good fortune in having her three daughters even though, she wrote home, 'the price for you is at times a bit high'.

Being away from Dublin was apparently giving Mary a chance to do a great deal of thinking and, of course, worrying. and she spelled it all out for Valdi. Had she imposed her money worries upon them all excessively, she asked? 'I think of you a lot and of Caroline,' she wrote, 'and I feel that in the past two years I have made such a poor job of bread winning but it was inevitable to begin to limp near the end of a very rough road.' She hated the thought that if anything happened to her 'all you would remember *clearly* was the rough bit of road and my complaints about having no money – and not the brave beginnings with the trips abroad, etc.' That might, she speculated, be truer for Caroline than for the others. But she was going to try to 'take a new course.

162

The secret of life is to be able *to change all the time* – to adapt, adapt, adapt to anything.' She concluded: 'I love you all so much and want my love to bring you nothing but good, as true love cannot but do, I truly believe. But it must be practised like an art and not abused by either giver or taker.' Sharing the blame a bit, she added, 'Let's make a tremendous effort to make our life more reasonable.'

Away from home, she was able to view the Valdi situation and her attitude towards it with a certain amount of objectivity. She seems to have been rationalizing what she now saw was her mishandling of the whole matter. She had come to feel that she was more exhausted than she had realized and that, had she been more fit, she would not have been so hard on Dermot. But, she added, he should have taken into consideration that she was an old woman, 'and that alas is what I suppose I have become', and have been more understanding. It is amazing that, at fifty-four, Mary was beginning to refer to herself as an old woman.

The ending of the Valdi-Dermot story is a tragic one. In 1968, Dermot, though an expert mountain-climber, suffered a bad fall on one of his trips and was very seriously injured. He was taken to the Provincial Hospital in Innsbruck and then flown home to St Vincent's Hospital in Dublin, where he remained unconscious. Every attempt to save his life proved futile. Dermot died on 30 May 1969. His funeral took place in the chapel of UCD, then a very short distance from where his home and his offices were located.

Mary's troubles seemed to be endless. The latest one was concerned with the fate of Lad Lane and the Mews. The firm of Goulding Fertilisers Ltd. was proposing to erect an office block that would replace the grand old houses on the canal: houses which backed on to Lad Lane. It would mean that the Mews would no longer face an attractive residential area but look out on an office block. Over the years Lad Lane and the area around it – Baggot Street, with its restaurants and studios – had become something of an artists' quarter. Now there would be, as the family saw it, mobile canteens and rubbish collections on the lane, with the consequent reduction in the value and the charm of the property.

When the building of an office complex became a certainty, Mary Lavin instituted a law suit. Never one for the quiet life, she rather enjoyed the subsequent excitement. In January of 1967 she wrote to Valdi saying that she had had a field day in the Four Courts. 'Went in innocently and created a sensation.' One of the notables 'collared' her and she was taken down to the bar, where they had 'real booze'. She had to go again the next day and was looking forward to it.

Mary won the high court case and was awarded compensation and costs. Gouldings, however, appealed the decision before the Supreme Court and won. The Walsh-Goulding case was one that would continue to be cited by preservationists over the years. To Mary's great disappointment, Lad Lane became a prestige office complex and most of the residents moved away. Mary and her family continued to live there, however, until she sold the Mews in 1983. One of the 1960s letters to Valdi is one long lament. Elizabeth had been turned down for a position she had been quite sure of and everything was 'in a low state generally'. She, Elizabeth, was trying to shake depression but Mary was finding living with her 'one terrible strain'. One of Caroline's teachers had had a 'terrible row' in class with Caroline about her mother. Mummy (Nora Lavin) was beginning to fail and it was uncertain how much longer she would be able to remain in the Mespil Flats. She had promised to sell a bond but had not yet done so. And the weather was miserable. Mary had just about decided that if possible financially she would close the Mews and go to a hotel in Dun Laoghaire for perhaps six weeks.

One of Mary's great concerns was that Valdi continue to further her career in law and to get her law degree. She suggested to her that it might be wise for her to go before the English bar rather than the Irish. 'You may love Ireland now away from it but when you come home you'll see how petty and small it will seem.'

Valdi did not follow that advice. Late in 1966 and with Mary's help, she began canvassing American universities for a scholarship so that she might go on to study for her ML. Letters were sent to Harvard, Yale and Columbia, and strings were pulled wherever possible. Mary's advice to Valdi was to 'paint a black picture' of her financial needs in her letters. Undoubtedly in reference to a letter of recommendation from one of Valdi's former professors, Mary wrote to Valdi: 'He is a *bastard* but humour him for your own sake.'

The University of Connecticut at Storrs had approached Mary with an offer to come there as writer-in-residence and she was giving the offer serious consideration. Her hope was that Valdi would be studying in the States during that year and that it would be possible for her to have Elizabeth and Caroline with her in Connecticut. For a time it appeared as if Valdi would be going to Cornell University in Ithaca, New York but, because of an error in timing, that arrangement fell through. Finally, however, all plans were made. Valdi had obtained a scholarship from Southern Methodist College in Texas, and Mary had accepted the University of Connecticut offer. She was working hard in order to get a little money ahead, and her 'Happiness' was going well. She was beginning to feel there might be, at last, a certain amount of stability in her life, and she was in great form.

It had been impossible for Mary to arrange to have both Caroline and Elizabeth at Storrs, but Caroline was going to be with her there. Elizabeth was to remain in Dublin, to stay at Buswell's Hotel, to continue studying at UCD, and to prepare for her finals in English language and literature.

Buswell's was truly 'home from home' for Mary and her girls and, as Elizabeth said later she had a blissful time during that year. She had a good year at the college as well, ending it by receiving her BA in English plus French with honours.

She obtained it, she says, 'at the lowest level possible to an honours student'. Looking back, she saw those as crisis years for her mother: years when she was attempting to see that the girls got a good education but were also taught what she referred to as 'the hard lessons of life'. These were things that Tom Lavin had tried to keep Mary from learning.

CHAPTER 7

A letter to Valdi, settled in at the university in Texas, opened this way: 'Dear Valdi, I hate my place.'

And that was the way Mary Lavin's academic year 1967–8 began. Fortunately, she was referring to her living quarters and not to the campus, her colleagues, or her students. The university had arranged housing for her and Caroline and they had chosen unwisely. She had rooms in the home of a graduate student and his wife, Dick and Marion Boyer, and was to share their kitchen. The house was dark and gloomy, the kitchen small and hopeless, and Mary made no attempt to use it. Instead, she paid one dollar a day for supper. She knew that was cheap but, she wrote, 'you should see what they call supper!'

She was not there very long, however, when Professor George Brandon Saul, on the faculty of the English department and the only member teaching Irish literature, suggested that she and Caroline move in with him and his wife, Eileen. Eager to escape from her Dickensian surroundings, she happily accepted. The English department did not have an Irish Studies programme as such, but Professor Saul, a self-professed Irish expert, taught Yeats and Joyce and Irish literature.

Professor Saul was a bitter, disappointed man. When young and handsome, he had wanted to live in Manhattan – as it was in the 1920s – and write poetry. Instead, he had come to the university when it was still Connecticut Agricultural College with four members in the English department and a total enrolment of 484. He remained there for sixty-two years.

The early years were fairly pleasant for Professor Saul but, beginning in the late 1940s, a New York University professor, Leonard 'Pete' Dean, was brought in as chairman of the English department. It was a blow for Professor Saul, who had expected the position would be offered to him. Quite naturally, the new chairman attempted to introduce forward-looking ideas. The curriculum was updated and older members were under attack, with George Brandon Saul as the principal target. Here was a professor teaching Irish literature who 'refused to take James Joyce seriously'. Professor Saul had found it impossible to change with the times.

Professor M. Kelly Lynch, in 'An Appreciation of George Brandon Saul', an article in the Winter 1994 *Eire-Ireland*, described conditions as they were when she enrolled in the Irish literature course in the autumn of 1963, four years before the advent of Mary Lavin. Professor Saul was teaching only one graduate course in Anglo-Irish literature and academic advisors were routinely discouraging students from enrolling in it. It met for three hours one evening a week and, when she enrolled, there were only seven students signed up. Before the semester ended there was only one left – the author of the article. She explained at length why, in her opinion, Saul, even long before her time, had taken on 'an extremely unpleasant, irrational, and vitriolic public persona'. He had been passed over for the chairmanship of the department, he was looked down upon, and he was disliked. Professor Lynch defended Professor Saul. She agreed with his detractors that he did have a 'need for control', but, in her opinion, when he was in command of a situation he was 'devoted, caring, loving – a perfectly reasonable human being'.

That must have been the side of him that Mary Lavin saw. To Valdi, she described Professor Saul as a gentleman and a scholar. In addition, he was a devotee of women writers, those who were well known and those who were not. Among those who were, he had kind words to say for Isak Dinesen and Elizabeth Bowen, but he refused to read better-known writers such as Virginia Woolf. His wife, Mary wrote, had a heart of gold. That was not exactly the way other members of the faculty saw the Sauls. Apparently they all thought his wife long-suffering and Professor Saul an intolerable bore. He was considered a poor teacher: one who enjoyed the sound of his own voice. It disturbed the other members of the department that any attempt to get young, capable instructors who knew Irish literature into the department was impossible, for Professor Saul stood in the way.

One member of the department felt that Mary Lavin accepted Professor Saul's invitation because of a need for some kind of home-like environment, but he could not imagine that she would find it with the Sauls. Yet Mary must have appreciated the fact that George Brandon Saul was a scholar and that, as Professor Kelly points out and proves, he did, through his scholarship, do a great deal to further 'the cause of Irish literature in the United States'. And he and Mary had a few things in common in addition to the love of Irish literature. He was a great lover of nature; he dwelled often on the thought of death, as she did; and he was deathly afraid to fly.

Perhaps Mary would have said that part of his trouble was that he was a teetotaller. The following story is still told on campus. One evening Mary was taken out to dinner by a colleague and, on the way back to the Sauls, she asked him to stop at a liquor store where she bought a bottle of Irish whiskey. The house, when they reached it, was dark. She cautiously made her way into the kitchen and was reaching for the light switch when Professor Saul, who had come downstairs silently, reached it first. A full bottle of Irish whiskey crashed to the floor.

As writer-in-residence at the university, Mary had only to give one course a term – a combined undergraduate and graduate level course in writing – and, since the university did not lack for funds at that time, she was paid rather handsomely. With her living arrangements more or less settled, and with Caroline in high school, life at the university seemed brighter.

The University of Connecticut at Storrs was an agricultural school with a widely recognized agricultural department. The whole atmosphere helped to make Mary less homesick for Bective. The campus and the village – which seems to be what Storrs was considered then – with its rolling hills, its woods and old stone walls, was a perfect environment for Mary, so responsive to the natural world around her. Though the village was quite remote and self-contained, Hartford was only a half-hour drive away and Boston could be reached within two hours.

One of Mary's great pleasures from the start was spending time with the other members of the English department. She discussed her work with them in a professional and technical manner, and she brought to those sessions a vast knowledge of Irish literature and literature in general. She liked thinking out loud and, with her exuberance and her wit, her colleagues found her a delight. She often said that for shop talk she preferred academics rather than other writers. It was what she was accustomed to at home. 'In Ireland there doesn't seem to ever be any shop talk with Irish writers', although being with them was 'in some extraordinary way' lots of fun. She cited her friendship with Benedict Kiely. 'Ben and I together are rather a bit much for anybody that's also present.'

She was pleased to see that there was considerable interest in the short story among American academics, and it was a topic, quite naturally, which she and her colleagues discussed at length. And yet she believed that, instead of making that genre more significant, the academics were making it less so and alienating readers by placing too great a stress on technique.

Mary's colleagues were interested as well in the rise and fall of the attempt in Ireland to revive the study and use of Gaelic. There Mary had her ideas in order. She thought the influence of continental Europe far more powerful and authentic than the revival of a language of which half of the country had a particular dread when it was compulsory rather than optional. Yeats and Lady Gregory wanted a Gaelic revival. She just wanted 'Joe Soaps to be educated.' That was enough for starters, she said.

To say that Mary Lavin was a welcome addition to the English department would be putting it mildly. As for the students, they worshipped her. She had merely to walk into a classroom and in minutes they became Lavin fans. Her method in assembling her class was to take the first ten students who applied, without having any knowledge of how well they could write. One girl had enrolled merely because she wanted to learn how to write a good letter to her husband in Vietnam. She obviously was not good material for a creative writing class but she intrigued Mary. 'Go home and write a description of the ground outside your window,' she told the student. The result was poor. Mary refused to give up. She learned that the student had an aquarium and was fascinated by the little creatures. She told her to go home and write about whatever she found interesting. The result was a vivid description of a newt, and then of a frog. She really wasn't a writer, but she was a good observer, she could write about what she saw and loved. That student wrote Mary later that she was a catalogue writer for a publisher specializing in flora and fauna and Mary was pleased.

Mary's teaching method was to assign essay topics, meet with the students individually to discuss their essays on those topics, and then discuss them further in class. She quickly established a reputation as a very responsive teacher and one with a good critical eye who was always on the lookout for emerging talent. But she was careful not to raise hopes unduly. 'Don't consider yourself a writer until you have proved you are to yourself and to others,' she cautioned her students. For them, she became not only a teacher but an editor and a friend. She cautioned her students against confusing

171

originality of expression with originality of content which, she maintained, was 'as rare as a white blackbird'. All a writer could do was to give his or her own view of what man had seen and done for a couple of million years in a way that was original to one's self, she told them. The writing, however, had to be plain, clear, and correct. 'In other words, classic.'

A time came when Mary grew tired of living with the Sauls. There was one member of the English department – Alex Medlicott – with whom she and Caroline had established a close relationship: one that endured throughout Mary's life and has continued on with Caroline. She was happy when the Medlicotts invited her and Caroline to stay with them and they spent the last few months of her stay in Storrs there.

The Medlicotts – Alex, his wife Sue, and their three children – lived about a mile from campus in a good-sized house set back from the road and surrounded by woods. Mary and Caroline shared a large, comfortable room over the garage, dined with the family, and became very much part of it. Sue Medlicott accepted Caroline as another one of her children and Mary as someone else to look after. It appears that Mary's clothes were often in need of attention and Sue Medlicott 'sewed, mended, and washed'. She had taken on an awesome responsibility but one that soon became a labour of love. At one point Mary said to her, 'Oh, we must be so much trouble.' Sue's reply was 'Yes, you are, but you're worth it!'

The peace and quiet of the Medlicott home, the many kindnesses of the family, and the companionship, proved to be invaluable for Mary. She liked to stay in bed in the morning, her tea beside her, reading students' essays and writing letters. There seems to have been one very good reason for this habit. She once told a group of students, in answer to a query about where she wrote, that she found it difficult to write when she was with people. Living with

172

people, she said, 'impinged' on her totally, causing her to have a reaction to them. 'You know, gratitude, and deference, and lots of less nice reactions. I am never in possession of myself.'

The letter writing took up quite a bit of her time. She had a long list of correspondents, but first on that list always were Valdi, Elizabeth, and Fr Scott. Dressing for the day, however, was never very time-consuming. Invariably, she wore a black wool skirt with a short-sleeved cashmere sweater under a black cardigan and black patent leather shoes with black grosgrain bows.

It was at dinner hour that Mary shone. Dinners, whenever time permitted, went on for hours and were always fun-filled. The Medlicotts remember that Caroline and Mary vied for centre-stage, with both wanting to tell their stories at the same time. The result was that they often did.

The Medlicott children – Alex, Peter, and Susan – were around thirteen, sixteen, and eighteen at the time and the middle child and Caroline attended the E. O. Smith high school together. E. O. Smith was a town school run by the university and located right on campus. Not all the students were 'faculty brats', but a large number came from families whose parents were connected with the university in one way or another. The standards were high, as was the number of students who went on to college.

Often Sue, Peter, and Caroline would study together in the evenings. The Medlicotts have a lasting memory of the evening when there was a power failure and the lights went off. The children lit candles and one of them burned down, leaving a hole in the Columbia Encyclopedia. 'We think of the kids always when we see that book – and that hole,' Alex Medlicott said.

Caroline, whom the Medlicott children loved, was a vivacious girl with long, dark hair. She made friends easily, was extremely articulate, took an active part in the high school activities, and was well liked. She seemed old for her years: not surprising in a child whose father had died a year after she was born and whose mother had had to raise all three of her children alone. On the other hand, she had a wonderful youthful vitality. All things considered, she resembled a typical American teenager. The Medlicotts, very early on, felt that Caroline would choose writing as a career and follow in her mother's path.

There had been times, during Mary's stay in her first lodgings, when she felt that perhaps bringing Caroline with her was a mistake. But soon she could see that Caroline was in love with the States, with the village, and with her high school and Mary was delighted to have her with her. Caroline, in fact, looked back on that year as one of the happiest of her life. Mary's only regret was that Valdi and Elizabeth were not there as well. Her two older girls were constantly on her mind and on her lips: so much so that the Medlicotts felt they were acquainted with them both.

In addition to teaching, Mary was giving readings both on and off campus. It had not taken long for her to earn a reputation for those readings, and she was in great demand. She gave them not only on campus but also in the town and always to overflow audiences. Although not a very tall women and a little heavy, Mary was a striking figure on the platform. It was difficult to judge her age. Listening to her or talking with her, she seemed ageless: a tribute to her personality and her demeanour. It may be unfair to compare her appearance, in her fifties, with that of an American woman of the same age and class but she would have been considered older and not as smart. Appearance was not a high priority with Mary: she simply didn't pay much attention to how she looked.

Mary read her stories with great sensitivity, and knew them so well that she scarcely needed to consult her text. An excellent mimic, she actually acted out some of the scenes. She liked the question periods and answered the questions graciously, even though some of them would have tried the patience of any writer. To be asked how many hours a day she wrote was a question she found particularly irksome and, for her, unanswerable.

She was in great demand for dinner parties as well as for readings. She was a raconteur and her anecdotes were based on what she had lived through: experiences that often became part of her fiction. Those dinner parties, like those with the Medlicott family, were marathon occasions, lasting often for three or four hours. No one was ever bored.

Socializing was very much to Mary Lavin's taste but it left very little time for creative writing and that bothered her. As she said, she might go weeks or months without writing but not without wanting to write. She was, however, never very good at fending off the innumerable distractions. The truth was that she enjoyed spending time with people. Undoubtedly, too, she allowed her students to take up more of her time than was necessary. Her readings required no preparation but there were the chats afterwards and the social engagements that they often led to. Nevertheless, during her time in Storrs, she appeared in the *Kenyon Review*, as well as in the *New Yorker* and Constable brought out her *In the Middle of the Fields* collection.

Whatever the university paid her, one of her colleagues said, they got more than their money's worth. She was a good teacher, a good critic, and a public personage. She didn't see it that way. In talking about that year later, she said 'I didn't give lectures. All I did was wander around the campus. I think maybe I was a disappointment.' She was wrong, of course. The proof was that the administration invited her to return during the academic year 1970–71. What had started out disastrously proved to be a good year for Mary Lavin and Caroline and she gladly accepted.

When Mary had left Ireland to take up her position at Storrs in 1967, Nora – Mummy – had been very much on her mind and her conscience. For Mary, as she had often said to her daughters, the greatest happiness on earth was for a mother to be loved by her children. She was saddened to think that her own mother had been denied that happiness. Nora had been failing for some time and, finally, had had to go into a nursing home. Mary and her daughters visited Nora faithfully and Mary brought her *The Irish Times* daily. Although Mary felt that it was the wrong time for her to be away from Dublin, she knew she was glad for the respite from the duty visits to her mother. On those visits there was generally some unpleasantness: some remark made by her mother that was cruel or, about Tom Lavin, disparaging.

It is difficult to determine whether Nora was really quite satisfied to be in the nursing home or whether, in a letter from her to her brother Leo and her sister Kathleen at the time she was admitted, she was just Nora being 'noble'. At any rate, the letter provides a clear picture of Nora Lavin's personality. She wrote:

> Pets! Wait till you here [sic] where I have decended [sic] to now! and you will die, but the matron of the place upstairs took my suitcase with a few necessary things in it & said she was putting it in a *safe* place & locked it up and I sent for her & no use so we had a small row but it's alright now – she came in and said I am putting you in a very nice room now, but I was on my guard. I have been thro [sic] so much that I didn't care, Kat.

Obviously Nora had very little regard for spelling or punctuation but her handwriting was distinct.

The matron had put Nora in a wheelchair and 'off we went!!' She was wheeled down the hall 'and into a lovely big rather bare but airy room windows *wide open* & a few nice bedsteads with 3 old people in them – very nice people indeed & very kind but old and feeble & this evening a social worker arrived & we were great friends'. She loved social workers, she wrote, and always had. This social worker was named

'Miss Bloomer!!! a very nice person & says she will come again to see me, very nice I liked her and best of all is a lovely little church & weekday Mass *every day!!!* nearly by my window! Just think and I have missed my Sunday Mass of late *so much.*'

She was apparently quite thrilled when Miss Bloomer said of the other residents that they looked upon Nora 'as a teenager!!!' She went on to say that they now had a nurse too who had 'just arrived with my tray of tea & marmalade! & I get all my meals too sent down and so do not worry about me love I am independent for the moment anyway so that means a lot and I can come & go as I like & the buses pass the door so you and Leo do not worry about me.' The ending was difficult to make out because Nora had written across the top of the letter, as Mary always did.

Mary was back in Dublin when, in July 1969, Nora Lavin, her health having deteriorated further, had to be admitted to St Kevin's Hospital. Mary was upset about her mother's condition but seemed to be almost as upset because she was going into a public facility. There was stigma attached to being reduced to becoming a patient in a public institution like St Kevin's. It seems that, had Mary felt able to afford it, Nora would not have spent her last days there. Similarities between Mary and her mother existed to a greater extent than she realized. Somewhat status-conscious, she had also inherited a bit of that imperious streak. It would be difficult to characterize her as someone who looked down upon anyone. She was the soul of kindness to graduate students, to young faculty, to aspiring writers, and to just about everyone with whom she came into contact. But she expected acknowledgement of her position, and, if she sensed she was not getting it, under that warm Irish manner there was a visible layer of displeasure.

By the time Mary returned to the University of Connecticut during the 1970-71 school year, she was free of the care of her mother. Nora Lavin died in December 1969 and burial took place in a Catholic cemetery in Navan, County Meath, in a plot purchased by Tom Lavin where he and William Walsh were buried.

Near the end of Nora's life, according to a letter Mary wrote to her daughters some years later, Nora had said that Mary had never loved her. That wasn't exactly true, Mary had written, 'I did but in a helpless way – and certainly without understanding her.' She had been unable to find a way to compromise between their incompatibilities or 'make her see they had to be supported'. One quite moving story is told, though it changes somewhat in various renditions. When Nora was in the nursing home, Mary had said to her: 'I love you, Mummy', and Nora had replied, 'Yes, but it's too late.'

In an undated letter to one of her daughters after her mother died, Mary wrote:

> I am reminded so sadly of my mother – poor little Mummy – I suppose she tried to make me good company for her, her little anecdotes and choosing my books when I was small (all sentimental and worthless) and I just grew up to be not good company for her at all. But . . . let's not think too much about it. I feel that the theory of putting everything sad or disturbing out of one's mind completely is to atrophy one's self – to be half dead in life – but one must only let those terrible shafts of sadness illuminate for a moment and not harm, damage, enter into one's soul and destroy.

During that first period at the University of Connecticut, as well as giving a great deal of thought to her mother's illness, Mary had been thinking too of her relationship with Michael Scott. In March 1967, she had written Valdi that a great decision had been reached in her personal life. She and 'Mick', as she and the girls always called him, had settled everything at last. She planned to join him in 'Buenos Ayres' (by then she might learn to spell it, she wrote) for three weeks, after which they would have one month in Spain. They were planning to have a year together in 1969. As for marriage, they were not going to worry about it until they could talk the whole thing through in Buenos Aires.

Apparently, they had no intention of violating the celibacy ruling. She was certain that was the right course to follow and she was very happy. Years later, talking with one of her daughters, she indicated her scepticism about 'this whole celibacy business'. They had made a mistake by going along with it, she felt. But they had not regarded living together 'as an alternative'. They wanted to be married, as her daughter put it, 'by bell, book, and candle'. Later she came to believe that waiting had been neither praiseworthy nor honourable.

Around the same time that Mary was disclosing her plans to Valdi, 'Scottie', according to Dr Gillen, had come to him to say that he had decided to leave the priesthood to marry. Dr Gillen tried hard to dissuade him. For years Michael had never had to worry about anyone but himself, he pointed out. How, he asked, could 'a selfish old bastard' (apparently fifty-seven was old to Michael's younger friend) take on the responsibility of not one person but three others as well? Michael, however, would not listen and even asked his friend to write a letter to facilitate his release from the priesthood. Dr Gillen had considered refusing. At the time he had felt that he would be 'saving a Jesuit from ruin', and that Michael would be sorry that he had not listened to his advice.

It was only later that Dr Gillen thought of the 'cold, draughty halls and barren walls of Newman', and understood how much Michael must have 'longed for the warmth that he found in the hot heads and peat-fired-up Walshes who eventually gave him plenty of distraction from the cold theoretical, theological abstractions and brought him facing up to life's realities with a jolt'. As for the responsibilities Michael would be taking on with Mary's children, Dr Gillen could see that for him that would be no drawback. He loved them so very much that whenever he spoke of them it was as though they were his own and their troubles his.

There had never been any doubt about the depth of Michael's love for Mary. As Dr Gillen wrote to her long afterwards, over the years every letter that arrived from Dublin had 'lubricated his [Michael's] larynx and dissolved his inhibitions'. And there can be no doubt either about Mary's feeling for Michael. Once, during the fifteen years of her widowhood, Mary had said to Dr Gillen that she 'had made a vow that she would get him back from the Jesuits come hell or high water'. Surely that was said lightly but just as surely it was what she hoped she could manage to do.

Early in 1969 she succeeded. Mary Lavin and Michael MacDonald Scott were married on 18 March 1969 in Bruges, Belgium. It was a civil marriage, with Valdi serving as her mother's sponsor and a Belgian bishop, the Most Reverend Burder, serving as Michael's. That civil ceremony was followed shortly afterwards by a Catholic service in a Jesuit abbey. Michael was now 'without a profession', as he stated on his marriage certificate.

The night before the wedding, Mary and Michael had a very pleasant dinner with Dr Garret FitzGerald, who, in the 1970s, became Ireland's Minister for Foreign Affairs and later leader of the Fine Gael party. His presence meant a great deal to them both. Dr FitzGerald's association with Mary had been a long one. Before he assumed his political role, Dr FitzGerald had been a lecturer at UCD and he and his wife Joan had met Mary in 1957 at the home of mutual friends, John Lovat-Dolan and his wife Elizabeth. The FitzGeralds and Mary enjoyed each other's company. They had visited with her at the Abbey Farm and also the Mews, and their daughter Mary and Caroline had become good friends. Subsequently, possibly 1978 as Dr FitzGerald recalled, Mary and Mick stayed with the FitzGeralds in a house they had rented in Les Arcs near Draguignan in the South of France.

The decision to marry had not been made lightly or hastily by either Mary or Mick. The difficulty of the decision for Michael and the toll it took is spelled out in the Newman College Collection of Art catalogue mentioned earlier. There is a description of Michael's appearance in 1967, when his portrait was painted by Clifton Pugh. According to the writer, his face shows visible signs of suffering. Of Michael's plight, he wrote:

> 1967 was a most difficult year in Scott's life. In early 1968 he resigned from his position as Rector of the College in order to leave Australia and the Society of Jesus after forty years in the Order. The laicization of a Catholic priest involves a painful dislocation at the best of times. In Scott's case it was made all the more difficult by the length of his time in the Society and by the prominence of his position as Rector of a major university college. Much of 1967 was spent agonizing over the decision, which he confided to a small group of close friends and associates.

When, on one occasion, Michael was asked for his opinion of the Pugh portrait, he had said that he thought he looked 'old and grim', much more so than he believed he actually did: 'but who can see oneself properly?' Perhaps that was the way Pugh saw him at that point, he added. 'Anyhow, I believe Cliff Pugh to be a great portrait painter, and I am proud to have sat for him.' Many of Michael's friends and colleagues were not quite so charitable in their reactions. They believed the work should have emphasized his 'more abiding qualities', which they list as warmth, humour, and compassion. One of his friends went so far as to call the portrait 'an insult to his memory'. Be that as it may, Michael Scott was certainly a troubled man during that period.

Rome had been slow in granting laicization. According to a friend of the Scotts, Michael hurried the proceedings along a bit by telling the authorities in Rome that Mary had a fine bed in the Mews with a much-admired headboard, and that he was planning to take advantage of the wonderful bed if they didn't hurry. That, Michael said, 'did it'.

Soon after Mary and Mick married, there was another wedding in the family. On 10 July 1969, Valdi and Desmond (Des) MacMahon were married in Dunderry Church, about five miles from Bective, and their wedding reception was held at the Abbey Farm. Valdi had met Des, a fine-looking young civil engineer, through Elizabeth: he was a friend of one of her men friends. Mary was pleased with Valdi's choice. In many ways he resembled Mick: straightforward, reflective, rather serious, and intelligent.

That period between Mary's first and second stints at Storrs had altered her life. She was once more a married woman, she had a married daughter, and her mother was no longer there for her to look after. What perhaps loomed largest was the sense that Valdi's marriage was undoubtedly the beginning of a break in the close relationship she had had with her daughters, or at least a change in that relationship.

III

Autumn

CHAPTER 8

For her second stint at the University of Connecticut – the second semester of 1971 – Mary was given a small apartment in the graduate housing complex, an architectually rather stark building adjacent to the library. It was not exactly a home-like atmosphere but her friends the Medlicotts were not too far away and she spent a considerable amount of time with them. Often, on mornings when Mary found time to write, she would do so at the Medlicotts. In their home she was very much part of the family and allowed to go her own way.

Before Mary had had a chance to become accustomed to having a married daughter, Valdi informed her that she would soon be a grandmother and on 2 April 1970, Kathleen, Mary's first grandchild, was born. Valdi and Des were living in Waterford, south of Dublin and on the coast, and Mary visited them there shortly after the birth of Kathleen. Back home, she wrote them about her visit, a visit which was without a doubt the inspiration for 'A Walk on the Cliff', a story which appeared in her collection *A Family Likeness and Other Stories*, published by Constable in 1985.

The letter written after Mary's visit read in part: 'The cove, and the charm of the house, & the haute cuisine, and the trawlers at the pier, made my visit so enjoyable, but most of all it made me so happy to see you both so happy.' And in 'A Walk on the Cliff', a young couple, married for a very short time, are visited by her mother. There are tense and trying moments and sharp words during the evening. The following morning, as the mother prepares to leave, all is pleasant and loving. There are in this story many beautifully descriptive passages. Driving towards home, the mother stops the car and looks back.

> The morning sun shone full on the small port, on bay
> and shore. As for the cliff . . . it was as if it had been
> struck by a magic wand and all its crags and rocks
> grown over by verdure, and, what was more, a verdure
> blonded by sunlight.

She drives on a bit and then stops and looks back once again.

> The stillness of it all! The waves that must be
> incessantly breaking on the shore, and the tumultuous
> waves that must still be dashing violently against the
> base of the cliff and sending their spray heaven-high
> into the air, seemed, all, all to have been stilled. From
> where she stood they appeared like a painted frieze,
> fanged but static, in the way that mountain cataracts
> in Connemara cascaded thunderously downward
> drenching the roads with spume yet seemed, when
> one looked back, from even a short distance away, no
> more than a veining of white marble in the black stone.

It was as though Mary Lavin were reflecting upon how, just
as the landscape changes in the light of day, relationships
change and become illuminated.

Another story in that same collection, 'A Family Likeness',
also concerns itself with the visit of a mother to a married
daughter and her husband and, in this case, a grandchild. In
both of these stories, the picture Mary Lavin draws of the
mother's efforts seem to parallel her own attempts to be the
kind of mother that, to her mind, Nora never was. And in
both, Lavin shows the sadness involved in the inevitable
conflicts in the mother-daughter relationship and the hurts
provoked unnecessarily. Both show, too, the difficulties
involved in such relationships: a grandmother trying
desperately not to interfere, not to criticise, and yet unable
to achieve either goal completely.

In 'A Family Likeness' the daughter, now the mother of

an active four-year-old child, is drawn as extremely tired and irritable. In an attempt to form a bond with her, the mother dredges up a memory from her own young mother-hood to form a parallel. Her mother, she says, used to annoy her by telling her that she would look back on those years as the best years of her life. Predictably, her daughter reacts in exactly the same way.

To Mary's great delight, in April Michael Scott came to Storrs to be with her. She had done her usual worrying about his flight. 'Please God he will be all right and get away in good order and arrive safely,' she wrote to Valdi and Des. And she added, 'Do you know I have had a letter from him almost every day. He is incredible.'

Mick was just in time to share news of the latest family upheaval: Elizabeth's marriage on 6 April 1971 to Diarmuid Peavoy, someone about whom Mary knew very little. It had all been very sudden. Alex Medlicott recalled that, when Mary told them about the marriage, her way of drawling *Pea-voy* seemed to indicate that she was far from elated. But she rose to the occasion. She turned to Valdi and Des for details. 'What do you make of it? I'm dying to hear the MacMahon version. Anyway the deed is done now and I hope all is for the best. They certainly looked a fine pair in the picture.' She was more eager than ever to get home now. 'I hope we can have a little party for her in Bective – a daytime one maybe – like a wedding – very special. What do you think?'

Michael Scott was something of a surprise to Mary's friends at Storrs. Those who had expected him to have Mary's *joie de vivre* were disappointed. It was obvious, however, that they were a devoted couple and well suited to each other. Although they did not exactly act like newly-weds, she would tease him with the verbal jabs which came very naturally to her and they would laugh together. He was well organized, quite methodical – with a wonderfully rational mind. He gave the impression of being a very serious man – quiet, modest, intelligent – but he had a dry wit much like Mary's. He wore well: the longer one knew Michael Scott, the clearer his admirable qualities became. He proved to be an asset at the numerous dinner parties given for the couple, though invariably Mary dominated all occasions.

Mary had once said that Mick had not known what a 'tough life' was like until they were married and to a certain extent that was true. Just as Dr Gillen had pointed out, Michael's life as a priest had been a sheltered one, financially and physically. By the time they were married, however, he had made a great many of the adjustments that were necessary for his new life. He was already accustomed to acting as a father figure for the girls and had spent a considerable amount of time with Mary. He took quite naturally to the role of husband and father and to that of grandfather as well when, by the mid-1970s, there were grandchildren. Kathleen MacMahon, Valdi's daughter and their first grandchild, spent fairly lengthy periods at the farm with them when she was around three or four, and she said in an 1994 interview that he – more than her grandmother – seemed to enjoy the little ones. He had the patience to watch television with them, according to Kathleen, whereas her grandmother wanted to talk. It was Mary, not Michael, who had to adjust during the early years of their marriage.

Michael had not taken very easily to being, as he had recorded on his marriage licence, 'without a profession'; he was not without one for very long, however. In the early 1970s he was named Dean of the School of Irish Studies, a highly respected non-profit educational institution, founded in 1969 and located on Merrion Road in Ballsbridge. Its purpose was to give overseas students – particularly those from the United States and Canada – an opportunity to become acquainted with the literature, language, history, archaeology and art of Ireland. Particular emphasis was placed on studying the forces which had shaped Irish writers. The student body was carefully selected and limited to forty in any one semester, and students were encouraged to live in an Irish home as part of the family.

Michael's duties included a certain amount of travel to colleges in other countries to acquaint the institutions with the School of Irish Studies and to interview prospective applicants. On one of his trips he visited twenty-five colleges in five states: Washington, Oregon, California, Colorado, and Kansas, successfully enrolling twenty-five students for the following semester. It was tiring work but it had its advantages. He could continue to pursue his study of architecture – his great love. And he could always look forward to the periods in between when he was at the school in Dublin or in Bective with Mary.

A letter Mary wrote to Mick during one of those periods when he was travelling is a good indication of how great her dependence upon his stabilizing influence was. That had been true from the time of William Walsh's death but with marriage it appears to have increased. The letter was never sent because, after writing it, she realized that it would not catch up with Mick in his travels. She decided, therefore, to hold it. He could read it upon his return, she wrote, and then she would not 'have to take time from later misfortunes to tell you those that have been overcome'. And they were numerous.

'My dear love,' the letter began. 'I miss you more than I knew I would.' She had received five letters from him and had loved them. 'I was beginning to think that there was an end to love letters when you got married to one you loved, but my faith has been restored.' She was writing in haste, she told him, because she was expecting a *New York Times* correspondent to interview her in the Mews, 'which is filthy'. She had bought 'a fiver's worth of flowers to distract an eye that I fear is not to be distracted'. She was nervous about the interview as the day had been hell – and she capitalized that – 'the only ray of light being that I haven't had time to clean the mews'. Her 'trials and tribulations' included 'fatigue, tension, and utter inability to finish the story as well as not paying bills or answering urgent letters'. She had also locked the car keys in the car and, at the time she was writing the letter, was waiting for the Automobile Association.

The conclusion of Mary's letter underlined not only her dependence on Mick but also a fear which she would express many times over to him and to her girls that she had not been protective enough of their love. She wrote:

> I have benefited in many ways by being alone – when I was let – but I'm sick of being parted from you. We need to quote that French poet (whose name we *knew* in those days) who said *'Partir c'est mourir un peu.'* Perhaps for lovers – for husband & wife it is not little – it is death, exactly the same. I have felt at times that you *were* dead. And then I got scared & thought it was a premonition. Oh, Mick. Your letters were so warm & loving. But, by and large, we have not tended our love very well. Let's be more watchful of it when you come home. And come home in two pieces, body & soul – a corpse only comes back in one.

Towards the end of her time in Storrs, she wrote home that she would never 'do a stint like this again'. Giving readings had helped to make the year fairly pleasant: she had given them at Vassar, Bryn Mawr, Boston College and the University of Pennsylvania. She longed to be with the family, however. 'The shortness and the preciousness of life was something I knew all about always but now it seems so short it scares me. So precious – oh so precious.' The one shining light during that period had been Mick's presence there for at least part of it.

At last the school year had ended. She was to sail from New York on the *Nieuw Amsterdam* and watching her pack her 'cases', the Medlicotts said, was a treat. Everything imaginable went into them: a growth from a tree, a torn scarf, scraps of students' essays, answered and unanswered letters. She could not bear to leave anything behind.

The trip home was enjoyable but she did become bored. She was beginning to think that she had had enough of ocean voyages but, of course, anything was better than forcing herself to fly. There was never any question of that and the family knew it. Asked once whether she would ever consider flying, her reply was only if one of her daughters was in urgent need of her. She believed that she understood – or at least could see one reason – for her fear. It came, she thought, from an intensity of love for her family, for life, and 'even love of the earth under my feet. It is because I put such value on it, that I quake and tremble at the mere thought of the smallest danger.' She knew as well as anyone that she was rationalizing. As she said, she didn't need to be told that a brick could fall on her head from the top of Clery's department store on O'Connell Street in Dublin.

On shipboard one evening she was persuaded to enter a dance competition 'with about 40 other so-called ladies in first class'. The ladies, she thought, 'looked as if they had learned the Viennese waltz from Strauss himself'. Mary won the contest hands down. She was so sure that the family would never believe that story that she had the people at her table sign an affidavit to that effect.

As always, Mary's greatest joy was coming home to Dublin – 'the most beautiful city in the world. You get light and shadow here like nowhere else.' A walk around St Stephen's Green upon her return upset her, however. It was being destroyed, she thought. Statues all over the place. She was sure that if the men who were being honoured could return they would feel that 'a single blade of grass was more valuable than all the stone'.

Back home, Mary settled down to her routine of writing,

socializing and giving occasional readings. Between travel assignments, Mick would occasionally accompany her when she gave a reading. There is an article in an undated issue of the *Athenry Journal*, signed Muriel Nolan, of a visit by the Scotts to Athenry in the late 1970s when Mary gave a reading of some of her works in Hansberry's Hotel. Apparently it caused quite a stir. Headed 'Mary Lavin: The Athenry Dimension', it reads in part:

> Many of the readers will remember Mahon's shop on Cross Street, subsequently owned by Sean and Carmel Torpey and now Iggy's. In Mahon's era paint, wallpaper, delph, and stationary were the main part of the business, while the pub was in a quiet little corner at the back. For a number of years, they had a small lending library which was a real boon as there was no public library in the town. I wonder if the lending library owed something to Mary Lavin's influence.

What Michael found eminently satisfying, whenever he had a bit of time, was writing. For some time he had been making an attempt to solve the mystery surrounding the death of Tony, a much-loved younger brother. Because their parents had died early, Michael had always felt responsible for Tony. Their affection for each other was so deep that when Tony, a flyer during World War II, went on a mission he always flew over his brother's college. Tony had been shot down in a raid on Blenheim in July 1941, but his body had never been accounted for and Michael was obsessed with the challenge of finding his grave. He tramped everywhere in Europe, living in the hope of finding it, and it seems that Caroline and Mary occasionally went with him.

He had compiled a meticulous dossier of information over the years and had decided to do a book about Tony, but it was not until he retired in 1980 that he was able to do extensive work on it. By October 1981 it was finished but he was unable to find a publisher. Many years later, his research was bound in book form and deposited in the British and Australian War Museums.

All accounts indicate that Mary had mixed emotions about Michael Scott, the writer. On the one hand, she appeared to be proud of his ability and desire to write. But on the other hand, she seemed to consider it an infringement upon her territory. After all, *she* was the writer. Her attitude may have been a reluctance to share the limelight: she needed always to have attention focused upon her. One of her sons-in-law recalled that, when they were all at Bective, Mary disliked having them spend too much time on the telephone talking with others.

When the Tony book was out of the way, Michael began work on a history of his family: the Rankin family. In this book, he wanted to tell the story of his great-grandmother Rankin and her six sons. They had emigrated from the Scottish Highlands in 1848, had spent three years, as he phrased it in a letter to Dr Gillen, on the Darling River, and then moved south to Tumut, New South Wales, where they managed to build up a holding of about 200,000 acres. Michael was trying to trace the descendants of the six Rankin brothers.

In 1982 he visited Australia to gather more material for the Rankin book and to make a further attempt to find a publisher for the book about Tony. Apparently he had felt the urge to go 'home'. His childhood had been a happy one. His father had been the Medical Superintendent of the mental hospital at Morisett on the shores of Lake Macquarie and Michael had said that 1914–18 were the most wonderful years 'for a boy' there. Mick was seventy-two when he made that trip, and he had not expected to live that long. His mother had died at forty-six, his father at fifty. The trip seemed to fill a need for Michael. He visited family and friends and spent a few days with the Gillens and, he said, he felt as if he had recovered something of what he had lost in fifteen years in Ireland: a sense of being an Australian.

Nevertheless, Michael had become very much part of Dublin life, was well known and respected there, and had even become accustomed to being referred to as 'Mary Lavin's husband'. They led an active social life, but social life aside, 'Mick' – as he was becoming generally known – was happiest when he was at the Abbey Farm. He once wrote: 'I am coming to resist every minute I spend away from Bective and am really looking forward to retirement.'

When Mary was at Storrs, she had written to the family to say that she longed to be in Bective where she could 'do nothing but write and read and read and write'. And she did love the peace of life at the farm. But, unlike Mick, she had to get away to the excitement of the city, and the kind of live she led there. Mary was on the guest list of most of the embassies in Dublin: Canadian, American, French, Italian and, as her daughters recalled, on the Russian and Japanese as well, and she and Mick were much in demand at embassy parties. The behind-the-scenes workings of the countries' leaders would have been known to Mary, for she did mix with the diplomatic crowd. There is no indication that she was greatly interested in politics as such, but she undoubtedly took a certain amount of delight in the gossip. According to V. S. Pritchett in his *Dublin*, the Dubliners, like villagers, thrive on gossip. Nothing can be said in a pub that isn't repeated and quite likely embellished.

Mary was present also at most meetings of Ireland's cultural and literary associations: often in an executive capacity. As one friend said, you would be hard put to attend any literary cocktail party without seeing Mary Lavin there, her full face, with its deep-set eyes and arched brows, wreathed in warm smiles. She was usually surrounded by an admiring audience and usually also, according to reports, somewhere near the *hors d'oeuvres*.

On those occasions when they had a free evening, however, Mary and Michael could be seen dining at the Unicorn restaurant on Merrion Row, a favourite place for writers and artists. Mary, a handsome woman and one whose appearance never went unnoticed, would stride rather than walk into the room with Mick by her side. There would be very few people there who did not know Mary Lavin and her husband and, in their case, the proprietor's effusive greeting was genuine.

At lunch time the Unicorn Minor, in a lane beside the main Unicorn restaurant, was popular. It was there that Elizabeth Shannon, the American Ambassador's wife, saw Mary Lavin for the first time. At home in Washington DC she had been looking forward eagerly to living in Dublin and, among other things, meeting people whose names had meant a great deal to her over the years. In her book, *Up in the Park: The Diary of the Wife of the American Ambassador to Ireland, 1977-1981*, she listed Mary Lavin, Benedict Kiely, Terence de Vere White, Dervla Murphy, Seamus Heaney and John Broderick. As she wrote: 'It's a long list for such a small country.' She had read Lavin's stories in college and afterwards and, to her mind, Mary was 'a woman who "understands the human heart" (to quote one of her colleagues) better than anyone writing in Ireland today'.

On the day Elizabeth Shannon met Mary Lavin, she and a friend were sitting at a counter in the Unicorn Minor having lasagne when she noticed 'a remarkable-looking woman'. She had 'piles of thick, iron-grey hair pulled back into a knot, heavy black eyebrows, piercing blue eyes that seemed to see everything in the restaurant, enjoying what they saw. Also, every time I wasn't staring at her, she seemed to be staring at me.' Apparently already well versed in the vernacular, Elizabeth Shannon said to her friend, 'Who's your one over in the booth alone, with the grey hair?' When she learned it was Mary Lavin, she didn't waste a minute. She went right over, said hello, and told Mary that she knew who she was and that she loved her stories. Mary smiled – 'a warm, natural smile' – and said: 'I know who you are, too. Sit down.' And 'within minutes' they were friends, and had arranged to meet again.

There is in Elizabeth Shannon's book a glowing account of an evening in the Mews, with her husband, the Scotts, and Caroline: just the five of them. They ate a delicious dinner in the kitchen with Mary protesting at every compliment that she really couldn't cook. Actually, Mary was a gourmet cook, who enjoyed cooking and eating as well. She was horrified on one occasion when one of her guests referred to her *crêpes suzettes* as 'lovely pancakes'.

It was a perfect evening 'with laughter and talk and the lively enthusiasm of new friends who have found soul mates but haven't yet heard each other's stories'. Benedict Kiely, another of the writers Elizabeth Shannon had been eager to meet, was mentioned and that led to conversation 'about every Irish writer we liked, disliked, had read, hadn't read, must read. It was a colourful travelogue through contemporary literature.' It was also the kind of evening that a great many people – writers, painters, and just ordinary folk – had had with Mary Lavin over the years. Her children had always been natural 'straight men' – to use Elizabeth Shannon's term – for Mary and her stories and now Michael Scott had been added to the group.

To see the Scotts together was visible proof of their compatibility, and yet there was a certain amount of friction. Both Diarmuid Peavoy and Des MacMahon saw quite clearly the friction and, almost as clearly, some of the reasons for it. Mary and Mick's relationship at UCD and during the years of Mary's widowhood had been idyllic. When, finally, they married, they were well into their fifties: in those days considered fairly old. They were already settled in their ways and their personality differences were more marked at that age than earlier. Where Mick's need for order, his administrative ability, even his abstemious habits, had all been advantageous during the days of Mary's widowhood, they now were the basis for discord and resentment. With marriage, reality had to be faced. But what Mary's sons-in-law also saw were the lively discussions between Mick and Mary, their enjoyment of each other's wit: a true meeting of two fine minds.

In 1979 Mary expressed her concern about their relationship in a letter to her daughters. 'It must be nearly fifty years since I first set eyes on Mick. I love him so much, girls, and I've not been as good to him as I ought. I'm trying harder now.' Whatever Mary thought she was doing wrong apparently did not alter Mick's need for her. Towards the end of the 1982 trip Mick had made to Australia, he had written Robert Gillen to say he would soon be going home and was pleased at the thought. He was tired and also, he confessed, 'lonely for that old girl with whom I fight so much'.

One area where, inevitably, there must have been a need for considerable compromising was religion. In 1978, Pope John Paul II had assumed the papacy. His conservatism troubled Mary so much that she wrote to Elizabeth about it. It seemed, she wrote, that he had just discovered virginity, unaware that it had been a subject of paramount importance since the eighth century and that it had been an ideal to strive for through all the present-day permissiveness. 'Mick says and believes that he is so good and true a man that he will learn.' Mary sincerely hoped so because he surely had a lot to learn, she thought. Mary went on to say that she had read that a great Jesuit theologian, Karl Rahner, had challenged the Pope on the issues of contraception, abortion, celibacy and, among other things, women priests. 'He [Rahner] says God ordained for man to advance and no one can stop him. Or something like that.' The issue of contraception, she told Elizabeth, did not interest her particularly except in relation to the Third World, or 'in huge black letters, spelled *Cambodia*'. It was unimportant whether 'Valdi has another baby or whether Joe Soap's teenager has sex without consequences'.

However, on the subject of celibacy, it appears, the Scotts

were in complete agreement. Dr Gillen recalled that, during all the years he had known him, Mick had believed in optional or voluntary celibacy: priests should have the right to choose to be celibate if that was what they wanted but it should not be a rule.

It would not have been unusual for the intellectual in Ireland during those years to see the need for reform in the church. That attitude may also have prevailed among some city dwellers, though much less so in rural areas because of the lengthy history of repression, lack of education, and poverty. For so many, especially women, the parish priest was the only one the people could turn to for advice and comfort. Religion offered their greatest solace.

That the church was becoming fearful of the changing attitude in Ireland – among the young especially – can be noted in the statements of the Pope during his visit to Ireland in 1979. He called upon the people to 'remain steadfast to the old faith, loyal to the Holy See and Papal teaching'. He urged the 'lapsed and careless' to reaffirm 'the historical destiny of the Irish as a Christian and missionary people'.

Declan Kiberd expressed Mary Lavin's attitude towards religion and religious oppression in this way:

> Insofar as Lavin protested against religious oppression, she offered the principled dissent of a true believer who detected that spirituality might, in a conformist community, move from living form to dead formula. Her fear appeared to be that the Catholic religion, even in Ireland, was collapsing into a matter of mere social decorum: so she was appropriately sardonic about those who treated their own celibacy as a heroic denial of appetite rather than a positive expression of spiritual value. At moments, she could be quite scathing about the degradation of ritual to routine.

It was not only her relationship with Mick that was worrying Mary in the early 1970s. She was greatly troubled about what she perceived to be drastic changes in her life. She was aware that Elizabeth and Valdi were leading lives apart from her, and, though Mick was there, apparently she needed to have all her 'girls' around her. Elizabeth's husband, Diarmuid Peavoy, had obtained a position with APSO, the Agency for Personal Services Overseas: an agency that had been inaugurated by the Scotts' good friend, Dr Garret FitzGerald, in 1974. Diarmuid's work would be what was called distance teaching at the College of the Air, funded by the Irish Department of Foreign Affairs jointly with the Cambridge Extension College, and he would be stationed in Mauritius, one of the Mascarene Islands in the Indian Ocean. Now Elizabeth and the children were preparing to leave Dublin to join him there. Mary was sure that once the Peavoys were in Mauritius Elizabeth's life would be so full that 'she mightn't even read my letters'. Valdi was in Nicaragua where her husband was working for an irrigation firm. They corresponded, but letters were far from satisfactory. Of course, Caroline was at home and their relationship was extremely close. But Mary missed the days when they were all together.

Despite her mood, Mary was turning out a considerable amount of work. She was managing to produce new material, although busily engaged in choosing stories for her collections. In January 1973, the *New Yorker* carried 'Tom'; in the spring of 1974, *Southern Review* brought out 'The Mug of Water'; and that same year 'The Shrine' appeared in the *Sewanee Review*. Making selections for the collections was time-consuming but they were appearing with increasing regularity. *Collected Stories* came out in the United States in 1971; *A Memory and Other Stories* in London in 1972 and a year later in the States; and the *Stories of Mary Lavin, Volume II* in London in 1974.

For *Collected Stories* – twenty-two stories dating from the late 1930s to the late 1960s – the novelist V. S. Pritchett wrote an introduction. In it he explored the Irish gift for the writing of short stories. The Irish, he wrote, had what he termed 'double vision': a gift that Mary Lavin possessed. She wrote 'most of the time about people who appear to be living, at first, in a state of inertia, in the lethargy of country life: then we notice that they are smouldering and what her stories contain is the smouldering of a hidden life'. Her short stories 'make the novel form irrelevant'.

> . . . They give a real and not a fancied view of Irish domestic life and it combines the moving with the frightening. She excels in the full portraiture of power-loving women, downtrodden women, lonely women, bickering country girls, puzzled priests and seedy shopkeepers who might pass as country types first of all, but who soon reveal a human depth of endurance or emotional tumult in their secret lives.

Pritchett chose one perfect example – 'At Sallygap' – as an illustration of his points. 'It is on the old Irish theme of saying goodbye, of leaving for a better life abroad,' Pritchett wrote. 'At Sallygap' is the story of a young man who almost escapes from Ireland to embark on what he is sure will be a better life in 'gay Paree', as he phrases it. But, as he is about to sail off on the mail boat, he looks at the girl who is waving to him from the quay and he cannot bear to leave her behind. He remains at home to marry and, growing old, is trapped in a marriage which is loveless and dead. 'Henceforth, he is the girl's prisoner and we shall see him turn into a meek dealer whose only freedom is to go to farms on the Dublin mountains to collect eggs every now and then,' Pritchett wrote.

The stories had been chosen well for all the collections which appeared in those early 1970s. In *A Memory and Other Stories* there are only five. One of them, 'Trastevere', appeared in the *New Yorker* in December of 1971 and that story, as well as 'Villa Violetta', also in the collection, was based on

Mary Lavin's Florence trip. The setting of 'Trastevere' is New York City but she uses the flashback technique to tell the story of a *ménage à trois* in Florence.

The title story, 'A Memory', which concludes the collection, is a vivid portrayal of the differences in people's natures and of the blindness to the reactions of others which often ensue as a result. James, the leading character in this story, is a no-longer-young professor: a bachelor and a selfish, quite unfeeling man. The opening sentence sets the tone well. 'James did all right for a man on his own.' It is the way James lives and the way he wants to live. There are two women in the story. One, Emmy, never appears but lives only in his memory; the other, Myra, is a professional translator, and a modern, independent woman: an intellectual companion to James. What he has with her is a marriage of the minds, a state perfectly suited to him but one, he is too insensitive to realize, not suited to her. His relationship with Emmy when he was young was the closest thing to love he ever seemed capable of feeling. The climax occurs when Myra reveals how unsatisfactory their arrangement is for her and at last accuses him of having 'denatured her'. Without some physical manifestation, their relationship is barren. Mary Lavin's portraits of James and Myra show a deep understanding of the celibate male and the woman for whom a career is insufficient, without in any way condemning or placing blame.

Edward Weeks reviewed the *A Memory and Other Stories* collection in the *Atlantic Monthly* in October 1973. Of the story 'Asigh', which appears in it, and of Mary Lavin, he wrote: 'It is her special skill to begin with a single clue and a single episode and, working now in the past and now in the present, to embrace the whole of life.' The writer Joyce Carol Oates reviewed the collection in the *New York Times Book Review* and Benedict Kiely wrote of it that it showed Mary Lavin 'at the height of her powers, and that, as we should all know, is very high indeed'.

CHAPTER 9

The bond between Caroline and her mother, with Valdi and Elizabeth no longer nearby, had strengthened and Caroline was well aware of how much the changing relationship with her older daughters bothered Mary. Because all three felt that involvement in her writing had always been Mary's salvation, Caroline urged her to do a critical evaluation of her work: a study that Mary would find absorbing, one that she was well equipped to do, and one that would prove valuable. In addition, literary criticism intrigued Mary and her library contained a fair amount of books on the subject. John Montague, the poet and short story writer, had once commented upon that. He distrusted the work of any writer who read so many critical studies, he said. 'I distrust the work of any creative writer who doesn't,' Mary had replied.

There is nothing to indicate that Mary took Caroline's suggestion very seriously. But when, in 1977, Alex and Sue Medlicott – Mary's good friends since the days at Storrs – visited the Scotts at the Abbey Farm, Alex and Mary spent endless enjoyable hours discussing the various aspects of her work: her techniques and her ideas on writing in general.

The Medlicotts' visit to the Abbey Farm that year was one they always remembered fondly. They were fascinated by the terrain and by the house, although like typical Americans they found it damp and cold and the method by which the living room was heated primitive. An electric heater heated a large slab of soapstone and was turned on during the hours electricity was cheapest and then turned off. The stone retained the heat and gave some warmth to the room but by American standards not a great deal.

The interior of the house reflected Mary's personality, they thought. The living room and the dining area – three steps up from the living room – were brightened by four

Jack Yeats oil paintings – brilliant and bold: *The Old Ale House*, *The Man in the Shooting Gallery*, *Secret Eyes*, and *The Hard Sailor Man*. The window in the sunken living room extended over almost the whole south wall and looked out across the lawn and the fields towards the Abbey, and the view at twilight resembled a Constable painting. The rooms were filled with flowers and everywhere there were books, journals, and newspapers. Mick's cocker spaniel was always underfoot and in the attached garage there were innumerable cats and kittens. It was Alex Medlicott's distinct impression that Michael Scott had brought as much order into Mary's life as she could tolerate. 'And God knows she needed order,' he said. Michael may not have won the battle to get Mary organized, but he had made a significant impact.

The periods when Alex Medlicott and Mary sat down to discuss her writing were stimulating for both of them, even though Mary said she found talking about her work rather embarrassing. 'You don't want to appear as if you think it's great but you don't like to be knocking yourself either.' Yet she knew there was much she had to say and liked saying it.

As she told Alex, she thought the talk about the quality of her work meaningless. She was always being told that her short stories were very good because they are so well written.

I don't think it matters. Nobody would read them if they weren't. I mean you wouldn't want a badly made pair of shoes, so why talk about how a story's made or why it's made. It's what's said that counts. One cannot aim at an impeccable style. What one seeks is faultless construction. I have an obsessive concern with words. I know the meaning is what matters, the essence of what's being said, yet the choice of words is a small hell, the search for accuracy, for the exact word.

Plot in the accepted sense did not concern her greatly, she

maintained. Had Alex Medlicott seen her MA thesis on Jane Austen, he would have noted that her stand was one she had taken many, many years earlier. There she had written that she could 'think of twenty novels where the character interest usurps plot interest . . . The plot must be strong, but it must not be so strongly constructed that the characters are mere puppets.' There is, of course, a particular pride for an author in coming up with what appears to be a really original plot but in reality the newness and freshness of any work is in the writer's approach.

The status of the short story concerned her greatly and she was deeply puzzled as to why that school was not considered more worthy of attention and was not more popular. As she defined it, 'The inner shape of the short story reminds me of lightning in which the zig-zagging flash seems to gather force when it goes back in order to go forward with even more deadly intent. Its course is ordained and the line of development from the beginning to its destination is a true line.'

To her mind, the short story was in no way inferior to drama, poetry and the novel. She used the short stories of Conrad, Thomas Mann, D. H. Lawrence, Hemingway, Faulkner, and even Tolstoy as examples. Was the genre perhaps badly named? So many of the great short stories were obviously complete stories, and what was often called a short story was really a novella. She cited her 'Cuckoo Spit' and two of her very early stories – 'The Becker Wives' and 'A Happy Death' – as examples. Often, too, the short novel was called a novella when, as she saw it, they were two different forms. By her definition, the distinction was that the novella was exactly the right length but the short novel was 'squeezed together'.

Her current reading, she said, consisted mainly of rereading. Since she did not have a great deal of leisure time, she had stopped reading purely for recreation: she read to stimulate her mind. Consequently, she had returned to the classics and to her favourite authors. Whatever spare time she had she spent with Chekhov, Tolstoy, Turgenev and Katherine Mansfield. She liked the stories by Katherine Mansfield in which Mansfield was 'homesick for New Zealand'. She never tired of reading some of the scenes in them. 'It is a *shock* every time I read the great scenes in literature. It's a fresh shock each time.' She listed other favourites as Racine, George Sand's pastoral novels, and Sarah Orne Jewett.

The contemporary writers she admired were Elizabeth Bowen, Willa Cather, Eudora Welty, and Katherine Anne Porter. Once it had been pointed out to her that her selections were all women, something she said she had not realized. But, in her own defence, she said that she had included Chekhov and Tolstoy on her list of those she admired. She added, however, that perhaps that was because they wrote 'almost from a feminine viewpoint'.

Eudora Welty was always high on any list of writers Mary liked to read and in 1950 she had been pleased to have her as a visitor at the farm. Valdi and Elizabeth had fallen in love with her. They had never forgotten that she sent them gifts from the States. One of the packages contained chewing gum and they were not quite sure what they were supposed to do with it. They were particularly pleased with the angora sweaters she sent them: a pink one for Elizabeth and a white one for Valdi.

Reading art criticism was one of Mary's great pleasures. It was both interesting and educational. It was for her 'a kind of recreation', and a good substitute for what, earlier, she had considered recreational reading. She knew many artists and delighted in discussing their work with them. And some of the fine art work in Bective and in the Mews – her Jack Yeats oils, for example, – had been presented to her.

She found it impossible, however, to read anything she had not herself chosen. If someone sent her a thesis to read, even if the subject of the thesis was Mary Lavin, the mere fact that she had not chosen it made it impossible for her to read it. 'I'll keep pushing it away, off, off, till it goes over the edge of the table and if anything falls off the table it never gets picked up.'

As much as she liked rereading the great writers, she heartily disliked rereading her own work. She was sure that she would never look at her stories again unless she had to use one of them in a reading or work on one of them for a collection. Sometimes, when she was giving a reading, she was appalled at what she had written. She knew that selecting stories for her collections might have taken less time if she had not been, as she herself said, a great reviser. She revised after the story was typed, revised again after it appeared in the *New Yorker* and before it went into a collection, and then once more before translation. And it was not unusual for her to read it again before she signed a contract and, even then, make minor changes.

Mary's *Happiness and Other Stories* collection is a prime example. Constable brought it out in 1969. The following year it came out with Houghton Mifflin but before it did Mary got busy with her pencil. A sentence which read: 'As long as she'd come, she might as well be put to use' became 'As long as she had come with them she might as well be put to use.' It was often hard to determine whether the change had been worthwhile or even whether it had been an improvement. Had a sentence lost something when she changed it from 'Iris was staring around her at the bleak shore, so lonely, with not a soul in sight', to 'Iris was staring around her at the bleak and lonely shore, with not a soul in sight'? One change would seem to be indicative, however. In a section where a discussion is taking place between a Protestant mother and a daughter who has become a Catholic, the mother says in the Constable draft: 'And you are willing to let your children grow up in the same bonds?' Mary changed that sentence to read 'And you are willing to let your children grow up in the same stupid bonds?' But, she told Medlicott, she never 'fumbled about with details'. She might 'chop and change the actual wording, but details nearly always remain unchanged. I may delete or add to them but I do not change them.'

The changes she made for the various editions were often relatively minor and mainly indicated her increasing experience as a writer: an exclusion of words to tighten sentences, or an elimination of extraneous phrases. But the understanding of her characters, the ability to reconstruct dialogue: all of these were there from the time the stories first appeared. Alex remembered that she had told him previously that nothing she ever wrote was *finally* what she wanted to say. 'Everything needs tinkering.' He had seen examples of her need to revise when at readings she would surreptitiously pencil a note. And, in their kitchen once, he had seen her 'do' 'The Becker Wives'. When she was finished, the book was almost unreadable.

She never could understand the expression 'lost in a book'. She *found* herself in books. It would be wonderful, she thought, if one had time to study subjects such as philosophy and, say, metaphysics, but 'you're only on the earth for a limited time. Where do you draw the line?' She wished that she had spent more time listening to music, for instance, to which she was totally indifferent. She believed that was because she didn't understand it. She liked popular music and singing well enough but if she had to go listen to a string quartet, she'd 'have a fit. I'd certainly kill myself.'

She was not particularly enamoured of reading poetry, she said, and she did not keep up with the modern poets and their work, although she liked the poets she knew. 'I love talking with Seamus Heaney but I don't read his poetry and I'm sure he doesn't read my stories either.' That last was a line a Mary Lavin could not resist: a good example of her customary exaggeration for effect. It is difficult to believe that she did not read Seamus Heaney's poetry and undoubtedly he had read some of her stories. At any rate, she would have gloried in what he wrote after her death in answer to an enquiry about their association:

> My sense of Mary Lavin is based upon many social encounters over the years, none of them very intimate or sustained. She had a wonderful radiance and force, a manner you might have called stately were it not for the vivid and mischievous intelligence which was always equally in play. I had a sense of something free and defined – at a certain expense; a genuine authority, a decisiveness and release. Gumption and subtlety . . . what one might expect from the writer that she was.

Mary had given a great deal of thought to a question which often arose. How did a story evolve? As she saw the evolution, an incident or an idea would catch her fancy. It would remain dormant in her mind until it was awakened by something she saw, heard or read. A certain amount of time had to elapse between an experience and the writing down of it. In her own case, it was often a decade. It was wise also to put a story aside for a bit before it could be considered finished. One point she wanted underlined. Ideas needed time to develop. It was something she felt young writers did not always understand. 'The reservoir has to fill up before a person has anything to say.' After that there is the job of trying to say it properly.

When, finally, a story was ready to write, she would get it down at breakneck speed with all the details and notes. After she had it all down – 'safely dragged out of the deeper recesses of my mind, and secure' – she began what she understood many writers considered the hardest part but the part that she enjoyed. She would do five or six drafts, each one more condensed than the other. It was not because she was seeking perfection, she argued, but simply because that reduction was her method. She wrote by reducing. 'Being a cook too, I know all about reducing fat and reducing pan liquor, and I think that's the way I do the stories.' A story might easily have started out with seven or eight characters but in its final form have only two. 'I like to know what the old uncle is like, and what auntie is doing, and what the maid is doing in the kitchen. I know that I'm not going to keep that in but I want to see it all.' In summary, she said:

> I have learned that to understand a character in a story fully and to understand how they may behave in the situations in which they are placed, I have to create all the necessary background information. Furthermore, I frequently place them in relationships with characters other than those which will be the sole protagonists in the final version. Each new experience gives a little more insight into the human heart.

She knew a story was finished when it approximated to her original vision.

Often the autobiographical nature of Mary's stories had been commented upon and it seemed to her that it was the technique, not the material, that was subjective. 'I have always said that the way you write is you.' What the writer does with the material and how he or she shapes it is, in general, the autobiographical element of the work. She explained her idea further. 'A character in fiction can arise out of the autobiographical self and lead an independent life.' She maintained that she had never written one single paragraph that had not had the imagination as its source. And she added: 'I cannot honestly say if my real work gained or lost by my scrupulosity... But I am curious about this and all other questions concerning the mystery of imaginative creation. Preoccupations of this kind continually fill my mind.'

She had never kept a diary because the temptation to use it later, she felt, would interfere with the necessarily spontaneous resurgence out of the subconscious. She did make notes at times of things that struck her as true, or beautiful, or perhaps significant, but she did not read those notes later. They had been written only so that they would be firmly fixed in her mind.

In Mary's opinion, becoming a serious writer, like everything else, required an apprenticeship. Some people believed that newspaper work fulfilled the internship requirement. But Caroline was now a journalist on *The Irish Times* and, as Mary observed Caroline's work for that paper, she wasn't sure. In the first place, there was no time to strive for perfection in a story. And always the journalist was aware that the story would only be read once, perhaps for five minutes on a bus. 'The little time the reader gives to it is balanced by the length of time the writer gives to it.'

She was often asked whether studying the technique of other short story writers was valuable in developing her own technique. It was a question she found difficult to answer. It was impossible to tell whether one was influenced by their techniques or not, she maintained. With very young writers she could generally detect who had influenced them, but influence was not aping and soon the young writer would develop his or her own technique. As for herself, she had studied English and French in college and read widely outside the curriculum among the Russians and the Americans.

Tom Kilroy's interpretation of some of the influences upon her and of what she had passed on to him add to the picture. When she gave him Turgenev's books and Flaubert's *Trois Contes*, she had told him that they had had a profound influence upon her at the very beginning of her writing career. 'It was as if she had instinctively understood the inadequacies of the UCD degree in English of the day as a foundation for someone who wished to write. She was dead right, of course. What she was saying, too, in giving me those much-loved stories was: This is where I come from, these are my models. Anything I wanted to achieve was in the tradition of world literature.'

She had seen O'Connor, O'Faolain and O'Flaherty as only a small part of world literature. She had not read the Irish writers, except perhaps for Joyce, until she had already dedicated herself to the short story. 'Then I would have been a fool not to have studied them, masters as they were of the medium.' She began to read critically those Irish writers she had neglected and to read them in a spirit of competition. Of the three, she had the highest regard for O'Flaherty. Reading the other two, she believed she could do as well as they did. When she heard people say: 'She's nearly as good as O'Connor and O'Faolain', she said to herself, 'By God, one of these days I'll be as good and maybe someday better.'

On a radio programme called *John Bowman's Saturday 8.30*, broadcast in August 1995, John Bowman suggested that Mary had been influenced fairly strongly by Joyce. As proof, he said that he had found a well-worn copy of *Dubliners* on the flyleaf of which was written 'Mary Jo Lavin'. He believed that had been written about 1934. 'The book clearly had been carried around in a handbag and read, and read, and read by the young girl at UCD,' he said.

Invariably Mary Lavin's name has been linked with the Irish triumvirate, O'Connor, O'Faolain and O'Flaherty, and that is quite understandable. Those men were writing in the same form for the most part. But when, on another radio programme, the poet Eavan Boland asked Mary if she identified with them, she said she did not. After all, she pointed out, she was twelve years younger than the youngest of them [in fact, Frank O'Connor, the youngest of the three, was born in 1903, Mary in 1912]. When she began to write, they were already famous. 'Twelve years is a long time in your own life but it's nothing when time rolls on so I can understand why I'm grouped with them.' But she did not see herself as being of their generation. They were already writing at the time of the civil war and the fight for independence. That was the period with which their work was heavily involved. But at the time when Mary and her mother settled in Dublin, the worst of the civil war was over. There might still be military patrols in the streets and the occasional sound of rifle shots but Mary, only about ten years old, would not have been particularly interested even in the talk of the conflict.

Had she believed firmly that she was going to make a career of writing, she said, she would have concentrated on the Irish writers sooner. But nothing could shake Mary in the belief that her choice of a writing career had been accidental. As a matter of fact, she remembered clearly that after she had written that first story, 'Miss Holland', on the back of pages of her thesis, she had thought seriously of 'rubbing it out'. After that and after her books began to appear, she realized that she was a professional writer. For good or ill, she was 'stuck with it. Unless I cut my throat or something, I was not going to be able to stop.' Once started, there was no possibility of turning back.

Since Mary depended upon her writing for her livelihood, Medlicott wondered if she ever sat down to write a story because she needed the money. No, she never did, Mary maintained. She believed that need, however, could *stop* her from writing. She would actually, on occasion, pick a subject that she was sure would not sell, and one that she really didn't like, just to prove the point to herself. Inevitably, however, the characters would start to intrigue her; she would begin to understand them. The result was a good story that would sell. 'But my insurance policy with myself, for my own integrity, would be to pick a subject I thought would *not* sell.'

The Lavin-Medlicott conversations bear out Caroline's contention that Mary could have done a valuable critical study.

It was very seldom that Mary was alone on the many occasions when there were visitors. On a taped interview with Zack Bowen in the 1970s, Caroline can be heard in the background, prompting her mother and arguing various points on which Mary's recollection had, according to Caroline, been mistaken. It pleased Mary that her daughters were so sure of themselves and perfectly willing to tell her when they believed she was wrong.

Caroline had written her MA thesis on Edith Wharton 'under that terrifying genius Denis Donoghue', and received her MA. She had then, after a holiday in the States, gone to work at *The Irish Times*. Until she became too busy with her own career, Caroline was there for Mary and so was Mick. Now that Caroline was more or less in her field, Mary was consulting her more and more, but in the main it was Mick to whom she turned. When, later, his health had deteriorated and Mary had succeeded in persuading him to retire, they worked well together on the interviews. When Mary was asked at one time whether she took all her characters from life, it was Mick who answered. She would take two or three characters and give certain characteristics to one and then to the other and take the events in someone's life and put a different character in the same place, he explained. 'I can spot often that some characters are mixtures of Tom Lavin, William Walsh, and myself.' Events from all of their lives would be recorded and sometimes even things they had said. He cited the death of the mother in 'Happiness'. That death, he said, was his mother's death as he had told it to Mary many years earlier. There was a basis in reality for her characters – 'an arm here, a leg there,' he said.

Indeed Mary would have been hard put to answer whether any of her characters were completely fictional. How could one be sure? You might imagine someone and then that character would become real. She had never known anyone like the character in 'Bridal Sheets', so far as she could remember. 'Maybe she was me.'

Mick was, she said, a superlative critic. It was not unusual for her to turn to him to say: 'Mick, I'm going to quickly read this. Would you ever take a carbon and read it too?' He would read it very quickly and it amazed her to witness how well he could edit a story which did not particularly interest him. He had loved reading in the humanities when young – 'before ever I knew him and when I just used to look at him across the classroom'. And he had written on the Jesuit poet Gerald Manley Hopkins – probably an obvious choice for a Jesuit novice. Mary never needed any advice about the motivation of a character. She understood people too well for that. But she might turn to Mick to discuss sequence.

In a radio interview in the 1980s, Mary was asked if she resented having so little time for writing. It was surprising, she replied, but she never did. She was often prevented from writing because of outside pressures, especially when she was raising her children, but her stories were always there in her mind. The proof for this was that the moment she returned to a manuscript she was totally back in the story. Even after months, she could go right on without rereading from the beginning. And, though she was well aware that changes would have to be made, she always wrote through to the end of a story before making them.

As Mary told the interviewer, she had a duty to her family and she put them before her work, but that had its advantages. 'It has made me think more about what I want to write about.' It had imposed a selectivity on her that she might not have been strong enough to impose on herself. She made a further point. As she saw it, her responsibilities were actually a plus. For example, men, usually protected by a wife or a secretary, wrote when they did not really want to, whereas women writers had so many demands upon them that they could not afford to waste time writing anything that they did not really feel it was necessary to say.

Early in 1978 Caroline wrote the Medlicotts that her mother was really 'gone mad on the work lately. Though outsiders say it is no life, I know that to be working madly is the only real thing for her. I hope it goes on for years and years and years.' She scarcely left her room, according to

Caroline. She began work at six in the morning and went on throughout the day. She would have 'the odd glass of wine', cook dinner or go out to eat, and then get right back to work.

This upbeat stage continued and by the late 1970s a letter from Mary to Valdi stated: 'You can now confidently refer to me as internationally known, with books translated into all major languages except Spanish and Portuguese.' Valdi could indeed. Mary Lavin's work had been translated into Dutch, German, Hebrew, French, Italian, Polish, Russian and Japanese. And Mary knew her rights. In her negotiations, she had insisted that translators would have to be acceptable to her, that they would have translated authors of note, and, if possible, authors with whom she could be said to have some affinity; for example, Hemingway, Flannery O'Connor and Joyce for his stories.

The 1960s and 1970s had seen Mary receiving awards, grants and appointments to high office in literary associations. She served two terms as President of Irish PEN, and also two terms, 1971–5, as President of the Irish Academy of Letters, an organization founded by William Butler Yeats and George Bernard Shaw in 1932 to fight against censorship. In 1972 she received the Ella Lyman Cabot Award; in 1975 the Gregory Medal, an honour that had been called by Yeats the supreme award of the Irish nation for writers of literature.

There were often accounts of her activities with accompanying pictures in the Dublin papers. On 29 March 1968 *The Irish Times* carried a photo of Mary in cap and gown with President de Valera watching as she signed the book after receiving her honorary Doctor of Literature degree from UCD. Two days later there was a report in the *Sunday Independent* of her receiving the degree which quoted her as saying, 'You do your best work as you grow older. If I did not believe that my next story was going to be an improvement on my last then I would regret ever having decided to become a writer.' In April 1974 at their annual dinner, the Éire Society of Boston awarded Mary the Gold Medal of that Society, an honour previously awarded to John F. Kennedy, Siobhan McKenna and Senator Eugene McCarthy, among others. The citation which accompanied the award read: 'Mary Lavin, Daughter of the Bay State, with fierce loyalties to all New England, she early fell under the spell of Erin, her home now for half a century. Mother, Wife, and Story-Teller of the First Rank, she has heard the heartbeat of her race and spoken Ireland's name to the Universe.'

In 1979 she was the recipient of the American Irish Foundation Literary Award, granted each year to an Irish writer, poet or playwright. At that time it carried a cash prize of seven thousand dollars. Mary's income, like that of many other writers, was uncertain and prize money was very often badly needed. 'Humble and all as I am,' she wrote to Elizabeth, 'by God, I deserve it.' She was not looking forward to the awards ceremony but, as she wrote, 'the joy of the money for a while eclipses the ordeal of the prize giving'. The money was to be paid in monthly instalments and 'the gloom and doom people' had told her that the amount would be affected by inflation. 'But who cares really. It was *so, so* great to get it.'

In 1981 Mary received the Allied Irish Banks Award for Literature which carried a prize of two thousand pounds. A photo in the *Irish Press* for 5 November showed Mary Lavin, flanked by Benedict Kiely, representing the Irish Academy of Letters, and Professor Patrick Lynch, Deputy Chairman of Allied Irish Banks, as she accepted the award. The decision had been unanimous, Kiely said, and he added that her work 'showed a warmth and extraordinary understanding of human beings'. The occasion was attended by an impressive number of dignitaries, among them Jack Lynch, former leader of the Fianna Fáil party. Mary's grandson Eoghan Peavoy, present as well, said that he had wanted to be an artist but after meeting Jack Lynch had decided to become a politician.

In the 1980s Mary had two of Ireland's highest honours bestowed upon her: she was named one of sixteen members of the Cultural Relations Committee for the years 1985 and 1986 by the Minister for Foreign Affairs, and she received an appointment to the prestigious Aosdana.

The Cultural Relations Committee advised the minister on the artistic and cultural merits of particular projects to be presented abroad, and recommended whether such projects should be assisted financially out of their 'Grants-in-Aid' programme. Those grants were intended 'to give support to Irish cultural projects of a high artistic standard with a view to the enhancement of Ireland's image and reputation abroad and the promotion of friendly relations and of mutual knowledge and understanding with other countries'. The recipients were selected by a means test. Mary was critical of some of the bursaries awarded but, her astringent remarks aside, it is more than likely that, had those writers come to Mary Lavin to ask for a loan, they would have received it and, if she had been consulted about the grants, she probably would have approved them.

Aosdána had been established in 1981 and funded by the Irish government through the Arts Council for the purpose of formally recognizing individual achievement in the arts by selected writers, artists and composers, and providing them with some financial support. Those who lived in Ireland and received no compensation except from creative work could apply for an annuity then set at five thousand pounds for a period of five years. Members were to be free of any political control and their work was not to be censored. They had to be born or have lived in Ireland for five years and be at least thirty years of age. Membership was not to exceed 150 persons though later an effort was made to increase the number to 200. Only on the death of one of the members could another be appointed.

The first meeting of Aosdána was held in April of 1983

in what was once the Irish House of Lords and at that time part of the Bank of Ireland. Garret FitzGerald, then Taoiseach, addressed the group of forty-six artists, thirty-four writers – Mary Lavin among them – and eight composers. Mention was made of absent members: the playwright Brian Friel, the poet Seamus Heaney, Samuel Beckett and the novelist Anthony Cronin. Dr FitzGerald began by saying, 'You are now an institution, established and underwritten by the State,' and he called this first meeting 'one of the most important developments in recent years in the cultural life of the country'.

In addition to being the recipient of so many honours, Mary's work was being lauded in the Irish press by top-flight reviewers and distinguished critics. Brendan Kennelly, reviewing her *Happiness* collection in *Books Sunday*, commented on the 'poetic quality of her work'. He believed that it stemmed from 'her faith in the essential goodness of life', while at the same time she did see, and cause her readers to see, that forces threatened that goodness. 'Mary Lavin pushes back the shoulder of despair with the shoulder of humour and compassion,' he wrote. 'She answers the despair that threatens the twentieth century with: "Look around you: there is hope in the ground at your feet, in the sky above you, in the faces you pass on the street, in the sacredness of your own feelings, in the wonder of others, but, above all, in the knowledge that though men die, man lives and loves and grows."'

In 1978 *Tales from Bective Bridge* was reissued and Benedict Kiely said in *The Irish Times* in November of that year that he had reread the collection twice since it came out in 1942 and had enjoyed it more each time. He had also read everything else she had written over the years and felt that Mary Lavin got better and better. But then he had looked at *Bective Bridge* once more and decided that one couldn't really get better than that. He was amazed at how well she understood people and how clearly she saw 'the details of the lives of various sorts of people in various places'.

Mary wrote an introduction to the 1978 edition of the *Bective Bridge* collection and Kiely praised that as well. In it she modestly attributed the collection's success not only to Lord Dunsany's help but also to luck. After the collection won the James Tait Black Memorial Prize, it had become a Readers' Union choice which, according to Mary, 'made it a commercial as well as a literary success'. She expressed regret that the stories in the collection had been accepted by reputable publications without any revision on her part. As Kiely commented, what she wrote on the subject of 'polishing' stories should be heeded by any writer, 'young, old, or in-between'. She wrote, in part:

> No manuscripts of those early stories are in existence today, but I am fairly certain that there would not have been more than one version of each story, with few corrections and no revisions. I do not think it entered my head that I could, or should, try to make them better. Now, more than thirty years later, their flaws bear witness to my carelessness . . . I wholeheartedly believed – as I do to this day – in the power of the imagination to arrive at truth, but I did not know that the imagination cannot be trusted unless it is fully disciplined. When it is so disciplined, its blinding light shuts out all that is irrelevant.

She concluded her introduction with a gracious acknowledgement of the debt she owed Lord Dunsany:

> When I was young my gratitude to Dunsany was overshadowed by my embarrassment at the extravagance of the praise he had given me. Now, when that Preface as well as the stories it introduced belongs to the past, I am able to be wholly grateful to him. Only an extraordinarily generous mind could make the

219

mistake of attributing more merit than it deserved to the work of a young and unknown writer.

Professor Augustine (Gus) Martin, talking with the poet Eavan Boland on a radio arts programme in 1985, spoke of what he felt Mary Lavin had managed to accomplish in her work. She gave a voice to 'a whole world of comparatively inarticulate people – small shopkeepers, lonely girls working in farms, widows, people living in dull small towns'. He believed that it was 'her peculiar gift' that she was able to find in their lives 'a kind of round poetry which a superficial aspect of society is constantly trying to blot out . . . a kind of romantic spirit, constantly striving against a world of dull conniving calculation'.

Declan Kiberd wrote of her style that it 'seldom drew attention to itself, working more by innuendo than by statement'. He went on:

> Though her focus was on individuals, often caught in autumnal solitude after a fulfilled passion, her values were those of her community. She thus became that most rare thing in Ireland: a writer who found expressive freedom in rather than from the available community; and one who somehow managed . . . to find within those constrictions a way of mapping the contours of the human heart.

The reissue of *Tales from Bective Bridge* had sparked one surprising review, carried on 5 October 1978 in the *Irish Press*. The author was James Stern, whose family had sold Mr Bird, Tom Lavin's employer, Bective House in 1926, as noted earlier. One day in the early 1940s, Stern had been walking down Fifth Avenue in New York City when he saw *Tales from Bective Bridge* in a bookstore window. He bought it immediately, eager to read how Mary Lavin, born in the United States, had reacted to his home and to Ireland. 'Of what would she have been thinking and writing as she looked up from her desk to gaze out over the placid river to the Hill of Tara.'

Stern was amazed to find Mary's stories about 'an Ireland reduced to its simplest, least sophisticated terms', with so many of her characters peasants and shopkeepers living in villages and small towns. The writer of the stories might never have lived in the United States. He called her prose 'as unpretentious as the characters it so vividly describes'. When, in 1978, he reread the stories in the Poolbeg edition, he was again amazed and then moved to write a review. He could, he wrote, 'think of no other living writer of stories whose first collection attains such maturity'.

Stern ended his review on a personal note. Twenty-five years after he left Bective, he had returned to Ireland for the first time and there 'the now famous author' welcomed him and his wife and gave them tea in 'our' schoolroom. He remembered thinking at that time that he had never felt so much at home. 'Glory be, what was I after saying! I was home!'

All the praise heaped upon Mary in the Irish press seemed far from adequate to her family, however. According to V. S. Pritchett, 'The Irish writer works best in his own country, but his countrymen are his worst enemies and he can succeed only outside it, either in England or America.' Elizabeth, and undoubtedly Mary's other daughters as well, could echo that sentiment. They have never felt that Mary received sufficient recognition, and they are not alone. People well qualified to judge her work objectively, such as Robert W. Caswell, Zack Bowen, Richard F. Peterson, Augustine Martin and Frank O'Connor, agreed wholeheartedly. They offered interesting and convincing arguments.

Both Martin and Caswell felt that she had been neglected for what they called 'extra-literary reasons': for example, her stories did not stress politics and nationalism. Peterson shared that opinion, but that reasoning, he believed, reflected 'preconceived notions of Irish literature'. He pointed out that Frank O'Connor emphasized the Russian influence, undoubtedly present in Mary's stories, because the stories did not fit the world of 'rebels and exiles', as his did. In his *A Short History of Irish Literature*, he had said:

> Only once has she written about Irish nationalism; this was in a story called 'Patriot Son', and from my point of view it was once too often. Like Whitman's wild oak in Louisiana, she has stood a little apart from the rest of us, 'uttering joyous leaves of dark green', but like Whitman I know that I could not do it.

Certainly, Peterson wrote, Ireland's political history has had a strong influence upon its literature but 'to deny Mary Lavin a place in modern Irish literature simply because her stories did not fit a preconceived literary pattern' was 'wrongheaded'.

The attitude towards women in her field was undoubtedly one of the reasons Mary Lavin's work did not get the recognition her family and certain critics felt it deserved. The prejudice against women writers – the lack of attention paid to their work – though fading, was still undoubtedly strong in Ireland during the years when Mary was doing much of her writing. But in the 1970s and 1980s notice was being taken of the neglect.

In the introduction to *Women and Fiction: Short Stories for and About Women*, which appeared in 1975, editor Susan Cahill commented on the meagre representation of women writing fiction and pondered on how much longer it would be before the 'litany of literary saints' – Bellow, Roth, Malamud, Mailer, Updike and other men – would be updated to include women like Joan Didion, Joyce Carol Oates, Flannery O'Connor and other women of equal stature.

In 1984 an anthology called *Woman's Part*, an anthology of short fiction by and about Irish women, 1890–1960, was brought out by Arlen House in Dublin. In her preface, Janet Madden-Simpson, the editor, lamented the lack of attention paid to the important part women had played and were playing in Anglo-Irish literary tradition. 'This book is an attempt to focus attention on a part of Irish literary and social heritage that has been too long forgotten and too often dismissed.'

In the introduction, Janet Madden-Simpson wrote that Frank O'Connor, in his *The Lonely Voice*, published in 1963, had remarked that 'the literature of the Irish Literary Renaissance is a peculiarly masculine affair . . . it is in society that women belong'. Although she assumed that he was being facetious, she still took note of the absence of any of the women writers, except Lady Gregory, who were part of what the writer Mary Colum had called 'the struggle towards cultural nationalism'. She pointed out that bibliographies, reading lists for courses in Anglo-Irish literature, and library collections in the same field, cite very few women. As exceptions, she mentioned Maria Edgeworth, Lady Gregory, Edith Somerville and Martin Ross (Violet Martin), Mary Lavin, Elizabeth Bowen, Kate O'Brien and Jennifer Johnston. However, the reason they were included, she felt, was because they had already achieved undeniable status. But even those she listed were often referred to in discussions with qualifications.

The novelist and short story writer Daniel Corkery used the term 'the hidden Ireland' to apply to eighteenth-century Gaelic poetry. It was equally applicable to women writers in Anglo-Irish literature, Madden-Simpson wrote. That neglect of women writers was, she felt, self-inflicted to a certain degree. Unlike male writers, they did not appear to view writing as a serious business. The result, as she saw it, was that their work tended to 'further constrict, concentrate and reflect stereotypical attitudes towards female thought and behaviour'. Some of the writers in her collection were exempted: Elizabeth Bowen, Mary Lavin, Mary Beckett and

Elizabeth Connor. Of those writers, she wrote:

> Their stories convey a deliberate sense of claustro-
> phobia, a portent of change as well as a reaction to
> the frustrations of a parochial Ireland where women
> still have little formal status but where they no longer
> submit in as docile a manner to the assigned role.

Madden-Simpson did take note of the fact that since 1960
there had been much more attention paid to writing by
women. Since that time, too, more women were writing,
being published and receiving critical attention. 'Deserved
critical attention has been focused on Mary Lavin, whose
work long suffered comparative neglect,' she wrote. Yet, she
maintained, there had been only a minor breakthrough.

As pointed out in an introduction to *Virgins and Hyacinths*,
a collection of short stories written by Irish women and edited
by the features editor of *The Irish Times*, one Caroline Walsh
– Mary's Caroline – and brought out by the Attic Press, it
was only necessary to examine anthologies of short stories
of the past to see how few women writers were represented.
In Caroline's introduction, she wrote: 'One has only to
remember the paucity of female contributions in the *Field
Day Anthology of Irish Writing* . . . or examine any of the
main literary collections of the past to see that a gender
balance simply didn't exist.' The point can be further
underlined by citing *Modern Irish Short Stories*, with an
introduction by Frank O'Connor, and published in 1957.
Fifteen writers are represented in the collection; only four
of them are women: Elizabeth Bowen, Mary Lavin and the
team of Somerville and Ross.

In 1996 *Tales from Bective Bridge* was once again reissued.
In an introduction to it, Evelyn Conlon wrote that she was
not taught Mary Lavin's work in school. She found her
eventually but she would have profited if she had read her at
what she considers the right time. 'Young femalehood in

Ireland in the sixties would have been greatly illuminated by the voice that examined the wars of relationships rather than those of countries,' she felt.

Invariably in discussions of women writers, the question would arise as to whether the author in question should be labelled a woman writer or merely be considered a writer who happened to be a woman. When the poet Eavan Boland was asked that question with regard to Mary Lavin, her reply was that in Lavin's case the matter was made more complex by the fact that at one and the same time she was writing as a woman and one whose writing was linked instantly in the public mind with the work of other men who wrote in the same form: and here she listed the inevitable triumvirate of O'Flaherty, O'Faolain and O'Connor. Mary did not see the matter as complex. 'I write as a person,' she said. 'I don't think of myself as a woman who writes. I am a writer. Gender is incidental to that.'

All the reasons given for the paucity of recognition of Mary Lavin's work – a paucity which undoubtedly existed – were valid. But there is one that can be attributed to Mary's personality. She was well aware of her ability as a short story writer and did not appear to feel that she needed to strive for signs of approval. She had learned early on, she once said, that 'the intoxication of writing comes from straining to write as well as one can and not from success'. She made no attempt to publicize herself but rather appeared perfectly willing to allow her work to speak for itself.

CHAPTER 10

As the year 1978 began, Mary was undoubtedly more worried about the country than about recognition. All through Ireland people were on edge. In February the papers were full of reports of the trial of four young men, supposedly with IRA connections, who had robbed a train in Tipperary two years earlier. That same month twelve people were killed by a bomb explosion in County Down. The violence in the North showed no signs of abating and the fact that the victims were, in the main, innocent – young married couples, teenagers and old age pensioners – added to the horror. Throughout the country unemployment was increasing dramatically and was particularly high among those under twenty-five.

In a letter to one of her daughters, Mary reported on the situation. The political scene, she wrote, as well as economic conditions and the mess made of things by the government, had the country nearing chaos. A cauliflower or a bunch of celery or a cabbage cost over fifty pence. 'Garret [FitzGerald] in a recent interview said that he would decline to say whether or not he could or would be able to form a government if asked because of the appalling mess the country has been got into.' He had added that 'anyone any good in Labour was going for the EEC jobs'.

The School of Irish Studies was being affected by a postal strike and Mary was afraid that, since they depended so heavily upon the mail, they might be put out of business altogether. She was feeling the effects of the postal strike personally as well. She had not received a cheque in three months from any source and there was the likelihood of cheques being lost or destroyed in the post office or rotting in a pillar-box.

As that year blended into the next, the list of strikes was

endless. There was a city-wide bus strike, Aer Lingus struck, dustbinmen struck, farmers said they might, taxi-drivers went on strike for a day, switchboard operators at the Department of Public Affairs struck, petrol truck drivers refused to move their trucks, and electricity was cut off, but, 'thanks be to God', as the Dubliners said, only in part of the city. The list was endless. As Elizabeth Shannon wrote, 'The strike against Aer Lingus, the post office shut down, and the petrol truck drivers' strike caused serious upheavals in the nation's economy, and hardships to almost every citizen of this country. If I were Irish, I'd protest. I'd strike!!'

It was all taking its toll on Mary and, by the spring of 1979, she was once more, as she wrote to Elizabeth, 'low in spirits'. She was even having difficulty making the effort to 'pour out the torrent of things' she wanted to say. She had advertised for a typist but, though she received a great many replies, they wanted 'three to four pounds an hour or a pound a page plus material'. She was sure that, with all the letters she had to write and with the 'insane amount' of drafts she did of a story, all the money she received for her stories would have to go to a typist. She considered going to a typing school. 'After all, if all those twitty wealthy women . . . are doing BAs for purposes of rejuvenescence or boredom or greed,' she wrote, she thought it might be 'legitimate' for her to make a fool of herself since her reasons were purely financial. Besides, she added, it might be good therapy. She proceeded to get out the typewriter her father had given her when her first story was published.

With economic conditions what they were, Mary was worrying even more than usual about money. 'Sometimes I think I've got cautious about spending money due to fear of age, etc.,' she wrote to Elizabeth. 'Don't worry, I'll fight it off.' Although the *New Yorker* continued to be a good source of income, they were taking fewer and fewer of her stories: one in 1971, another in 1973 and a third in 1976. Though she saw no obvious reason, she was not blind to the difference managing editors could make, and, in addition, what would hold for one period might not hold for another.

The question had often arisen as to whether or not there was such a thing as a typical *New Yorker* story. Mary did not believe that there was. She found the idea absurd. To prove the point, she mentioned Mavis Gallant, Benedict Kiely, Frank O'Connor, J. D. Salinger, Elizabeth Taylor, Eudora Welty and herself. They were all published in the *New Yorker* and they were all different. And yet she could see that their stories were getting shorter and a bit more slick and she was beginning, late in the 1970s, to feel that perhaps her stories were now too long for that magazine's taste and not slick enough. Well, if slick and clever stories were in vogue, she felt she could not write one as such: 'I think I can write a not clever story cleverly, but not a clever story.'

A new farm tax had been levied which Mary feared would 'totally destroy' them and exemptions for farms over sixty acres had been removed. There was going to be 'a great and possibly violent protest', but she was not at all sure how effective it would be. The upkeep of the farm was becoming something of a nightmare. A lengthy letter Mary wrote to the Board of Works of the county in June of 1977 illustrates one of the problems. Two or three years earlier a section of the boundary wall between Mary's property and the road had collapsed. In the past, though the Board of Works was responsible for the upkeep of the adjacent Abbey, much of this chore had devolved on Mary. 'I can safely say that between damage to our property, our land and our stock by hikers and vandals – apart from the damage to the Abbey itself – we had our hands filled.' The letter went on to list four reasons why she was writing:

1. The rest of the wall was leaning and in danger of collapsing.
2. A private owner should not be responsible since the place was a 'public amenity. Certainly visitors to

the Abbey regard our whole farm as theirs and go so far as to come up to the house and look in our windows at times.'

3. She was very worried about the cost and she knew that if they were 'ordinary farmers, and not conservationists' they would 'stick an old bedhead or spring mattress in the gap and that would be the end of it'.

4. The damaged wall 'took greatly from the beauty of the area', one of the most beautiful spots in the Boyne Valley and one frequently visited by coach tours.

Upkeep aside, the value of the property had risen beyond belief and Mary was giving serious thought, as she had from time to time, to selling it. It was not a step she would take hastily but she did feel that, at the very least, she should have it appraised. Yet, as she looked about her that spring at the green grass and the buds and the daffodils, she knew that she would have to 'fear for her sanity' if she sold.

As a stopgap measure and with the thought that it would add to the value of the property if she had to sell, she had plans drawn up for two self-contained wings to be added to either side of the house and applied for 'planning permission'. The family was almost unanimous in its disapproval but, as Mary told Mick, she had lots of ideas for the farm – not simply the addition. 'I feel we should *not* sell it – or the Mews either – but if we are going to work ourselves into skeletons (me?!) before we're coffined at all, at least we should have comfort and quiet and rest and not the crazy existence we've been living. We nearly killed our love. I dare say we would have done if that kind of love hadn't proved itself nearly immortal.'

The possibility that the farm would have to be sold loomed larger when, in March of 1979, Mick went into the hospital for nine days for tests and, a month later, had a back operation. For a period after the operation he was unable to drive and Mary was envisaging what the future might be like for them. The winter of Mary Lavin's life was setting in. There would be many autumn days interspersed with winter but the likelihood of illnesses and other uncontrollable episodes had to be faced.

The best way to handle the mounting troubles, Mary knew, was to push them aside and turn to her writing. That, however, required the kind of concentration she was unable to give it just then and she had written nothing for almost a year. But since, for her, keeping busy was the only cure, she found a cause she could devote time and attention to almost immediately.

The most controversial local issue at the time was the Wood Quay dispute. The four-acre Wood Quay site ran along the river Liffey between Winetavern and Fishamble Streets and the proposal had been made that the houses and other properties on the site be acquired and demolished for the erection of a municipal office building there. The building would be directly in front of Christ Church cathedral, an appalling thought for many Dubliners. Fr F. X. Martin, Professor of Medieval History at UCD and an outstanding figure in his specialty, acknowledged – in an article in the *Belvederian* – that there was a need for modern offices for the expanding Corporation staff but pointed out that the choice of a site had not taken into account that there might be 'substantial and invaluable archaeological remains underground'. As early as 1961, when the Office of Public Works began reconstruction at Dublin Castle, Viking remains were uncovered which indicated that beneath the buildings in the neighbourhood there was evidence of the earliest days of Dublin as an urban settlement.

When, in 1974, the plan was first initiated for the building of an office block, a group of National Museum archaeologists, aware of what had been revealed earlier on, felt that there was no time to lose and began to dig for artefacts. What they soon found were the remains of a Viking settlement dating as far back as the eleventh century. The archaeologists unearthed bones, jewellery, clothing, pottery, bronze and gold ornaments, and even the prow of a Viking ship. As they continued to dig, the outline of houses and streets emerged and innumerable relics, well preserved by mud and water over the centuries, were uncovered. The results gained worldwide attention. Experts came from Poland, Germany, the Scandinavian countries and Great Britain to examine the Wood Quay site. But already the bulldozers were being brought in and the archaeologists had to fight to stay ahead of them.

The first real action against the developers was sparked by Fr Martin. Under his guidance, an organization was set up called the Friends of Medieval Dublin, which received surprising cooperation from the Dublin City Council. As Fr Martin remarked, the Vikings had become the 'in thing' in Dublin. The organization had a dual purpose: to put pressure on the Dublin Corporation to give up the idea of using the Wood Quay site and to encourage the Museum group to continue digging. The newspapers were behind Fr Martin. An article in *The Irish Times* of 4 June 1979 read:

> Now that we know more clearly the facts of our past, all the greater is the onus on us to respect that which has been left to us. Whether the remains are Viking or Celtic or Anglo-Irish (or Shankill Irish) in bull-dozing them as if they were Sunset Strip hamburger joints, we are leaving a miserable, craven, cheap inheritance to succeeding generations.

One of the forms of protest was a sit-in to deter the bulldozers. The participants in the demonstration were professors, students, trade unionists, writers, artists and representatives from all walks of Irish public life and, Fr Martin wrote, 'a nun and a priest to give it an Irish flavour'. They began occupation 1 June 1979 and from then until nearly the end of the month took turns manning the site. The occupation was covered fully by the newspapers and was obviously welcomed by Dubliners. As Fr Martin commented later, 'We hung out a banner which passing motorists could see: "Hoot for Preservation". The trouble was that we could get no sleep at night with all the cars and buses which were hooting enthusiastically!'

Mary and 'Frank' Martin had been friends for some time and it was at this stage that she became involved. She was one of twelve 'prominent citizens' asked to take part in the occupation. It was, she wrote to Elizabeth, 'very scary with the guard dogs baying in the huts and the big quarries and cranes'. She was embarrassed by the praise she received because, as a matter of fact, she had enjoyed it. It was reminiscent of the days when she and the children had gone camping. 'It wasn't half as rough as when you put up the tent single-handed in Le Touquet!'

Late in June the Supreme Court ordered the protesters to quit the site. But by then it was obvious that the move to save Wood Quay had solid backing. By the end of June, Mary was able to report to the family that they had won the fight at Wood Quay – 'for the moment anyway'. An indication of her pride in participating can be noted in this line to Elizabeth: 'Tell the boys.'

Her triumph was dimmed by the death that month of Elizabeth's third child, a daughter. Eliza was a lovely baby but, a victim of cerebral palsy, she was destined to have a short life. She was born 19 March 1978 and died on 30 June 1979 in Mauritius. 'What a marvellous little fighter she was,' Mick wrote to Elizabeth. 'Fourteen months fighting for life all the time. For you and Diarmuid we are glad that you had such a baby daughter – of whom you can always be so proud. I believe you were all enriched by her – not least the two boys.'

Mary's letters to Elizabeth reflect the depth of her grief. With one of them she sent a photo of herself as a baby, sitting on a skin of some sort and raising her right hand. 'People say Eliza looks like me & it is only partly true,' she wrote. 'She was so beautiful. But there is a strong resemblance of some sort.' In letter after letter she mentioned Eliza and some years later she wrote from the Gramercy Park Hotel in New York City to say that she was troubled about that. Did it bother Elizabeth to have her mentioning Eliza so frequently, she asked? If so, she would try not to but she found herself thinking of the baby so often. She had never, she wrote, taken a photo of the girls on her trips but on this one she had taken two of Eliza and kept them by her bed all the time.

During the months of Eliza's illness, Mary made every attempt to get help for her. She wrote to Elizabeth that she had obtained a book through International Library Services which had listed Ireland as 'the bottom', in terms of any advancement in work on cerebral palsy. It had listed Sweden as 'the tops'. Mary's hope was that she might be able to spend a few days in Sweden in order to check on specialists and hospitals and then they could see about getting Eliza there. But, of course, Eliza did not live long enough for any of Mary's plans to materialize.

Diarmuid Peavoy's family, grief-stricken, offered to take care of all expenses connected with having Eliza's body shipped back to Dublin for burial but Elizabeth felt that she wanted her buried in Mauritius, partly because of the beauty of the area and partly so that she might visit the grave. 'I think you made the right decision to leave your darling daughter in that warm and flowery island and, as you said, you can visit the grave while your grief is still vivid and can be assuaged by that,' Mary wrote to her. 'The pain in your heart will never really go – nor would you want it to – but it will change & be no worse than any sorrow – even the sorrow for the passing of youth or love.'

Mary searched desperately for whatever solace religion could give her, with apparently some measure of success.

She wrote: 'You know that I try to believe in God and indeed would probably find it harder to disbelieve than to believe except for the rubbish we have been fed – not just by our own church but almost all religions – even those of the other hemispheres.' She had, she went on, always 'longed to believe in a hereafter where we'd meet those we loved again, but it was made so hard by all the stupid holy pictures and prayers'. She had felt that it might be possible, but only in a way that their minds could not comprehend:

> Then after Eliza's death I suddenly had a most extraordinary reconciliation between my beliefs and disbeliefs due *entirely* to her having grown to be so beautiful, but not having grown to know us or us her beyond the beauty really. And I felt it was *owed* to me to know her and her to know us. And it gave me not only a great comfort but also a feeling that such comfort was legitimate.

The following account, written by Mary to Elizabeth on the day of Eliza's funeral, indicated at least a desire to believe in the supernatural as well. On that evening, when Mary was getting ready for bed, the house was filled with the fragrant smell of roses. She looked in the drawing room, thinking that perhaps Mick had put some roses there, but found none. The rose garden was a considerable distance from the house and yet, when she went up to her room, the perfume of roses was almost overpowering. Noting that one of the garden seats had been left out, she went outside to bring it in. It was a lovely evening and outside, too, the scent of roses was strong. Suddenly she thought of Eliza and of Mauritius, which she had been told was a paradise of sun and flowers. She felt 'the most extraordinary peace, even happiness'. That night she fell asleep immediately, as she had not been doing, and slept soundly. Shortly thereafter she learned that legend had it that, when a person asked for the intercession of the Mauritius saint Père Laval, 'there was found to be what you could only call a celestial perfume'. Recounting that tale to Elizabeth, she knew, would give her great comfort, for Elizabeth's reactions were much like her own. As she once wrote to Elizabeth:

> For people like us, intensity is always near the boil – other people are all their lives making spills out of newspapers and down on their knees blowing into cold and even damp grates, to try to raise a spark of fire. We have to keep the chimney from going on fire – that's our problem. We are all of us all the time on high seas and in peril of our lives and who'd want it to be otherwise.

Mary was certainly 'on high seas' those days with Mick's ill health and the thought of selling the farm in the back of her mind. Her mood was considerably brighter by mid-August, however. The weather was 'unbelievable' and the garden had never been so wonderful, she wrote to the Peavoys. Probably the best news was that she was working hard on stories. Between writing and the garden it was 'round the clock'.

As much as she hated to leave the farm just then, Mick and Mary were planning a trip to London so that he might finish research on his 'Tony' book. Any trip had a reviving influence upon Mary. She had often said that, for her, trips were the secret of surviving. They stayed at Duke's Hotel on James Place, Mary's favourite on all her London trips, and she did nothing except stay in bed and read, take walks and sit in pubs and parks writing and stopping for tea in Fortnum and Mason's. She was looking forward to another trip in 1980 to do a reading in London for ICA, the Institute of Contemporary Art, at Poetry Society headquarters. She would be reading with Sean O'Faolain, Liam O'Flaherty and the novelist Francis Stuart, and she was 'thrilled, honoured'. And she was going to get expenses and forty pounds.

Undoubtedly in an attempt to cheer the Peavoys up, Caroline made a trip to Mauritius at the end of July. In a letter to 'My Two Darlings', Mary commented on how strange it seemed to think of them 'both together so far away – in the Indian Ocean no less'. She dwelled on how far two of her 'little birds' had flown: Valdi for years in Rio and Managua. For Mary, no matter how great her triumphs, nothing made her as happy as having 'the three graces' at home.

The year Eliza died, Mary received an invitation to give a reading at Harvard and at the Library of Congress in Washington. In Washington she was scheduled to stay with Ireland's ambassador, Ambassador Donlon, and that pleased her. At Harvard the poet Elizabeth Bishop was to be reading on the same occasion and Mary looked forward to that as well. The whole idea cheered her up considerably. She planned to accept the invitations if she could be sure that she would make enough money on the trip to pay her fare on the *QE2*. It was unfortunate that money worries sometimes interfered with her availing herself of the opportunity to set sail for the States, for she loved the sea voyages and the sea. Her letters home from shipboard were always full of references to being 'up on deck'.

By early in August 1979 Mary could see her way clear to book passage and all arrangements were made for the trip to the States and for her readings. She wrote the family from mid-Atlantic that the *QE2* had cancelled two sailings and she was on the Russian ship SS *Mikail Lermontov* which had departed from Tilbury on 8 September and was to arrive in New York on the 18th. The Russian ship was not only cheaper but also more interesting and different from any other she had sailed on, she told them. There were no luxuries and no service in the cabins, but the food was good and the drinks were cheap. Some passengers complained about the lack of frills, but they were forgetting, Mary commented, how much they were saving on fares. There was one distinct disadvantage, however. The passengers received no news except from Moscow. They had no idea what was going on in Rhodesia (now Zimbabwe, where there was violent unrest at that time) or Dublin – 'the two spots upon which most interest is focused at the moment'.

Dozens of nationalities were represented on board and the entertainment was provided by passengers and crew. The day she wrote home, she had been watching an exhibition of Russian dancing. The films were educational and more or less propaganda but, she wrote, 'I buy a lot of it.' Mary took advantage of everything available. Always eager to learn and with a keen interest in cooking, she went to the kitchen for a lesson in Russian cuisine. She thought the kitchen – though small and with a small staff – was incredibly efficient compared with other ships' kitchens she had visited.

She marvelled at the military discipline. The crew members seemed a little tense and fearful of getting instructions wrong. 'You have to be clear in asking for things, never change your mind, obey all rules no matter how petty, and never question them.' She had witnessed a couple of 'shocking rows in the bar between pig-headed Germans and Americans trying to get their way and really baiting the barman'. She had to restrain herself from joining in because she thought the passengers were stupid and the barman right, patient, and clearly nervous about failing in his duty to his superiors. She was delighted when the involved passengers were booed by the others.

She was invited to the captain's table on the one evening when he ate in the dining room with the passengers. Three passengers were invited in addition to Mary, and one of them was the foreign correspondent for *Pravda* who was on her way to take up a year's assignment in Ottawa. Of the six officers at the table only two spoke English. Never had Mary eaten such food and in such quantities. There were nine courses: caviar sturgeon, asparagus, pâté in aspic, soup, fresh salmon, chicken Kiev, swans made of apples, then cheese, ice cream, brandy and coffee. Both red and white Russian wine was served with the chicken or the salmon, but vodka was served with the other courses. Glasses were refilled after every toast and there were three toasts for each course: 'To the captain, to his health, to his ship, to his crew, to his passengers, and to each of the guests, with a speech in Russian.' The guests stood and clicked glasses for all toasts and Mary was thankful for the exercise. She tried taking only a sip at each toast but as soon as she did her glass was filled up again.

Mary always put her heart into descriptions of food. In one of her letters to Elizabeth she mentioned that she and Mick had had dinner at the home of the novelist J. P. Donleavy. 'Champagne for drinks before dinner! With the champagne, smoked salmon. To my horror Mick *ate* the smoked salmon which he loathes. Then vichyssoise (heavenly), with Chilean bottled Burgundy, and then roast, etc. Dessert was a stupefying pears in port with a bowl of whipped cream.'

There were very few passengers on the ship who were as happy as Mary was when a storm broke out. She had said on one occasion that she enjoyed bad weather: rain and wind. 'Things are breaking all around the tea room, and people think it's bad,' she wrote home, but 'after hurricane Flossie on the QE2 this is nothing'. Up on deck, she was having a fine time. 'I'll have to be more careful than I'd be when I was a young lass,' but she saw no need to forego it 'if I hang on to things'. She described the spectacle:

The sea was an incredible colour in the storm – pure sapphire, with white tops on the waves. When the ship hit a large wave it smashed it down until it was as fine as snow and pushed back the other waves until it seemed as if it were ploughing through snow and in the air the spray flew like snow in a snowstorm.

There were arcs of rainbows everywhere in this spray,
little ones, hundreds of them. It was oh so beautiful.

But, except for the storm, she was finding the ten-day trip
monotonous.

When at last they docked in New York, it was heart-
warming to be met by the Irish Consular Service and by
good friends: the playwright John Beary, an old and cherished
friend; Elizabeth Cullinan, now a regular contributor to the
New Yorker, and Mary's friend since she had come to the
Mews in the 1960s, and John McDonagh, Mary's cousin
from Hartford. Mary had been first off the ship and, when
Elizabeth Cullinan found her, she was sitting on her baggage
'a la Florence long ago'. Later they all gathered at Elizabeth
Cullinan's home bringing wine, flowers and chocolates. The
Embassy had booked her into the Gramercy Park Hotel,
small but nice, and a great favourite of hers. Expensive
though, she wrote to the family: fifty-six dollars a night and
no breakfast. She spent two nights there before going on to
Washington.

The trip appeared to be off to a good start but, as it
developed, the two months in the States turned out to be
irksome, in many respects disappointing, and 'pretty much
of a washout'. She had reluctantly signed with an agency –
she'd been talked into it, she said – to handle her trip and
they had made a mess of it.

Mary left Washington as soon as she possibly could and
went back to New York to meet Mick, who was now well
enough to travel, at the Algonquin. Many years later John
Beary recalled that he had had drinks at the Algonquin with
Mary and Mick and Eudora Welty. He remembered Eudora
Welty's 'extraordinary good manners'.

After a night at the Algonquin, Mary went on to Boston,
where she was to share the stage with Elizabeth Bishop at
Harvard. There she joined her old friend, Anne Francis
Cavanaugh. That evening Mary talked a great deal about

her crossing on the Russian ship. 'The Russian captain was wonderful to me,' she said. The next morning Mick joined Mary and Anne Francis for breakfast. While they were chatting, there was a phone call for Mary. Elizabeth Bishop had died suddenly during the night, Mary was told, and the readings had been cancelled. While they were trying to absorb that news, the phone rang once more. Her reading would go on, Mary was told, and friends, students, faculty and writers would read favourite passages from Elizabeth Bishop's work. The first half of the evening would be devoted to those tributes and then Mary was to read. 'We all sat in silence,' Anne Francis wrote later. 'Then Mary . . . stood, pulled herself to full courage and stated "I will wear my new black dress."'

At the appointed time they all went to Sanders Memorial Hall where Elizabeth Bishop's admirers read favourite passages from her works. There was a moment of silence and then a young poet introduced Mary. She rose, walked to the podium, looked out at the audience and began: 'I will read "Happiness", a story about death.'

What Mary discovered while in Boston, she told Mick later, was that her agents had never done agency work before but were trying out their hand on her. Mary had informed them clearly that she did not want to do more than three or four readings and those for a high fee or free for a friend, and only at universities. Instead, they had arranged for her to read at two colleges for a fee of one hundred and fifty dollars. Her fee normally was a thousand dollars or at the very least seven hundred and fifty and she was furious. They had booked her for an intensive schedule and told her, furthermore, that she would not be paid until she returned home. She had been booked to read at 'little colleges', where the students had never heard of her and during classes at eleven o'clock in the morning. The list of her complaints, as she detailed them to Mick, was a long one. She told him that she was determined *never* to read again anywhere but in theatres at night. She wanted it understood that she didn't read as a writer but as an actor. Acting was another part of her, she claimed. And that was that.

At the end of that speech, Mick took charge, as he so often did after one of Mary's outbursts. He told her to stop whining about the agents and to act. Whereupon she followed his advice and 'lacerated' the agents. She demanded their own cheque for a thousand dollars and made them cash it and then, as she reported to the family, 'once my temper was up, I tore the lights and livers out of them'.

Letters from home during those two months away had done a great deal to sustain Mary. In one of them Elizabeth had written that they, her three graces, regretted that they had never really told her how much they loved her. 'Mick and I nearly died laughing,' Mary wrote to her:

> You never needed to tell me – any of you – you showed me almost every day of your lives – but as well as that you *did* tell me. Mick said he was sick and tired of hearing you all say how much you loved me. I was *not*. I could hear it every minute and like the old tear jerker Danny Boy I think that 'I shall hear though dead I well may be' even in my grave.

Apparently Mary did not suffer from the whole experience, because she was told by Mick and friends when she returned from Boston that she looked better than she had in years and had never seemed more in command of herself. 'Indeed, I think that I seemed to find myself – to come into more possession of my identity than I ever had in my life.'

She had always felt that she lacked self-confidence. Her use of the word 'honoured' earlier because she was going to appear on the same platform with O'Faolain, O'Flaherty and Francis Stuart tends to bear out the authenticity of her assessment. And a June 1973 letter to the writer Kay Boyle adds to the picture. Kay Boyle had apparently written a letter of praise to Houghton Mifflin then and another earlier. Mary began the letter with 'Dear Kay Boyle' and then apologised for addressing her that informally. 'I do not know if the surname you have made so familiar to all lovers of the short story is in fact your maiden or your married name.' After going on to praise Kay Boyle's work, she concluded with 'I must also send my humble tribute to your art.'

Her reverence seems excessive, given the fact that Mary must have been well aware of Kay Boyle's assessment of her stories. In *Women and Fiction*, the editor Susan Cahill, in her biographical sketch preceding Mary's 'In a Café', quoted Kay Boyle on the subject. She had written:

> I am very much moved by her writing. Her stories speak to us from a far, green world – a world whose freshness we have desperate need of at this time. Mary Lavin's characters are living people, all of them, who speak directly from the spiritual setting of Joyce's *Dubliners*. But this time it is a woman's voice telling us with eloquence and compassion of other women's love, and pride, and courage, and despair. Mary Lavin has given us in these stories an entire country, and surely there is no greater gift a writer can make to his time.

As well as lacking confidence in herself, Mary considered herself shy. There is no indication that she gave others that impression, however. To see her the centre of attraction at social gatherings and to witness her poise on a platform would defy her own interpretation. But it was an honest and undoubtedly an accurate one.

It may be that needing to take charge of the situation after the catastrophe of the Bishop death – and no one there to back her up – had given her a kind of confidence she had not had previously. At any rate, she believed that she was changing. She reported proudly that now she informed Mick of an action she planned to take, instead of asking him if she should take it. 'I am going home determined to be more in command of my life,' she wrote. She felt that she had been in command of herself but not of her life, under the mistaken belief that the two things were one and the same. She had learned that they were not and 'that's worth all the time and money I lost'.

CHAPTER 11

In Mid-October 1979 Mary was again on the Russian liner SS *Lermontov* and on her way home. She was finding the trip more tiresome than usual. 'The ship is restful but boring as hell,' she wrote home. 'God in his goodness to *me* (not the rest of the passengers) blew up a bit of a tempest yesterday and another – I hope – is on its way.' That reduced the boredom a bit but she was beginning to feel that she could enjoy the sea without its stretching from continent to continent and with a depth of thousands of feet. It was actually far more beautiful 'breaking on the rocks of Connemara'. She believed it would help if she could write lengthier letters but it was difficult with the ship pitching and people stopping by to chat. 'I really think I'll never come alone again – it's too long and I miss you all. Wouldn't it be nice if I stayed young enough for Eoghan and Kathleen [her grandchildren] to come with me places. For me I mean.'

Summing up the whole trip in a letter to the family, Mary tried to list positives. She and Mick had spent a night with her relatives, the McDonaghs, at their home in Connecticut. It had been lovely and John had driven her to Boston – 'a great kindness.' She had had a good meal with Rachel MacKenzie, her *New Yorker* editor, at the Algonquin. And she had had fine meetings – all too few – with Elizabeth Cullinan.

It had been bothering her that she had had no opportunity to write or to work on the manuscripts she invariably carried with her on trips. A briefcase full of her stories, finished and ready for editing or unfinished and to be worked on, had gone untouched. 'Please God I'll get to work soon after I get home. I long with all my heart to be home and think of how short a time I may have to enjoy it – or enjoy it to the *full*.' Once again there was the hint of impending doom.

But the trip had not been wasted, she finally concluded. She had 'lots of thoughts in mind, the only activity worth a damn'.

One of the areas she had had time to think about was her daughters' chosen careers. 'It's only an idea but I think you girls should make your livelihood from books,' she had once written them. Caroline was obviously taking that road. As for Valdi, friends believed, as mentioned earlier, that Mary had encouraged her to go into the legal profession because her father had been a solicitor. Mary had always maintained that they were wrong. If she had tried to encourage Valdi in any direction, it had been towards a career in the arts. But now Mary realized that Valdi had made a wise choice. She was a capable barrister. An item in the *Meath Chronicle* of 23 August 1979, headed 'Lady Barrister Complimented', read:

Mrs Valdi MacMahon, BL, daughter of the distinguished Meath short story writer, Mary Lavin, made her *first* appearance at Trim Circuit Court and was complimented by Judge T. F. Roe on her handling of the case. He said he was impressed and he congratulated her and wished her every success at the Bar. Mrs MacMahon fittingly returned thanks.

And then there was Elizabeth. While in the States, Mary had started to write a letter to her suggesting that she give up trying to write stories. 'They are so, so hard & so hard to sell,' she had begun. Elizabeth, Mary was sure, had the ability and apparently the desire to write, and Mary's advice to her was to devote herself to writing poetry. 'Poetry makes much more money now – really it does.' But that was not as important as the fact that she *was* a poet. 'I wish I was,' Mary had added. She compared a poem to a neat whiskey, nothing added, while a story was more like a cocktail, with at least one other ingredient added and then shaken and stirred.

She had not posted the letter, however. When at last she was home, she wrote to Elizabeth. She was happy not to have posted the earlier letter, she wrote, because she had changed her mind. She had just read 'An Irish Girl', a short story that Elizabeth had written, and had liked it very much. 'You have improved so much,' she wrote. 'You have got such mastery over your prose.' She had to admit that it had surprised her. What she was witnessing, she believed, was maturity. 'I was afraid you'd go in for that splattery kind of writing that is so common, even fashionable today – especially among young Irish women writers,' she wrote to Elizabeth. 'You know, "Rain, Drenching, Bashing against the window. Jesus, I can't stand it" kind of thing, as if all writing since Time began and till Time ends does not depend on uniting a noun to a verb.'

It is too soon to determine whether Elizabeth should have concentrated on prose rather than poetry but at times she voiced the opinion that she may have turned to poetry because she felt overshadowed by her mother when she was writing. If that is so, her mother cannot be blamed. She treated Elizabeth as an equal. At one point she commented on Elizabeth's use of the expression 'right as rain' in one of her letters. 'What a title for a story,' Mary wrote. 'Bags it or better still let it go to whichever has a story to fit it first.'

Elizabeth herself attempted to analyze her reasons for turning to writing in any form. She said at one time that, if she had realized more clearly the extent of her mother's brilliance, she would not have attempted to compete, as it were. She would have done those things she wanted to do: either become an actress or taken up nursing as a career. 'But in the end, you see, mother was determined that I would compete with her. She needed this.' Her use of the word 'compete' seems strange, since there is no indication that Mary thought at all of competition. She was a good judge of writing ability and she could see that Elizabeth possessed considerable talent, a vivid imagination and a real love of

246

words. Rather than a competitor, Mary may have seen Elizabeth as a daughter created in her own image.

Apparently Mary had meant it when she made that point about her own desire to write poetry. As reported earlier, she had had some of her poetry published in the *Dublin Magazine*, and in 1995 Elizabeth read an untitled poem by Mary at the Botanic Gardens in Dublin:

Christ if you wanted my shining soul
that flashed its happy fins
And splashed in the silent seas of sin,
Then Christ, keenest fisherman
On the Galilean shore,
If you wanted to catch my shivering soul
Why did you let down nets that were worn,
Unravelled and floating light?
I slid along the ribbony web
In and out
And when the nets slim-wet and black
Crawled over the prow of your boat again
Empty as nets that sway all day
In an empty sea
My sly soul waited
And swam aloft
To play at leaping the ripples
And showing its silver dapples
To the silent floating fishes
On the outer-side of the wave
The little silver minnows of the moon.

She had written that poem when very young and, she wrote to friends, 'before the short story cast its spell over me'.

In 1981 the Peavoys returned to Ireland when Diarmuid's position in Mauritius came to an end, and also in that year Caroline married James Ryan, a young man Mary had known since the early 1970s. While he was a student at Trinity, he and some of his friends – all in their early twenties and interested in writing – were regular visitors at the Mews and in Bective. It was a tribute to Mary's agelessness and personality that she was still very much the centre of attraction with these young people. James's first impression of Mary is still fresh: the way she wore her hair, her black clothing, and, as he said – her way of looking at a person with a sort of stare which was very inviting and very judgemental at the same time. 'She had a larger than life persona,' James said.

It was not until the late 1970s that he began courting Caroline. By then he had graduated from Trinity College and was teaching history, English and creative writing at Newpark Comprehensive School in Blackrock. He was a staunch Lavin fan and was using her stories in his classes. Quite naturally, he became increasingly involved in the life of the family and of the Abbey Farm after he and Caroline married.

The Peavoys were happy to be back in Dublin and Mary and Mick were pleased to have them there but, unfortunately, both their return and Caroline's marriage were overshadowed by illness: Mary's and Mick's. In the early 1980s their illnesses began to assume major proportions, and although barely seventy, Mary was feeling the pressure of advancing age.

The nine days that Mick had spent in the hospital and the subsequent surgery had had disastrous results. Mary blamed a good bit of it on Mick's 'contemptible effort at appearing noble and unselfish'. He had been issued and had worn a steel brace – around his neck instead of his groin – for an upper dorsal operation, when the problem had been at the base of his spine. Apparently the error had occurred because a staff sister wrote the wrong prescription for the brace and Mick, who Mary believed must have realized that a mistake had been made, did not complain. The surgeon did little to cool Mary's anger when he said – blithely according to her – that he hoped they hadn't done irreparable damage.

After the surgery, Mick had gone back to work for a few hours a day, though still in a great deal of pain. It was even painful for him to put on his socks and Mary had to be on hand to help him. 'It is no wonder that I am nearly crazy and I cannot go away,' Mary wrote to Elizabeth. 'Going away', of course, was always Mary's salvation. It was obvious that Mick should retire but he hated the thought and put it off for as long as possible. When, however, driving back and forth from the school to the farm became too much for him, he was forced to accept it. He retired in 1980 and was appropriately honoured by the staff. Mary was present on that occasion and accounts indicate that she spoke movingly.

Mick's days after retirement were spent working on his Rankin book and doing occasional chores at the Abbey Farm. It was apparent that retirement was made more than palatable by the thought that he could spend so much more time in Bective. His interest in the farm and its workings had always been total. In the mid-1970s he had written Valdi's husband, Des MacMahon, 'We hope to sell some of the cattle next week (10 or so) and the remainder in June.' If the 'good prices' held, he expected they could do very well and get the farm completely out of debt by July. He told Des that he was thinking of retiring and spending most of his time in management of the farm. 'I think that under certain conditions one could make it earn enough for us to live on. Here's hoping anyhow.'

It was Mary's lack of a goal that Elizabeth worried about during the period following Mick's retirement and Caroline's marriage. Visiting Mary, she found her gardening. It troubled her to see her mother, whom she believed to be sorely in need of some kind of emotional and intellectual stimulation, unable to find it. Her premise was correct but, in actuality, Mary was not feeling well enough to do a great deal more than she was doing.

The Peavoys left Dublin once more in 1983, this time going to live in Brussels. Diarmuid had obtained a position as a public relations expert with the LOMÉ Convention at Centre de Développement Industriel, a joint venture with African, Caribbean, and Pacific states for the development of industrial projects.

That same year, Mary was hospitalized and her gall bladder was removed. She received daily calls from Brussels and, as she told Elizabeth, 'I cling to your voices, yours, Eoghan's [Elizabeth's son] & Diarmuid's.' Elizabeth thought of sending her mother flowers, possibly daffodils, but was afraid that Mary might think of her 'Happiness', and fear that, like the husband in the story, she was at death's door. When finally Mary was at home she wrote to Elizabeth: 'You'd have been mad to send flowers. My room was like a funeral parlour. Did anyone tell you Garret [FitzGerald] sent me the most truly exquisite pot of some glorious kind of blooms?'

With Mick retired, with both of them unwell, and with the couple spending most of their time in Bective, the decision was reluctantly made to sell the Mews. Money, Mary's constant worry, must have been an added consideration. With economy in mind, she had given up her American citizenship in July of 1981, fearing taxes on money earned there, although at one time she had told the Medlicotts that, on his death bed, Tom Lavin had told her never to give up that citizenship. Even allowing for Mary's flair for the dramatic employed in this deathbed scene, it was undoubtedly her father's advice.

In order to have a base in town, the Scotts bought an apartment at 5 Gilford Place in Sandymount in what might be called a condominium complex. It was located in a residential area, a very short walk from the sea, and was a well-maintained building.

Their apartment, on the second floor, had a good-sized entrance area, with the rooms circling around it. The living room, with a dining area, was fairly spacious. Sliding doors opened out onto a small balcony which looked out on a street that led down to the sea, and, of course, there were always flowers growing on the balcony. They furnished the living room rather sparsely, with a comfortable-looking sofa and a very large desk and work table, both of which had been designed for the Mews. It was not a room that lent itself to conversation; it appeared to be a work place for Mick and Mary. The dining area, however, was book-lined and the walls throughout the flat were covered with pictures. When, some years later, the Abbey Farm was sold, the two portraits of Mary – the young Mary Lavin, done by Ernest Hayes, and the other of the older Mary, done in 1960 by Sean O'Sullivan – would dominate the living room. Straight ahead from the entrance were two rather small bedrooms and a kitchen. Off to the right of them was a large, walk-in closet, lined with book shelves, where some of Mary's and Mick's papers and books were stored. All in all, although rather pleasant, the flat resembled an artist's studio rather than a home. To Mary, it seemed claustrophobic and was not a place for which she ever developed any great fondness. But she did try to make a life for them in their new surroundings. She cooked lavish meals there for the family as she had in the Mews, but, according to Elizabeth, there was an underlying tension about those occasions: 'like a time bomb about to explode'. And, she added, 'it did'.

Selling the Mews and buying the apartment had, the family understood, been a necessary move and they heartily approved, knowing it would simplify life for Mary and Mick. To have to worry about both the Mews and Bective was too much. But it had been a wrench for them, in particular for Mary. The Sandymount location was not as accessible to friends and, thanks to its size, their apartment did not lend itself readily to entertaining. No longer living in Dublin proper had, to a great extent, cut her off from people, and being with people was of vital importance to her. One of the greatest deprivations was the loss of a garden in town. Being outdoors and spending time in a garden was for Mary the perfect way to relax. Mary Mew, who had worked with Mick at the School of Irish Studies and who lived in the Sandymount area, said that often Mick and Mary would put lawn chairs in the trunk of their car, go to Sandymount Green, set up their chairs, and sit in the sun. Occasionally they would go further along to Herbert Park and follow the same ritual.

The year after her hospitalization, Mary suffered another fairly severe bout of depression. In an undated letter to Elizabeth, she wrote: 'I feel I cannot go on living, but I suppose you just try – not one day at a time but one hour, one month at a time.' And in January of 1984 she wrote: 'They bested me in the end and I am going (in five minutes) to St Gabriel's Nursing Home.' She went on to explain. 'Just before Christmas I began to spin like a top – inside and out.' She was sick of everyone, including Mick, telling her that all she had to do was pull herself together. She tried calling all her friends to see if someone might be able to recommend a competent doctor. Everyone was 'out shopping', she complained. At last a consultant was recommended and he saw her 'there and then, at dark on the eve of Christmas'. He gave her 'chemicals, not tranquilizers' and she got through Christmas. A short time later, however, he persuaded her to have a series of tests and to go into St Gabriel's for a rest as well. 'I feel a fool. I know I am as strong as a bull and only need the tests.' And she added bitterly, 'if you put yourself in their hands they are capable of doing pregnancy tests at 71'. She was sure that a week or two of rest in the ten years preceding would have prevented the whole business. But her strongest complaint was that she didn't have anything to take with her to read – at least nothing that she wanted to read. Her letter concluded with 'Life is lousy but we're stuck with it, and deep down hope it won't come unstuck.'

Elizabeth urged her not to be cross with people who told her that she was all right and that there was nothing wrong, and that she should just pull herself together. 'They are only trying to get you over whatever it is, and not understanding quite what it is, etc.' She assured her mother that she could sympathize with her because she herself suffered confused feelings from time to time. And, after all, moving into the apartment had been a major upheaval. 'Maybe it was best, labour saving, wise, etc., but who ever thought making life easy was solving anything.'

Apparently Mary's stay in St Gabriel's was not lengthy and soon thereafter Elizabeth received a letter from Mick giving her the results of the tests. Low blood count, he wrote to her, and glandular fever causing utter exhaustion for months. Reassured, Elizabeth replied that she was happy that it was 'such a simple complaint, and a dignified one, not an undignified feet up kind of one'.

Summarizing for Mary the family's reaction to her illness, she wrote:

> The whole point is that both Caroline and I and also Mick knew that there wasn't much wrong with your mind, brain, etc. In fact we thought you were putting it on . . . in the hope of gaining time and attention. What we did not count on was that there was something physical that was dragging you down, further into the abyss . . . We thought you were in the hands of capable men who could pinpoint your strengths and unstrengths, and it came as a shock to find out that your physical health was not so good. But we were confident that nothing would keep you down for long.

Elizabeth was writing her mother often. Diarmuid was busy and, although she had her three children, she was lonesome. Letters from home were a blessing for her: a substitute for the conversation she longed for. 'Oh how I miss you,' she wrote, 'I don't want to be away at all.' The life of an expatriate was a lonely one. Diarmuid was back and forth to Dublin and London on his assignments, her two elder boys were busy with their own lives, and her youngest was far too young to be a great deal of company for her.

There was a genuine similarity between Elizabeth's letters to her mother and those of her mother to her. One began, 'I'm as jumpy as a jack-in-the-box. Not spinning like a top, because I think you must have patented that one.' She had sat down to write a letter, thinking that would steady her. 'Can you imagine anyone contacting you to steady themselves . . . Oh, Mother, what is life, its ups and downs are so topsy turvy that sometimes you don't know whether to walk on your head or on your heels.'

During the January following that unhappy Christmas, the news that Elizabeth received from home was confusing. On the one hand, Mick's letter had been comforting, but word from Valdi was far from cheerful about Mary's condition. Late in the month Elizabeth wrote to Mick that it was his opinion, rather than Valdi's, that she was willing, and actually needed, to accept.

It was a comfort for Elizabeth that Mick was so organized and good and kind but she was concerned about how well he would be able to cope or for how long. As she wrote to him, she and her sisters had from time to time seen Mary in a distressed state during the many years before she remarried. They knew well how difficult it was for those around her. She feared that seeing her mother in her present condition would be too much for him to bear: the whole situation might be too trying for him.

> Loving mother as you do, so much, you are maybe sometimes a little too kind. You and Mud have been and are a wonderful couple and have times of great happiness ahead. Most of your life has been spent in helping others. I hope now that you can spend a bit of time enjoying what you have achieved.'

And to her mother, now that Mick's news was somewhat reassuring, Elizabeth wrote:

> Do not expect great things, just hope and *pray* in that kind of worldly wordy way you mentioned in a previous letter: dear god who has made me, with all my gifts and *ungifts*, who has caused all these problems to be, get me up and doing, to solve them.

She told her mother of a friend in Brussels who was seeing a marriage counsellor and 'undergoing a course of marriage therapy', and added, 'Of course we in Ireland are so hide bound we imagine all sorts of wrong things and end up doing nothing about them.' She advised Mary, now that she knew there was nothing especially wrong at the moment, to rely on her 'psyche' to get her through.

The question had been raised as to whether Mary should turn to psychotherapy and Elizabeth hoped that she would. She reminded Mick that, after William Walsh's death, a psychiatrist had advised Mary to take immediate action if she ever again had trouble coping. But her mother, she knew, was not receptive to the idea. It was Nuala O'Faolain's impression that Mary, during her days as a widow, had resisted any kind of psychoanalysis. She, Nuala, thought that it might be because Mary felt that it would damage her creative powers.

Elizabeth's involvement in her mother's work as well as her health was complete. As for her own writing, she had 'almost' decided to give it up, 'having missed out as the horses got out of the stalls and went around the first bend in the fence,' she told Mary. She was content to let her writing consist of letters to her. Those letters were profusely interspersed with comments on clothes. 'I am wearing your blue Nellie Mulcahy. It's so pretty, Mother.' But there was pride as well. 'Diarmuid and Adam were at the Brussels book fair and who was on the W. H. Smith stand? Mary

Lavin with her *Selected Stories* in paperback.'

She was busily rereading her mother's stories with an eye to which of them might be included in the next collection, but she was also rereading the stories with a friend merely for pleasure. 'I love "Villa Violetta" so much, for obvious reasons,' she told her mother. She had read most of the stories at least three times and she was fully aware that she was not reading them as a critic might but rather for the insight they gave into herself, her mother, and life in general. And, too, when she was away from Ireland, they were a kind of cure for lonesomeness. One of her favourite stories was 'The Young Girls', which, since it appeared in the 1944, 1964 and 1971 collections, must have been a favourite of Mary's as well.

Sometimes Elizabeth questioned her memory. Did she really recall the actual occurrences? 'You know what they say about remembering. It's hard to say which is the memory and which is the story told often enough to become a memory itself.' It was becoming more and more difficult for her to distinguish the real Mary Lavin from the Mary Lavin in her stories. 'Do I remember the you of our adolescence, or the you of "Happiness", "Trastevere" and "Villa Violetta"?' she asked her mother. 'I know we walked the stones of Rome, Florence, Venice, but it's the stories that recall it most.' But surely her memory was not playing tricks when she thought of the pensione in the hills outside Florence that the padrone had built for his fiancée, the apartment they stayed in and the waiter she fell in love with. It was all in 'Villa Violetta'. But one thing she was sure of: her love for that waiter had been real. 'I know I fell in love at every turning of the stagecoach but that was different.'

Diarmuid, as well as Elizabeth, was playing a substantial role in Mary's literary life. Mary had written to them that RTÉ was planning to televise five of her stories. Elizabeth, was annoyed that Mary was not getting more money for the stories. She advised her mother to act through her agent. RTÉ could 'afford to pay a leading national figure like you

Bective 1965: Mary Lavin leaning on a sundial

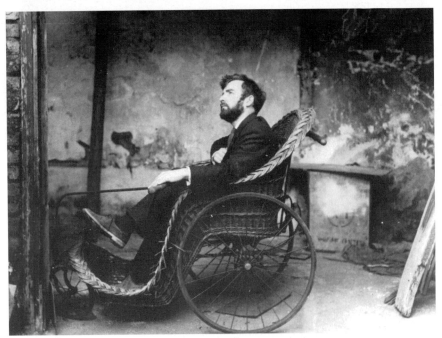

The architect Sam Stephenson seated in the wicker carriage found in the coach house, just prior to its conversion to the Mews in 1959 (photo by Dick Deegan)

Williamsburg, Virginia, in 1977: Mary Lavin, Michael Scott and Anne Francis Cavanaugh

Mary Lavin in the garden of the Mews, *c.* 1981

At the Wood Quay site, June 1979: Father F. X. Martin, Sister Benvenuta (Margaret MacCurtain) and Mary Lavin. Christ Church Cathedral can be seen in the background

Valdi, Mary Lavin, Caroline and Elizabeth at Caroline's wedding in 1981

Mary and Michael Scott, *c.* 1985, standing in front of the Town Hall in Bruges, the town in which they were married

Mary Lavin with her good friend Father F. X. Martin, at a Newman House reception to honour Father Martin (photo by Frank Miller, date unknown)

Mary Lavin and the distinguished writer Francis Stuart at an Aosdána meeting

Through an archway at the Bective Abbey ruins,
the Abbey Farm can be seen

for the glamour attached to those stories, to say nothing of the literary content'.

Elizabeth's letters to her mother exude love and worry in almost equal proportions. She knew from past experience that part of her mother's difficulty was depression and she hoped Mary could manage 'to curb this now, to nip it in the bud once and for all, and finally start to relive your existence, with Mick to share your life, and your work to interest you in small doses, like medicine'.

Mary's letters during that period indicate that she was doing little creative writing. She had signed with Constable to bring out Volume III of her stories, and choosing and editing the stories was demanding and time-consuming even though Mick was there to help her and the Peavoys were lending a hand from Brussels. A portion of a letter from Mary, undated, read: 'I'll send you copies of all my stories as soon as I can.' Compiling the collection was not, however, creatively difficult, since all of the stories had been written in an earlier period.

As usual, Mary was finding it difficult to control her editing. Commas were being added; periods removed. At last a deadline forced her to make final decisions and Constable brought out Volume III in 1985. Thirteen stories had been selected: five from *Happiness and Other Stories*, six from *In the Middle of the Fields*, and one each from *Bective Bridge* and *The Great Wave*.

The stories from the *Happiness* collection – 'Happiness', 'The New Gardener', 'One Evening', 'A Pure Accident' and 'The Lost Child' – had all been written in the 1960s and three of them involved priests and the Catholic church in one way or another. In 'A Pure Accident' and 'The Lost Child' the teachings of the Church are shown as harsh and unfeeling. In 'Happiness' her portrayal of the kindly, understanding Fr Hugh bears a strong resemblance to Michael Scott and balances out the other two.

'One Evening' had first appeared in the *Kenyon Review*

in September of 1967. The central character of the story, a young boy suffering the pangs of his first love affair, is witness to the unhappy marriage of his parents. Mary Lavin, in very few words, manages to convey fully to the reader the despair of the boy and the hopelessness of his parents' situation. It is a heart-rending picture. At the beginning of the story, the dialogue between the young boy and the girl he is courting seems weak. And yet very possibly it was intentional so as to portray the young boy's shyness. Certainly a clear picture of the two young people emerges and sets the stage for what follows. The young girl, Eileen, says: 'It must be queer having your father away all week.' He replies: 'What's queer about it? Lots of men are only home at the weekends.' And Eileen: 'It's hard on your mother though, isn't it – if they get on well together, and all that?'

As a young girl, Mary had gone to the seaside with her mother. She never forgot her sadness that her father was not with them: the feeling of loneliness experienced by a child whose parents were not often together. 'One Evening' is another story where the autobiographical is not far from the surface.

The six stories chosen from *In the Middle of the Fields* – 'In the Middle of the Fields', 'The Lucky Pair', 'Heart of Gold', 'The Cuckoo Spit', 'One Summer' and 'The Mock Auction' – all, except for 'The Mock Auction', deal with the pangs and problems of widowhood and of loneliness. And, except for the latter, all appeared in the *New Yorker* in the early 1960s.

'The Mock Auction' is a novella which depicts the life of Miss Lomas, a glorified housekeeper of Brook Farm, a country estate. Mary Lavin draws Miss Lomas and her pretensions (the natives call her the Regent of Brook Farm) with such skill that the reader finds her sympathetic rather than objectionable. Adversity strikes, it almost bests Miss Lomas, but she has the strength and the courage to overcome what appear to be insurmountable obstacles. Zack Bowen summed it up well. In both 'The Lucky Pair' and 'The Mock Auction', he wrote, 'It is as if Lavin herself had considered all the facets of death, struggled with the possibilities of her own future and that of her family, and was announcing a triumph over her own problems.'

The two remaining stories in the collection are 'Lilacs' from *Bective Bridge* and 'Lemonade' from *The Great Wave*. 'Lilacs', written at the very beginning of Mary Lavin's career, leaves no doubt as to her understanding of country folk and her ability to bring her characters to life. She draws an unforgettable picture of Phelim Molloy, who deals in horse dung: Phelim Molloy who, when he tells his prospective bride Rose Magarry that he is going into the business of selling dung, describes its charms. 'When I was a young lad, driving along the country roads in my father's trap, I used to love looking down at the gold rings of dung dried out by the sun, as they flashed past underneath the horses' hooves.' And Rose thinks, 'Who else would say a thing like that? It was like poetry.' Rose, who understands that there are all sorts of ways of making a living, and the couple's two daughters – one of them suffering from the smell and the other from the social stigma – are equally fully portrayed. As always in *Bective Bridge*, Mary Lavin was writing well beyond her years.

As mentioned earlier, 'Lemonade' had given her readers a rare picture of the very young Mary Lavin and a picture of her mother almost as rare in her stories. Only in 'A Bevy of Aunts', written much later, do the early years of Mary Lavin's life emerge as clearly. In both stories the portrayal of a very young person, seeing the conflict between husband and wife and made to suffer from it without the maturity to understand, is vivid. Long afterwards Mary said that, when she had written 'Lemonade', she had intended it to be the story of her mother and father rather than the story of the child, which was what it became. Though part of the story is set in East Walpole, Mary acknowledged that it was a world which was dimmer than the world of the imagination generally was for her. 'I don't think I could have sustained myself in it for long, and yet I felt a whole world was there, intact, but just beyond the threshold of recall.'

Volume III is a strong collection and her selections range widely enough to give a good picture of her work in the period prior to her second marriage as well as of her skill. By the time the selections were made for that volume, Mary realized that writing was becoming more difficult. Her 1979 letters reflected her worry. In one she wrote, 'I wonder if the frightful depression and nervous exhaustion of last winter, as well as being caused by tiredness, may not also have been a flinching from work: flinching from trying to write a harder story.' The only advantage seemed to be that she understood more clearly exactly what she was attempting to achieve. She believed that, as she grew older, she was getting better. She realized, however, that it would not go on forever. 'I just wonder, will I notice when the crack comes, or will I outlive that moment? Will I die before I crack?' It was a pity, she lamented, that writers couldn't have two lives: one to just live and another to just write. 'Writers do have to live two lives – suffering more than others at times, happier at others, but it's a waste of time to have to live the two lives in the one span.'

The same year that Volume III appeared, Constable brought out *A Family Likeness and Other Stories*. Those stories, though they may have been written earlier, had never appeared before. The collection contained 'A Family Likeness', 'A Walk on the Cliff', 'A Marriage', 'The Face of Hate', 'A Bevy of Aunts' and 'A House To Let'.

Understandably, Mary was often asked why she didn't write about the problems in the North. As distressed as she was by the violence, she saw no reason to do so. 'You don't have to write about the problems of your time,' she maintained. 'Your attitude towards the problems in your country must reflect in your work but your work doesn't have to reflect the problem.' In 'The Face of Hate' she made an exception. It is concerned with the Protestant-Catholic conflict in the North and is the only story in Lavin's collections placed there. It is an excellent portrayal of the division between the two groups. The two main characters are Johnny, a bright, sixteen-year-old Catholic boy, and Eileen O'Grady, a Catholic girl of about the same age. Neither knows any Protestants but, while Johnny is hard-bitten on the subject, Eileen has a far more open mind.

The story opens with these lines. 'Johnny knew the other boy only by sight, but he hated his white Protestant face and his sedate Protestant step. It was 1957 in Belfast. Johnny was sixteen.' Each weekday morning the boys pass each other on the way to school and 'It galled Johnny to think the little Protestant was then within a stone's throw of the grammar school, while he himself had yet to get across the city to St Mary's.'

In Johnny's opinion, all Protestants are filled with hate for all Catholics but when he says that to Eileen, she says:

How do we know what hate is if we don't have it in our own hearts? . . . Do you realize, Johnny Mack, that in other countries, civilized countries, people don't know, don't care, what religion you are? Do you think in England if a fellow liked a girl, he'd want to find out what church she belonged to before he'd speak to her? It's only in Belfast you get that muck.

As the story ends, the young people are taking their first walk together on the Twelfth of July, the day of the Orange Order parade, held each year to celebrate the anniversary of the Battle of the Boyne. They encounter three Protestant boys walking abreast towards them. Eileen's reaction is to cross the street; Johnny's is one of anger and defiance. When one of the Protestant lads steps back to allow them to pass, Johnny – sure that the boy is 'trying to show his superiority'

– punches him in the face, knocking him to the ground and drawing blood. To Johnny's amazement, Eileen kneels beside him and uses her handkerchief to stop the bleeding. When Johnny tries to get her to join him and walk away, she turns on him and on the Protestant boys as well. She accuses the Protestants of sneering at them and trying to provoke Johnny. 'You stupid fools. You think you're great, don't you? With your drums and sashes and your Union Jacks.' And then, turning on Johnny, 'And you. You, with your Green, White and Gold. Soon there will be only one flag in Belfast . . . There will be only one flag flying over this city soon.' And she 'walked away, going as steadily as was possible in her cheap papery shoes'. The story leaves no doubt as to the author's sentiments.

Speaking to an American friend, Mary compared the hatred in the North to the hatred between races in the United States: like the attitude of its citizens towards blacks and Indians. As she saw it, only time and intermarriage would solve the problem. 'When your son brings home a black girl or your daughter marries a black man and you swallow it, you advance the whole thing by a hundred years. The parents who accept the blacks are the bridges.'

'A Bevy of Aunts', a novella, is written in the first person. The narrator is a young girl, an only child, born in the States of Irish parents, who is taken to Ireland to live when very young. As in 'Lemonade', the comparison with the young Mary Lavin is hard to miss. The characters, clearly the Mahons, are drawn with memorable and moving intensity as well as wit.

In this story, once again, Mary's narration underscores the pain she must often have felt as a child with regard to her looks. Once again, too, the reader senses the delight of the child in the Irish countryside, a delight Mary never lost, and also the joy of being part of a large and, to her, very romantic and exciting family. Her character-drawing is superb and, as Benedict Kiely wrote of her characters, they 'stay with you for a long time after you end the reading'.

The strongest story in the collection and one which may very well rank with the best of Mary Lavin's short stories is 'A Marriage'. Here Mary shows her remarkable ability, so often mentioned by the critics, to see into the hearts of her characters. It is the story of an ageing college professor called James, his wife of many years, and their life together. The professor's love of their farm and the countryside is central to the story. The drive from the college to his home is long and wearing but when he reached the entrance gate to the farm 'his jangled nerves were immediately calmed by the broad expanse of unfenced pasture under the immense dome of sky'. His wife Emmy is waiting for him but he feels the need to walk across his fields before going into the house. In fact, he is reluctant to join her, to hear the list of chores she will have ready for him, and even to have the delicious dinner he knows will be waiting. There can be no doubt in the reader's mind as to James's love for his wife. But Mary qualified that love. She wrote:

> For some time now he had a real wish to feel more deeply for her, but she didn't make that easy with her unbelievable carelessness about her appearance . . . That soft, loose way she wore her hair used to be very attractive, but now that her hair was grey she really ought to make an effort to control it. He had always respected, and shared, her belief in being natural, but perhaps now that she was getting on in years, she ought to have something done about her looks like other women.

But when he remembers how beautiful her hair was, he feels disloyal. It had 'the living darkness of a bird's wing, with flashes of blue and green and even glints of gold'. Later in the story James is recalling his feeling when he received letters from her: the 'extraordinary sensation' when he had

263

touched one of her letters. And he asked himself:

> Oh, where did it go, that magic? To think that for
> years he had not noticed that it was gone. For years
> he had complacently accepted the substitutes of good
> living, companionship, affection, loyalty and perhaps
> above all care, good care, and had only lately faced
> that these things never made up for the delirium of
> first love.

In page after page in 'A Marriage' the couple's love for each other over the years comes through, as well as the regrets that time has inexorably made its changes. 'Oh James, what is the matter with us? I know we can't expect things to be like when we were young,' Emmy says. 'We're no different from other couples of our age,' James replies. And Emmy: 'Oh James! When we were young would it have satisfied you to think we'd end up like other people?'

Just as James is seeing flaws in Emmy, she is seeing flaws in him. The way, for example, he put his trousers over a chair at night. Year after year, she has hated 'the way you spread your trousers out on that chair, with the fly open, it's so – so obscene'.

Very worried about how tired he is at the end of a day and how irritable he can become and knowing he will not go of his own accord, she goes to see a doctor on his behalf. When he mistakenly believes she has been to see the doctor about herself, he is terror-stricken and guilt-ridden for his disloyal thoughts. 'Oh God, what a fool he was! If anything were to happen to her, it would be like the amputation of a limb.'

In this story Mary draws a picture of a lengthy relationship with great understanding. She manages successfully to expose and encapsulate all the hurts, the sorrows, and even the joys crowded into a life. The story's climax is powerful and Lavin's ending, with the death of the husband, is superbly written. Perhaps Kiely's summary may go a bit too far but it is not wide off the mark. He wrote: 'This particular story may well rank among the great stories from anybody, anywhere, or any time.' But he did not go too far when, of her stories in general, he wrote that she 'measures up to greatness because of art and craft and style and vision, and of understanding of the heart, because of a ruthless addiction to truth and, also, because of pity and humour'.

'A Marriage' adds considerably to an understanding of Mary at that point in her life. It touches on her fears with regard to Mick's health, her distaste for all that goes with ageing, her worry about her attitude towards Mick and his towards her. It is characteristic of so much of Mary Lavin's work that she was able to stand aside and study her own experiences.

Mick's friend, Dr Gillen, read 'A Marriage' in 1995 and wrote about his reaction to it. 'I read it nostalgically,' he wrote, 'because it was as though I was reliving a visit to the Abbey Farm.' He remembered how he had felt as he drove towards the farm:

> An outer and an inner gate and a Springer to welcome me. The crunch of the gravel and seeing, as in the story, the picture of Mary herself 'with her unbeliev-able carelessness about her appearance', and hearing her say, as in the story, 'Oh, James, think of what life would be for me without you', and seeing 'tears in her eyes'.

The theme of 'A Marriage', as well as that of 'A Family Likeness' and 'A Walk on the Cliff', indicates that these are works of an older Mary Lavin. Nevertheless, the stories in this collection are in many respects as strong as anything she had written previously. But she was growing tired and feeling her age beyond her years. As one of her friends said, she had never been kind to herself or sparing of her energies.

Before *A Family Likeness and Other Stories* had gone to Constable for 1985 publication, Elizabeth, desperate to have her mother start writing again, had tried to get Mary to do a preface for it but without success. She then suggested that perhaps working on a gardening book during the winter months when she had no gardening to do might be a worthwhile idea. Mick could work with her on it if he felt so inclined and, if not, she would be willing to pitch in. 'Please try to advance faster, not slower, try not to crawl but jump.' Jumping, she believed, was easier for someone with her mother's temperament than crawling. 'I know how much you've got on your mind. Well, get it off your mind and onto the drawing board.' Her advice was solid but, from a distance, it was difficult for her to see that at that point her mother was clearly unable to cope. During the years of Mary's decline, Caroline was the surrogate for her sisters, who were away from Dublin for lengthy periods. And it was Caroline who appears to have seen the situation more clearly at that time.

The whole situation was never far from Elizabeth's mind. Now she wondered if perhaps, after Mary married Mick, she had established a new pattern: one in which she did not feel the compulsion to write. In addition, her friends were urging her to 'put those damn things away', just as they had after William Walsh's death. That would have been fine advice if she could have been happy without her work but her daughters doubted that she could. 'It was part of her life.'

There is a possibility that Mary had already started to drink more heavily than she had previously but that possibility was something that Elizabeth was more than reluctant to face. Mary, however, did not mind discussing the whole problem. She recalled that Nora Lavin had had a fear of drink, possibly because of Tom's drinking, although there is nothing to show that he drank more than a great many Irishmen of his class. Certainly he enjoyed drinking with his pals in the States and in Ireland as well and, as Mary wrote in 'Lemonade', the little daughter had witnessed the mother's disapproval. When, after William Walsh died, Mary would take a drink at bedtime so that she might sleep, Nora disapproved, and cautioned that it might become habit-forming. Mary had rebelled against her mother in this as in many other things.

When William Walsh was alive, Mary had not taken more than the occasional glass of wine and neither had he. They did keep a bottle in the house for guests, however. But, she once said, 'when I was a widow for what – fifty, a hundred years or whatever I was a widow for', she had envied the households she visited where the man of the house would offer a drink to a guest. When she married Mick, she had looked forward to sitting down with him and having a sociable drink and a chat. But Mick did not drink and, furthermore, had what she considered very moral views on the subject. He disliked seeing anyone drinking to excess. He had once said that to see a man drunk was bad enough but a drunken woman was a 'terrible sight'. Mary's reply to that was that the remark was sexist. As she saw it, it was not very pleasant to see anyone drunk, no matter what the sex.

Mary had often wondered whether for some writers in particular drinking wasn't part of the performance. She cited Brendan Behan, whose audiences in the States, she maintained, expected him to be drunk. Declan Kiberd agreed. The 'stage Irishman', he wrote, had been replaced by what he called the 'stage writer': Brendan Behan's, Flann O'Brien's and Patrick Kavanagh's drinking had become legendary. Caroline, present when Mary advanced this idea, added that she had actually heard an editor say that a certain writer couldn't be much good since he had never seen him in a bar. Among Mary's miscellaneous notes now in the University College Dublin archives is this commentary on the subject:

Why does the world put up with its artists, tiresome, troublesome, often drunk, sometimes mad, occasionally suicidal? Why does the common man accept, even condone, or pity their behaviour? It must be that preoccupied though he may be the artist is a kind of Christ figure giving his life for others. That may sound arrogant, but is not, because the artist himself seldom knows what he is doing, seldom knows his motives, is often abashed by his own egotism, his self-interest, and this abasement speeds him on in his sacrificial self-destruction.

Mary's description of what went on when she and Mick had guests undoubtedly became one of her prize anecdotes. The last thing Mick would think of, when guests arrived, was offering them a drink. Mick would offer them a cup of tea and Mary would give him 'a daggers look'. But he would rush off to make the tea. 'Tea is such a paraphernalia, tea cups, saucers, sugar basins, cream jugs, and you can't give someone tea without a bit of cake or, if we didn't have cake, we had to give them something, a bit of buttered bread, make toast, you know.' On those occasions Mary would say, 'For God's sake, give them a drink.' As she put it, with drinks you didn't even have to wash the glasses: 'the damn stuff evaporates'. But tea didn't evaporate, and the sugar at the bottom of the cup solidified and it took a week to get it off. The whole scene made her 'take six drinks! It's an irritation.' She sometimes wondered whether it was Mick's disapproval that made her drink more heavily. 'I had nothing else to do but to bloody well show that I was me.'

She had developed an elaborate theory and one which, given her temperament, may have had a certain amount of validity. Sometimes life was too hard for her, she thought. She would be overwhelmed by people, hired hands, children, grandchildren, visitors. It would keep her from writing and she felt put upon. 'I don't think I drink as a writer. I drink as a housewife. It's when I'm peeling potatoes, washing a floor.' She would be 'half crazy' wanting to work, to write. She drank to bring herself down to a normal level. If she took a drink, she would then be 'just like everybody else. In my book I'm twice as sober as I would be without the drink. I drink to get sober.' That did not necessarily mean, she explained, that she would be able to work. It simply meant that she could stop worrying about not working.

Once, when Mary was expounding on the subject of drink, she was asked whether she believed wife-beating was often the result of too much drink. She admitted that on that subject she was a little unclear. Did the husband come home drunk and did his wife say something about not being able to put up with this any longer and then did he beat her up? Perhaps it would be advisable for her to say, 'Oh, God, what terrible thing happened to you that you come home like this?' And he would say something like 'the boss doesn't need me any longer', and then he would cry and she would put her arms around him and the result would be 'sixteen kids instead of fifteen'. On one point Mary was crystal clear. The alcoholic, she said, was not the one to be pitied but rather the one who had to live with the alcoholic.

Since Mary was finding it difficult to start to write anything new, she was giving serious consideration to a revision of *The House in Clewe Street*. The Peavoys urged her not to even consider a *Clewe Street* alteration. They thought that the idea of an afterword was far better than attempting to alter the novel, but, of course, if that was what she wanted to do she should go ahead. But wouldn't an afterword be easier to do? And if not an afterword, why did she not, the Peavoys asked, give some thought to 'a non-creative *joint project* type of venture, *on your work, you and it*, as your material is so rich.' What they were thinking, they told her, was of a kind of prelude to her later work, not an altered ending but more a critical study of *self*. They believed she richly deserved to make herself heard: 'to put your final stamp on the literature of your day'.

It was somewhat the same suggestion that Caroline had made earlier and Elizabeth urged her mother to start on it right away. She should count her blessings, Elizabeth wrote, and then sit down and try for something really difficult. Instead of merely trying to survive, as she seemed to be doing, she should try to 'overreach' herself. 'Do not throw it all away so easily. I don't care how bad you feel, how impossible the proofs are, the corrections, why don't you really try to explain your way out of it, the only way you know how, in print? Write a critique of what is going on in your work, and where you are going. Only you can know this.' That was the tone of all Elizabeth's letters at that time. 'Begin to be a bit of a Pollyanna,' she urged her mother. 'No matter how badly you feel, can you not think of something worse that you could suffer.'

In the ongoing crisis concerning Mary's depression, Diarmuid tried the praise approach. She was a survivor. She should now concentrate on her achievements under difficult circumstances. She had turned out an impressive body of work, she had managed the farm, she had raised three daughters who were all happily married, and she was herself happily married for the second time. There was, too, the added blessing of grandchildren. Like Elizabeth, he wanted her to count her blessings.

The Peavoys had from time to time urged Mary and Mick to visit them in Brussels, feeling that the change would be good for them. It was not entirely altruism on Elizabeth's part, however. She was well aware of how lost she was for the intellectual stimulus her mother provided – a kind of face-to-face communion which can be achieved sometimes without speaking a word. Diarmuid's position had its bad times and, at one point, he had actually resigned but had taken it back the next day. 'Very Irish,' Elizabeth commented. She had hoped that the resignation would be firm and that they would be coming back to Dublin.

Mary and Mick did visit twice in 1984: early in the year and again at Christmas time. Both visits may have done a great deal to convince Elizabeth that her mother was not quite up to resuming anything like a normal writing schedule and she modified her advice. Very early in the new year she urged Mary to 'fill your mind with coffee and buns and picture postcards, or become a do-gooder or a Pollyanna'. She no longer seemed to feel quite so sure that, for Mary, work spelled survival. She compromised and suggested that perhaps her mother could set up a schedule for herself. Limit her writing hours to one or two at a time, or one in the morning and one in the afternoon, and try to put out of her mind all the workload of publishers, editing, letters. Perhaps she had been doing too much and because of that her fears and worries had got the better of her as they had done previously. Now, perhaps, she could prepare for another period of fruitful existence but this time make it at her own pace. 'Mother, you used to love going to town. I know it's not the same, cheap and trashy now. But could you not go to the Shelbourne and walk down once a week to Grafton Street?'

She was on shaky ground. There was in her mind the fear that Mary would assume that her girls felt her writing career was over. She hastened, therefore, to say that she believed, as did Caroline and others, that Mary had a lot of writing life left. When, during that period, Mary was nominated for the Nobel Prize for literature, Elizabeth hoped that that would convince Mary that her writing was a real 'offering to the world' and nothing anyone could do would make that achievement any the less worthwhile.

Elizabeth showed an understanding of her mother which perhaps could not have been possible had she not been so very much like her. She too felt excited and then done in, she too had so many fluctuations of mood. Perhaps her mother could get a psychiatrist to explain this, Elizabeth wrote Mary. 'Should one not allow oneself to get excited? Is that it? And yet the excitement of writing is what you draw on to get you through the drudge of day-to-day.'

So much of Mary Lavin lives on in her children. Elizabeth's letters are full of references to her comments, her teachings, and the need they all felt to be with her and to learn from her. Mary's 'girls' would always remember the joys of the years when they were growing up and they did not hesitate to tell Mary so. As Elizabeth once wrote to her, they would never forget the 'rich abundancy' of the woods in Bective and the days of their childhood when they literally lived in those woods, and the people who would gather round in those days – the Dunsanys among them. 'In all the days of your writing life, the things which remain most clearly in my mind are the days when your publishers came to lunch in Bective, and Mrs Rahill was making fruit salad, and the time you wrote the preface.'

Another one of Elizabeth's abiding memories was the 'little old Christmas' they had spent with Mary and Mick somewhere in Germany 'was it, or where', when they had walked over the bridge to midnight Mass, with the snow falling, and Caroline, like the little match girl, lighting her candles on the washbasin. 'I think that hotel Christmas, somewhere out there in continental Europe, twinkling and glowing, amid the myriad lights, will never leave me.'

So very often Elizabeth had longed for the days when they had all been together even though sometimes, when they were, it was, as she said, 'stormy weather under the canvas.' So many times it had been Mary's love that had guided them. 'I think of you now,' she had written to her mother, 'when love builds up like a swell to guide us to harbour and all the times you were there to bail me out. Now I feel that I should do some of the bailing.' They would all, including Mick, need to do a great deal of bailing during that period in Mary's life.

CHAPTER 12

Despite family opposition, Mary's plan to build additions to the Abbey Farm had prevailed. Her persuasive argument had been that it would add to the value of the property when they were ready to sell. Therefore, with her application for permission to build granted, she had added two self-contained wings at the side of the house at a cost of eighteen thousand pounds. As the family expanded, Mary was glad to have the extra space. Her sons-in-law were now very much part of the family scene and each was in his own way a valuable addition.

Des MacMahon, Valdi's husband, was someone both Mary and Mick could turn to for practical, carefully thought-out decisions and in the family circle he was a stabilizing force. He and Mick got on famously. Mick had a splendid collection of slides and, even more than the others, Des enjoyed viewing them. He was, too, impressed by Mick's architectural background. There was, however, a more important basis for the fellow-feeling between Des and Mick. As Des saw it, it was because they both understood Mary. They recognized her complicated personality, her pretensions and the chemistry between her and her daughters which, in many ways, excluded outsiders. And Mary appeared to appreciate, admire, and in a sense be amused by his ability to understand her.

Des and Mary liked each other. His ability to see her clearly did not in any way dampen his enjoyment of her company nor his admiration for her. She was, he thought, not only interesting and stimulating but also challenging. 'She was someone you had to be on your toes with. She had remarkable insight and, at times, gave a laser-like demonstration of it.' At the same time, with her mercurial temperament and his fairly stolid reactions, there was a limit to how deeply they could enjoy each other.

What troubled Des was the relationship between Mary and her daughters. He had given it a great deal of thought. She was not a domineering mother in the conventional sense. 'I can't ever remember her saying "you must do this" or "you must do that",' he said. And yet she had a tremendous amount of emotional control over the girls: over Valdi perhaps a bit less than over Elizabeth. It did not surprise him that, after marriage, they had difficulty to one extent or another in loosening the bonds, nor did they have any desire to do so. It was a kind of psychic dependency.

Des examined the possibility that, as youngsters, they had led a life divorced from the norm. There was much less emphasis on pragmatic, practical things that might have permitted them to acquire living skills in the same fashion as other children. In addition, the family was financially insecure. Surely they did not feel poverty but Mary's livelihood was precarious. Then, too, they were the children of a celebrity, someone they looked upon as a genius. As the children of such a personage, they were in a special category. They had to live up to it: their mother would expect it of them. They felt no need for a father figure. Apparently Mary's larger than life persona filled any void.

As they all did, Des looked forward to the weekends at the Abbey Farm, with the family gathered there and Mary's generous and delicious meals. There was always wine on the table, and that lent an *avant garde* atmosphere to the occasions. Des's father had been a professional: a county engineer. The family would have had status in the modern Ireland, but people who came to the house would not have been served wine. It would have been tea. 'And these were hard men who'd been gunmen in their day and might have served jail terms,' Des said. 'It was the odd person who would have been offered whiskey, but that would be in the 1960s.'

Diarmuid Peavoy also saw the closeness of the relationship between Mary and her daughters which, as Des had felt, bordered on an exclusion of the outsider. In one sense, he felt it more keenly perhaps than Des did because of Elizabeth's more obvious need for Mary and, actually, Mary's need for her. As Diarmuid once said, 'Mary was a personality, she was on show, on stage. She was very conscious of her image as a writer, and her daughters abided by that image.' When at one point Diarmuid found that once again he would have to be away for an extended period, he had been in two minds about taking Elizabeth so far away from her mother. He knew that they both needed their long chats. So much of Elizabeth's conversation centred around Mary that, as he said, at times he felt he was living with them both.

Mary was very fond of Diarmuid, as he was of her. That had not always been true. Early in the Peavoys' marriage, Mary had seen Diarmuid as unable to support Elizabeth in a style Mary considered worthy of a daughter of hers. Elizabeth had taken a position with the *Irish Farmers' Journal* and had continued working there until her first child, Eoghan, was six months old. Despite the fact that Elizabeth – as she said later – was 'uproariously happy' and that Diarmuid's mother was caring for the baby while Elizabeth was at work, Mary blamed Diarmuid. Her displeasure was characteristically not passive. Years later Diarmuid recalled with amusement that Mary and Mrs Peavoy had had a heated conversation about the matter and Diarmuid's mother had reported to him that Mary had shouted at her like a fishmonger. But over the years Mary had come to have a great deal of respect for him and for his ability and they had established a genuine bond.

James Ryan, as mentioned earlier, had developed a friendship with Mary before his marriage to Caroline. He liked being with her, and he and Mick enjoyed each other's company as well. James had grown up in the country and, like Mick, he loved the farm. Often he and Mick would do the necessary chores together. James Ryan's recollection of dinners at the farm is vivid. Dinner table conversation was very lively and always fun, with Mary and her 'girls' attempting to shout each other down, he said. They would have fillet steaks, baked potatoes and salad. At Mary's it was served 'off at the side and on blue, quarter-moon salad plates.' There was always wine with the meal. Mary, James said, used to buy her wine by the case from the Unicorn restaurant – one-and-a-half-litre bottles of Italian wine – and, as he said, she was very generous with it. It was all 'very sophisticated'. The extraordinarily close and intimate relationship between Mary and her daughters impressed James. They 'disclosed' everything to her. She listened to every detail about their romances and their college life: she lived every moment with them. And it was not one-sided. Every detail of her life and of her work was equally important to them.

Valdi and Elizabeth, married within a year of each other, were having their children virtually in tandem. Valdi's daughter Kathleen, Mary's first grandchild, was born in 1970; Elizabeth's son Eoghan in 1971; Valdi's son Kevin in 1974 and Elizabeth's Adam the same year; Valdi's daughter Margaret (Meggie) was born in 1983, as were Elizabeth's son Tadhg (Tiger) and Caroline's first child, her son Matthew (Matt). Her daughter Alice was born in 1986.

By the mid-1980s the older grandchildren in particular were spending some time with the Scotts each year. Kathleen MacMahon and Eoghan Peavoy were coming to Bective – separately and on their own – for lengthy visits. Kathleen can remember going to Bective as early as when she was four and staying there very happily for three or four weeks at a time. She recalled that, when she was in her teens, the whole family would go to Bective for a Sunday or for a weekend and it was family tradition for all those available to spend St Stephen's Day, the day after Christmas, there. Kathleen's memories echo those of the other family members. Her grandmother cooked 'beautiful' big dinners and all the children and the grown-ups sat down together, she said. The family gathered around a big table, eating roast beef, with the children occasionally being given a sip of red wine. At one time there were eighteen people at dinner. A 24 December (probably 1980) notation in the ledger of Donnelly's Victuallers, the local butcher, lists a fourteen-pound turkey as well as fillet steaks purchased by Mrs MacDonald Scott.

Kathleen, too, saw that her grandmother preferred to spend her time with the older children and tended to become somewhat intolerant of the younger ones. Weather permitting, they had picnics on the lawn, and it was Mick who enjoyed playing with the younger children and doing all the childish things. He was very gentle, very kind and it was obvious that the father and grandfather roles suited him. 'Grandmother wanted someone to sit down and have a drink with her,' Kathleen said with a smile.

Kathleen was too young to remember much about the Mews days but she often met people who had visited there and who talked at length about its glories. She had no recollection of her grandmother writing – only gardening and cooking – but, as she grew older, she studied her grandmother's stories and developed a keen knowledge of her work. It is difficult to say how much she was influenced by Mary Lavin but she did major in English at UCD, earned her undergraduate degree with honours, and less than two years after her grandmother's death had turned to creative writing.

It was a source of great regret in the family that the younger children had not known their grandmother at the height of her powers. Caroline felt this especially strongly. Because she was so much younger than Valdi and Elizabeth, she had really only known the highly successful Mary Lavin, the glamorous Mary Lavin of the Mews days, the Mary Lavin always surrounded by an admiring entourage, and it was distressing for her to realize that her children would never know that Mary.

In 1995 Eoghan Peavoy recorded his recollections of the

early days of his relationship with his grandmother and Mick. Those memories began, as he put it, 'as does life itself, at a pre-rational, sensory level'. He saw her 'stout and familiar figure, always shrouded in black shawls and capes, more traditionally Irish in her way than her American background and cosmopolitan tastes would suggest'. She always insisted on the children calling her 'Grandmother'. To Eoghan, that lent her an aura of grandeur and stateliness, but even when quite young he appreciated the way Mick would always humorously cut the ground from under her pretensions as well as her anecdotes.

It was not only Mary's style that made his grandmother such a special person for Eoghan. There was her 'Big Yellow' – a bright yellow station wagon that they always had difficulty starting. Though he was quite young when the Mews was sold, he remembered it as a place where people led an esoteric kind of existence, totally incomprehensible to one as young as he was. And then there was Bective, with its beautiful wide-open spaces, where his grandmother was to him a person of warmth and magnetism. He also recalled that she was always surrounded with all sorts of peculiar and mysterious objects, such as bidets and cod-liver oil capsules, whose usages the children could only guess at.

It was in the 1970s that the Peavoy family left Ireland for Mauritius but Eoghan had one very vivid memory of the Christmas before they left: the Christmas he spent in Bective. At that time his father had already been working in Mauritius for six months and, as they always did when he was away for an extended period, the children missed him dreadfully. Rather than spend Christmas in Dublin without him, he and his mother and brother went down to Bective. There his grandmother's surroundings and her personality gave him a sense of security and stability which amply compensated for the absence of his father.

After the whole family moved to Brussels, they spent their holidays in Ireland and often Eoghan and Adam spent a good part of the summer there. Those summers were precious to them both. What the young people may not have realized was how much it meant to their grandmother to have them with her, to go with Mick to meet them at trains, buses and planes. For Mick, of course, it was the thrill of being a father and a grandfather. For Mary it was one more binding link with her daughters.

Life at the Abbey Farm fell into a regular routine. Eoghan recalled grand dinners in the evening, brack and tea in the study after the day's work, arduous tasks such as shifting turf by the barrowload from one corner of the garden to another. They took trips to the races at Bettystown, fished in the Boyne, amd went to Navan, the nearest town, for shopping or to Dublin for the theatre.

Both the boys felt that, during those summers, they established a deep and abiding relationship with both grandparents. Mick and Mary seemed to have an understanding of and to be able to relate to young people. 'In their company we were always free to air the issues which were foremost in our minds,' Eoghan wrote. They were willing to converse with the grandchildren as 'mini-adults' and to treat them as people. It was one of their most endearing characteristics.

Eoghan's most cherished and enduring memory of his grandmother, however, was of the lengthy chats he had with her on those summer mornings when he was approaching college age. He rose around ten and went down to the kitchen where pots of tea were ready. Mick would already have gone to his study to work and Eoghan would go upstairs to bring his grandmother her second pot of tea. There she would be, 'welcoming and gay, working with her papers on her board in the bed'. She would stop for her tea break and have a long talk with him. She seemed to be amazed that he was never bored by the conversation, when as a matter of fact he was enraptured and stimulated by those talks.

As Eoghan saw it, his grandmother had a 'somewhat

Victorian attitude to matters moral, social and domestic'. He related one incident which bore this out but did not seem to jibe with Mary's rather carefree attitude towards housekeeping. Apparently she considered it 'a heinous crime' for members of the family repeatedly to fail to fold their towels in the bathroom. She finally decided that what was needed was to post a sign and delegated Eoghan to make one. The whole family knew that Mary was addicted to the American TV series *Dallas*, then at the height of its popularity. Since all devotees of *Dallas* were waiting to find out who had shot JR, its main character, the sign read: *1985 – Who Shot JR? 1986 – Who Shot Bobby?? 1987 – Who Didn't Fold the Towels???* 'The sign worked,' Eoghan wrote, 'and a new chapter in family lore was completed. Grandmother's capacity to make an issue of state out of a technicality was now beyond doubt.'

Eoghan believed that his grandmother's somewhat Victorian outlook extended to the marriages of her daughters. It was percipient of young Eoghan to sense that side of his grandmother. It can be seen in Mary's attitude towards Valdi's early love affair. And it is not coincidental that Elizabeth insisted that the tone in the Mews was bohemian, but it was conservative bohemian: no run-down heels. That censorious attitude never seemed to carry over into Mary's stories, however. Her 'Sarah' is a good example: Sarah, the cleaning woman, with three sons all born out of wedlock and all by different fathers, whom Mary understood and did not condemn. Mary's inner conservatism appears to have been at war with her outer progressivism for much of her life.

Eoghan had always planned to go to UCD, where his grandmother and Mick had met and where there had been the 'romantic triangle' of his grandmother, Mick and William Walsh. Continuing the family tradition at UCD had a strong appeal for him. The status of being the grandson of an honoured alumnus appealed to him as well. When, arriving at the college for his first lecture, he found his grandmother's picture looking down upon him from the Famous Graduates area, he felt as if he had come home, and was filled with pride.

The summer before he enrolled at UCD, his grandmother and Mick gave him a tour of the Belfield campus. He was well aware that this was not the famous Earlsfort Terrace campus where the college had been located earlier and where his mother and her sisters had 'run the gauntlet of the writer's daughter's reputation in the sixties'. Still it was UCD.

With all the problems plaguing the Scotts in the 1980s – ill health, Mary's drinking, the loss of the Mews – Mick's salvation was the work on his family history: the Rankin family. As he once wrote to Dr Gillen, working on the family memoirs 'kept my sanity'. Even though he had gone to Australia in 1982 to gather material, in the mid-1980s he was coming to the conclusion that another trip would be valuable. Mary hated the thought: to have him away seemed to her a kind of death. But she could see, as could the whole family, that the trip would be good for him. He was beginning to make plans when everything came to a halt at the beginning of February 1987.

After Mary's gall bladder operation two years earlier, they had thought that was the end of it. But, as Mick wrote to his friend Dr Gillen, she had begun to have severe stomach pains and had started to 'waste away'. She was hospitalized and surgery was performed which revealed extensive bowel cancer. Two-thirds of the bowel were removed but, to Mary's great relief, a colostomy did not have to be performed.

Early in March and after the operation, Mary wrote to Elizabeth a few details of her hospital experience. 'Oh, Elizabeth, I went to hell and back,' she wrote. Her surgeon, quite young and blunt, had told her that she had a 'very strange and rare growth' that had spread to much of her bowel. The only way he could see to save her from a colostomy was to do an exploratory examination, and it would have to be done without anaesthetic. Even then, he could give her no guarantee. She consented and the examination was performed. 'I got through it by being a writer and most writers are ham actors as I'm sure you know. I just set myself to show them – everyone – that I could bear *anything*. I did it and I was very proud of myself.'

After a week of probing, her letter went on to report, she felt that the actual operation would seem mild but she did have a setback. For three hours she had to sit upright with needles in her arm while they gave her 'a long slow laborious blood transfusion'. The unexpectedness of it was shocking. However, the good news was that her surgeon was sure that he had removed all the cancer and, as he told her, whatever she finally died of would not be cancer of the bowel. He planned to do a colonoscopy every six months.

While she was in the hospital, she had sensed that something other than her illness was wrong: that something was being kept from her. Finally, she phoned Valdi to ask her what it might be. Valdi was silent for a moment and then said: 'The others will kill me – the doctors – because we were all sworn to secrecy. But I'm going to tell you.' She had seen Mick in town and he had looked ghastly. When she accused him of hiding something from them, he tried to lie to her, but finally admitted that he had a heart problem. It had been diagnosed as angina.

Mary, temperamentally always sensing tragedy and in addition in a weakened condition, immediately confronted the doctor, demanded the absolute truth, and then said they were to get the best heart man they could find. On second thought, she said, perhaps a GP with a well-earned name for treating heart patients might be better than a cardiologist. She knew Mick so well that she knew he would not want life at the cost of being a guinea pig. That, she feared, was something beyond a cardiologist's comprehension. As she wrote to Elizabeth, she had great faith in the power of will and of love, and of happiness and care. With all of that, she believed Mick could be 'got back from the brink':

> I love him so much. Love for a husband is so complex
> and so powerful. I have been able to put out of my
> mind for the moment all the selfish thoughts and fears
> I had of losing him and being alone. Who knows
> what is yet to come for any of us. What use worrying
> about anything in this life except trying to make a go
> of it – make it viable at least. Whatever that means.

She concluded her letter with the news that Mick seemed
to be feeling quite well, and she herself felt quite cheerful.
A message to Diarmuid had been added to this letter. She
was, she wanted him to know, 'still without much belief',
but while she was in the hospital she walked to the chapel,
miles away from her room, and went in. There was no one
there.

> I went up close to the tabernacle and had an inspir-
> ation. A name, that's all I wanted, for something to
> trust in through all my disbelief and my detestation
> of most religions but especially Catholicism and I got
> it – in a flash – and I prayed 'Mystery of Mysteries',
> I believe in *You*. I didn't ask for help for us. After all,
> I think of Ethiopia and Auchswitz and Belsen and
> the terrors in the north.

All of this she had written on her lap board two days after
she returned from the hospital. She was amazed at herself.
'Dear God, I cannot credit I wrote all this,' she wrote, for
when she was leaving the hospital she had been too weak to
sign the books she had given the nurses as presents.

She was expecting a visit from an agent to collect any of
her books he did not already have, and she suggested that
Elizabeth gather up her poems so that he might take those
as well. He, she reported, is a Welshman who wanted to

come home: 'shades of the British Isles or maybe just the triple crown!' No other agent would take her but this one had said that he would make money for both of them 'out of the wreck of what's left after my neglect of the business end'. It was one of the most upbeat letters she had written for some time.

She had in fact come through the operation surprisingly well and Mick was delighted. As he wrote to Dr Gillen, she was very much her old self, 'full of desire, at least, to write, even though she has not yet got down to it'. He felt that whether she did or not was unimportant. 'She has done enough and is now just on 75.' What was important was that she was not just sitting and moping, which was what she had been doing. He reported that he, also, had 'had a couple of scares just to even it up'. He had developed a growth on his thyroid which had been removed and which, thankfully, had been benign. His letter indicated that the angina attack he had suffered when Mary was at her sickest was controlled with medication and he had been assured that no damage had been done to the heart itself. The whole business, however, had ended his 'gallop' so far as physical work was concerned, but he could still potter around the garden at Bective and cut the lawn with his ride-around mower.

For Mick, one positive thing had emerged from all this. He had more time to write and was putting together his notes from material he had been collecting over the years from both Australia and Scotland about his great-grand-mother Isabella (MacDonald) Rankin. Already he had the first part of his manuscript finished, beginning with the Scott background and up to the death of his grandfather, Angus Rankin.

Mary's upbeat mood lasted only about six months, and by August she was once more falling into the old pattern of anxiety and depression. Everything worried her, first and foremost Mick's heart problem but, increasingly, her own mortality. She was giving serious thought to getting her affairs in order in the event of her death. First, she felt it was important to choose a literary executor and Elizabeth seemed to her the logical choice. Not only was she well acquainted with every facet of her mother's work but her family was concerned as well. 'Diarmuid and the boys, I feel sure, would feel that my literary remains would be up your alley and allow you to do it – even help'. Mary's conversations with Eoghan at the farm had convinced her of the soundness of his judgment and his deep interest in her work and, thanks to long talks with Diarmuid about literature, she was now equally impressed with his ability in that direction.

It had often been brought to Mary's attention that her work suggested a certain preoccupation with death. She recalled that a student at Merrimack College in Massachusetts had pointed out that even in her titles the emphasis was apparent: 'The Cemetery in the Demesne', 'A Visit to the Cemetery', 'The Green Grave and the Black Grave', 'The Small Bequest' and 'The Will'. At the time she had answered lightly. 'Perhaps it's because I'm Irish,' she had said. In a late 1970s interview, the recurrent cemetery scenes had been brought to her attention. She had not noticed the frequency of those scenes, she said, but she was quick to acknowledge her preoccupation with death in her stories. Searching for reasons, she concluded that perhaps it was because she resented death so much. 'I've resented death all my life. My husband accepts death. I do not. I resent leaving my children and the people I love. I resent almost everything that separates me from things that are important to me.'

As Mary dwelled on the whole problem, her depression and her nervousness deepened. Her first instinct was to get in touch with her doctor but Mick cautioned against it. He felt sure that the doctor would immediately put her in the hospital. Once more, he told her to pull herself together, a suggestion that never failed to infuriate her. To try to calm herself down, she suggested to Mick that they go out for a walk. Apprehensive and frightened as she was about so many things even when she felt well, she didn't want to go too far because it would be dark and there had lately been a number of muggings in Dublin. When they left the apartment, however, she saw that it was light, that there were a great many people out walking, and her fears subsided. She and Mick walked as far as Sandymount village, a considerable distance.

On their walk they encountered a friend who, when Mary talked about her inability to sleep, suggested that she stop in to see her doctor, whose office was close by. He could probably give her an injection so that she could get some rest. As he had earlier, Mick vetoed that suggestion. They talked next about the advisability of psychiatric help. About that Mary was as adamant as she always had been. She would have none of it. Her doctor had already told her, she said, and the surgeon had agreed, that she did not need that kind of help. She reported her doctor as saying 'They are all either mad or bleeders out for your money.' The tragedy of the last eight years, to her mind, was that she had listened to doctors even when she knew they were wrong.

And yet Mary understood that she needed more help than her doctor was giving her 'with his little pills that might as well be out of a jar of sweets'. He was young, he was giving her various types of sedatives, they were not helping her at all, and she had lost confidence in him. At that point, she was finding fault with everything and everybody. The decision was finally made to change doctors. Fortunately, she found a mature and sympathetic woman doctor with whom she got on immediately.

Six months later Mick was able to send his friend Dr Gillen a good report. Mary had been given Gamanil, an anti-depressant, and told to take it for six months. Within only four days she was feeling well again. She was full of energy and, in a remarkable reversal, maintained that she even liked housework and proved it by doing it. She was not back to writing but was 'playing about on its fringes'. Her friends could not believe the change in her and the whole thing seemed like a miracle. Mick had almost given up hope of ever seeing her like her old self again but now he felt confident. Mary had already had two colonoscopies since her release from the hospital and all seemed to be clear.

Once again Mick started to plan another trip to Australia to do further research. He wrote full details to Dr Gillen, assuring him that he realized his physical limitations. In his opinion, and both his GP and the cardiologist agreed, the heart condition had been brought on by stress. It had come on quite suddenly within about a month after Mary's operation and at a time when she was physically and emotionally at her lowest ebb. He was not too troubled by the ailment but any excessive physical exertion meant he had to stop and take a pill. That meant that he would have to curtail his activity in Australia. Nevertheless, he was determined to make the trip. 'This will be my last opportunity,' he wrote to Dr Gillen. His brothers and sister were seventy, seventy-six and eighty respectively and he was soon to be seventy-eight. They were, as he said, 'well into what the sportscasters call "injury time".' Mick, sure that these remarks would worry his friend, promised him that he would check with his doctor about travelling and medication.

Dr Gillen was delighted by all the good news. He urged Mick to tell Mary that she was never to come off the anti-depressant medication if she wanted to go on enjoying life. Like the diabetic and angina patient, he wrote, once you were treated properly it was essential to keep on with the medication. As for Mick's trip, Dr Gillen urged him to organise the trip carefully so as to have plenty of time for rest.

Once again, however, Mick had to postpone his trip. By 1988, travelling back and forth from Sandymount to Bective had become too much of a strain. Reluctantly, the Scotts put the Abbey Farm on the market. Late in April, Mick wrote Dr Gillen the news. Because the farm was up for sale, he wrote, he would have to change his plans and put off going to Australia until at least the autumn. They would have to find a buyer, settle the deal and arrange the move to Sandymount. It was, of course, hard to say how much time all of that would take.

Dr Gillen's 'knee-jerk response', as he termed it, was to say 'How much?' and make an offer. 'However, it's a bit far for a weekender.' With the farm sold, he wrote, visits to Ireland were never going to be the same. 'Still, we are all never the same, even though I find it hard to believe I have really grown up.' Abbey Farm held so many memories for him. His introduction to the Walshes had been at the farm and his son had autographed the oak dining table with the prongs of his fork. It would be difficult to estimate the number of people, both in and outside Ireland, who were saddened when news reached them of the sale of the Abbey Farm.

During the first week the house was on the market, there were two potential buyers, one of them from England. The English market was the Scotts' best bet. The price of a property like the Abbey Farm would be prohibitive there and, as a consequence, Englishmen were turning to Ireland to buy. If, Mick figured, they could get around £250,000 for the farm, that would give them an annual income of about £20,000. It was not a great deal in Ireland at that time but sufficient to live on, and there was a strong possibility that it would be all they would have. He was not at all sure that the School of Irish Studies could continue to pay his pension or, for that matter, survive. In its attempt to get students, it was facing formidable opposition from the universities – including the English ones – who were competing for the same market.

All of this Mick related to his friend, writing from his study in Bective, which looked out over the Boyne:

As always, I fee

I love its strange

far from the road

traffic and yet pre

horizon. I have had

contentment (and occ.

here and shall miss it m.

There was no doubt in Mick

broken at the thought of giving

her father, the Dunsanys, her lif

the children growing up there. A

those factors was sufficient to ke

lengthy periods. She had to get away

time. It was, as he wrote to Dr

relationship'. She was lonely there. She ha

to have lengthy conversations, to gossip, a

had 'no one to talk to or at except myself

good a listener as I once was!'

Mick was right about Mary's feelings, of

soon as the decision was made she began ha

'My heart is broken for Bective & I cannot unde

I let them persuade me to sell it except that I was

very very ill.' She seemed to derive some solace from

the blame for the decision to sell on to Des MacMa.

fact, it had been obvious to all of the family that it w

longer practicable to keep the farm. That decision had

been Des's but, once it was made, it had indeed been I

who had looked after the details and organized the auctio

for the sale. Mary's ambivalence was obvious to him. For a

few years before the farm was to be sold, she would say she

hated the place though it was obvious that she loved it. It

was his opinion that she had mixed feelings about a great

many things, however. Selling the farm apparently was only

one of them.

Unlike Mary, Mick was content in the Sandymount

s well as at the farm. He realized that it was a
phobic and that he and Mary were indeed too
ch other's pockets'. His hope was that they could
ugh from the sale of the farm to get a larger flat
dy for each of them and with a small garden.
le, he was spending as much time as possible at
, getting lawns mown, fences mended and the
hedges trimmed. There was a great deal of work to
e to get everything in order for prospective buyers
was enjoying himself enormously. Mary had refused
him and to take advantage of the joys of Bective for
me remaining. She had gone off on a holiday with an
chool and university friend but Mick had no doubt at
hat she would soon come racing back. She had only
n gone two days and already word from her indicated
t she was bored to death.

There is a letter from her to Elizabeth, dated 23 May, no
ear, which must have been written around that time. She
wrote that she seemed always to be waiting for something
bad to happen as it does in her stories. As examples, she
mentioned, 'A Memory', 'A Marriage' and, she added,
perhaps 'Senility'. She wished that she could learn not to
plague herself in advance. Here she was, unhappy at the
thought of Mick's leaving her alone to take a trip to Australia,
when his plans to go had not yet been made. And for some
time she had worried about Mick's dying and Bective's being
sold. Now Mick had a great many things wrong with him
and Bective was 'as good as gone'. Since Mick was two years
her senior, she had to face the fact that when he was gone
she would once more be alone as she had been when William
Walsh died. But she was very aware that this time – and she
brooded about it – she would not have the girls around her
to fill her life.

She had once said to Mick that they both had a visible
question mark over their lives while other people had an
invisible one over theirs. She imagined that Mick was worried

about the increasing loss of his physical powers and of death while she, because she had almost succumbed to cancer, no longer feared death. It was the loss of her mental faculties and becoming senile that worried her. 'I am trying to accept it – to face it – and to know that it would have to come soon,' she wrote. 'I am even trying to tell myself that if I take it well my life may open out into some better vista than I have ever known.'

Her letter continued in that vein. The apartment, although pleasant enough, was contributing to her depression. It was not only the fact that she did not have a garden there that was troubling her, though she was sure it was that in the main. It was the lack of space as well. As she wrote, 'in this apartment with *no* garden where I once had two, I am so debilitated and dispirited. I cannot bear the claustrophobia of it, which I cannot cure.' And she added:

> Living in a closed box with Mick, I have lost the fun of being with people – almost any kind of people. Only once in a long time do I go to something or meet some people that distract me from myself and I have fun. Mick does not know what fun is like and he has turned my life into a copy of his own. I realise now that that has been so for a long time and that only in Bective when we were just married did we have my kind of life.

But she should, she realized, be thankful for the earlier days. 'I don't forget our years of love before we even spoke to each other in UCD and in the garden together – a beautiful quiet loving!'

The MacMahons were back in Dublin during that period and, on occasion, Valdi would stop in to take Mary to read a story before one of the younger children's classes. It was something that, for a brief hour, took her out of her periods of despondency. Elizabeth recalled her mother reading to

Adam's class: stories such as 'The Widow's Son' and the 'Story with Two Endings'. Mary had delighted in the questions the children asked. The indications of the development of the 'emerging brain' intrigued her. Quite often, too, Valdi would stop in briefly or have them visit her for a cup of tea and occasionally for a meal. Her visits did not make her mother happy, however. They were too reminiscent of her own visits to her mother in the Mespil Flats.

At last Elizabeth was able to admit to herself that this was, as she put it, 'the beginning of the breakdown in the network of family'. Mick and Mary were semi-invalids, and she, Elizabeth, was 'well and truly' out of their lives except for holidays when she could come home and take over from Valdi and Caroline. She tried to make those trips often and to stay as long as she possibly could. Caroline was busy with her job, her family, her home and her country place in Athabo, County Laois. Valdi had had a bout of serious illness – breast cancer – and, though she felt very close to Mick and Mary and loved them very much, she could no longer count on herself being able to cope with the situation. In some ways, Elizabeth could agree with Mary that it was reminiscent of the days of her visits to the Mespil Flats to see her mother. There was, however, one basic difference and Elizabeth wished that her mother could see it. There was Mick.

Mary had been able to end the sad letter to Elizabeth on a happier note, however. She was beginning to write again 'and I can, and in the same old way, but it's terribly, terribly hard (maybe it always was)'. Although she said that she was writing again, it is not clear how much attention she was able to give to it. At that juncture, she was relying upon alcohol increasingly. Mick, his health deteriorating, was worried about her and was finding handling the situation almost impossible. And it was clear to the family that his predicament would be aggravated by the sale of the farm.

Without a doubt, it was that 'breakdown in the network of family' that Mary was sensing and finding so difficult to accept. All three of her girls now had their own lives to live: their own families to concentrate on and to worry about. But Valdi, in an unfortunate attempt to think things through, had said aloud that to live outside their children's lives was the fate of all ageing parents. It was true, but Mary had not felt like 'an ageing parent' until these last years when she and Mick had suffered illnesses, when she had begun to have such difficulty writing and when the sale of her beloved Abbey Farm was imminent. She did now, however, and, as she said bitterly, she did not need Valdi to remind her.

IV

WINTER

CHAPTER 13

Within a comparatively short time, a buyer was found for
the Abbey Farm. When that was settled, Dr Gillen wrote to
Mick that he had decided to come to Bective in September.
He was looking forward, he said, to 'sharing the sadness of
saying "Goodbye" to the Abbey Farm and, with so much to
be done, to give them a hand with the moving. He hoped
that they had got a 'mint' for the farm. While on that subject,
he mentioned that he had been thinking about the Jack Yeats
paintings which had been given to Mary. How did Jack Yeats
stand in the art world, he wondered? It seemed to him that,
if they could bear to part with them, they should be able to
get a considerable sum for them. 'My fantasy was that you
could sell one of those and keep the farm.'

He left the length of his stay in Ireland open. Certainly
he would stay for a week but longer if he were needed. 'As
we both have hearts and they are still beating we may as
well enjoy what time there is left to both of us,' he wrote to
Mick. He suggested that they put him up in a pub somewhere in Sandymount or, if it proved convenient for him to
stay at the farm, he would be happy to do the cooking, 'if
your digestion has cast-iron characteristics'.

As he thought of earlier visits, Dr Gillen grew nostalgic.
He wrote to Michael that he recalled fondly the view from
the sitting-room picture window 'across the green grassed
paddock to the Abbey and the lovely old stone bridge behind
it'. He would never forget his first visit to Bective. 'The first
time we all went there from London, before Mary bought
the Mews, we heard of Michael and how God got him and
she didn't. Hell hath no fury . . . as no doubt you've found
out now and again.' And he added: 'What happy days you
must have spent in the garden. You were so proud of your
vegetables and your roses. You will miss it all for all the

reasons that Mary will too. Because it has been so much of her life, it'll be like losing a part of her.'

Dr Gillen's reason for coming to Bective was not wholly to give the Scotts a hand or to visit the Abbey Farm once more, however. Mick had indicated that Mary was growing very anxious at the idea of his leaving her to go to Australia and for that reason he was afraid that he might not be able to make the trip as early as the autumn. That Mick was troubled and needed to talk to him, and to do that privately, was unmistakable.

His plan to come to Bective pleased Mick. That, he wrote, would give him two chances to be with his friend: in Bective and in Australia. He echoed his friend's thoughts on the subject of the shortness of their time. Mick had written, 'Time is marching on, Bob, and I have a feeling . . . and a perfectly calm and contented one . . . that a year or two will see me out.' He had had a 'great' life and 'in spite of mistakes, would not change it'. He now looked forward to making the most of the time he had left and in particular to his friend's visit and, after that, to the trip to Australia. That trip was something he could not bear to think of giving up.

Mary, too, was delighted that Dr Gillen was coming over to give them a hand and, while Mick was down at the farm trying to get it in shape, she wrote to Dr Gillen to tell him so. Just as she had often done when jotting down bits and pieces of her stories, she wrote the letter 'on her bag' in a restaurant in Dublin. First, she was happy to report that Mick seemed to be doing quite well physically. She was, however, worried by his apparent lack of interest in all the details connected with the moving. She cited his unwillingness to go through books and possessions of his which had accumulated in the apartment. It had to be done in order to make room for what would be coming from Bective but, when she spoke with Mick about it, he said that he would wait until the sale was final and all papers signed. It appeared that she would have to handle the Sandymount end of the move alone, she complained, and she was 'almost buried' under all the work. His, Dr Gillen's, help was going to be invaluable. 'Stay as long as you possibly can – or can stand. We'll see lots of people and do lots of things and go lots of places, as well as sorting out Bective.'

She then went on to complain to Dr Gillen about Mick's inability to have fun, just as she had in her letter to Elizabeth. After elaborating on that theme, she wrote that lately she had made 'amazing discoveries' about the changes in Mick's temperament. That twinkle in his eye in the UCD days and his spirit during the hilarous times they had had on trips had, in the last five years or so, vanished. He no longer seemed to know what relaxation and fun – just 'sheer fun' – was. And she feared that, as he lost the ability to enjoy himself, she was losing hers as well.

Having made that diagnosis, she had decided to change things. 'More of this by a fire,' she wrote. Her first move, although she remembered what he, Dr Gillen, had said about continuing to take her pills, was to throw them all away, except for the odd sleeping pill. Next, she arranged for them to go out a lot and, she was happy to report, Mick enjoyed it and 'became more and more alive'. But Mary may have misinterpreted what appeared to her to be Mick's renewed enjoyment of life. It may simply have been pleasure at seeing her happy. He had so often proved that her happiness was and always had been his greatest desire. It is hard to believe that anyone as percipient as Mary failed to fully understood the basic difference in their temperaments, unless, pre-occupied with her own needs, she had refused to recognize it. Mick needed and cherished a certain amount of solitude and the peaceful, quiet life he had known for so many years as a Jesuit priest. He was not naturally gregarious or outgoing. In many ways his personality resembled William Walsh's. There was a world of difference between their temperaments and Mary's and, undoubtedly, that was one of the reasons they were attracted to her.

At any rate, Mary obviously believed she understood the problem. Some years later, sitting alone after Mick's death and trying once more to comprehend what she thought of as the change in him, she scribbled a note on a scrap of paper. Her mistake, she wrote, was to enter into Mick's world, whereas she should have brought him into hers.

As scheduled, Dr Gillen came to Ireland in September. Mick had arranged for them both to drive to Bective from Dublin. That they should make the trip alone would, he felt sure, seem normal to Mary since, while they were getting ready for the move, she usually remained in Sandymount while he went to Bective. It did not work out that way, however. On this occasion Mary insisted on going along.

At the farm, Dr Gillen hoped that he and Mick could talk privately but, as he remembered well, Mary had joined in and had monopolized the conversation. At that time Dr Gillen saw this as another example of Mary's self-centredness, which, in his opinion, had been clearly revealed in her letter. Mick, characteristically, had left the field to Mary and gone out to mow the grass with his Toro: his 'ride-on' mower, as he termed it. With his great affection for Mick, Dr Gillen found the whole situation upsetting. 'I had watched him consider her every little whim, and wondered why he wouldn't frustrate her and attend to or insist on some of his own needs being met, or at least confront her,' he wrote later. 'This was the Achilles' heel of the relationship. He was just too polite, and that was his downfall.'

In the house, Mary talked on, once more explaining about her relationship with Mick and how she felt about it. As she talked, Dr Gillen was conscious of the noise of the mower as it circled the house. Suddenly there was silence and then the sound of a car horn. He went outside immediately and found Mick sitting in the front passenger seat of his Honda, 'looking ashen'. He had put the Toro in the shed that housed it and, when he was leaving, the wind had slammed the door of the shed against him and knocked him down. He had struggled about a hundred yards to his car after, in his usual meticulous fashion, taking time to lock the shed door. His hip was paining him, he said. Dr Gillen could see by the position of Mick's right leg and the rotation of his right foot inwards, that he had broken his hip. He knew that he was going to have to get him to a hospital.

Mary went with them to the Navan hospital, some five miles from Bective. She was so agitated during the trip and in the hospital that the surgeon who was examining Mick had asked Dr Gillen to 'get her out of here'. Dr Gillen, annoyed at the fuss she was making and quite worried himself, felt that she was more concerned with her own reaction than with Mick's pain and he was 'both surprised and angered'.

Looking back on the whole episode later, Dr Gillen observed that often 'the more creative some people are, the more self-centred they might become'. But it would not have been like Mary – the Mary Lavin who didn't take even minor matters calmly – to take this state of affairs with composure. As she looked at Mick, all her fears of losing him and being left alone must have surfaced, but that did not necessarily lessen her suffering for Mick's pain. Pictures which Dr Gillen took in the hospital during the whole episode show plainly Mary's anxiety as she sat by Mick's bed. And in a picture of Mary sitting at a table with Valdi and Kathleen, Valdi's daughter, taken very shortly thereafter, the tears in Mary's eyes are visible.

During the remainder of his visit, Dr Gillen watched Mick with a heavy heart. 'It was sad to see him walk on his broken hip . . . after he had ridden his favourite Toro with the love and enjoyment others would have had from riding a favourite horse.' Dr Gillen had somehow known that, after this visit, he would never see Mick again. He could see how that same fear was affecting Mary and, as he wrote to her later, at last he sympathized with and understood her. 'You retreated into your way of dealing with your fears, and I into mine.'

As the 1980s drew to a close, the problem of the couple's ill health was foremost in the minds of all the family. When at last the moving was over and those things they could not bear to dispose of were in the apartment, it became more apparent than ever that they needed larger quarters and also that they needed help. Mary and Elizabeth did, in fact, spend some time looking for a larger apartment but, as hard as it was to accept, they could both see that Mick's health – and Mary's as well – made another move almost impossible.

In 1990 Eoghan Peavoy, Elizabeth's son, left Brussels to enter UCD. He looked forward to having his grandparents close by and knew being near them would add considerably to the joy of his college years. It was arranged that every Sunday he was to meet them for lunch at the Kildare Street Club and Sundays were something he looked forward to eagerly. He would leave the Belfield campus and speed into town on his bike, wearing a jacket and tie to conform to both the standards of the Kildare Street Club and his grandmother. He had to admit that the 'aristocratic atmosphere of a gentlemen's club' never failed to charm him. Lunchtime conversation consisted of Mary's stories, Mick's 'usual litany of wisecracks' about them, and the banter between the two of them.

It was sad that this routine they had set for themselves lasted only a short time. Mick was becoming increasingly ill and Eoghan began to visit them at the apartment on Sundays instead. One Sunday when Eoghan arrived there, Mick was lying down. That day Eoghan saw the sadness in Mary's eyes and he sensed that already his grandmother was anticipating what life would be like without Mick whom she loved so much and whose support she sorely needed. Mary was extremely unwilling to leave Mick alone but Eoghan prevailed upon her to let him take her out for a few hours. 'There was a pall over our conversation that day,' he said, and a feeling of helplessness swept over him. He knew instinctively that Mick was dying and there was nothing he could do about it. Only four months after Eoghan entered college, Mick died, on 29 December 1990. But Eoghan felt that his relationship with both of them during that brief period sustained him throughout all his college years.

During the period of her husband's last illness and when he was in St Vincent's hospital, Mary found it impossible to go to see him. As she expressed it, she 'cracked up'. But on the day he died she went with Elizabeth to the hospital and she, with Valdi and Elizabeth on either side of her, was at his bedside at the end. 'We lost a father for the second time,' Elizabeth said. That Mary had not been able to spend more time with him during those last days caused her considerable anguish later.

Michael Scott's death represented a loss to a great many people. One of them was the scholar, writer and founder of the School of Irish Studies, Maurice Harmon. He wrote a fitting tribute to Michael which was carried on the editorial page of *The Irish Times* on 15 January 1991. 'The death of Michael Scott has removed from our midst a man of integrity and distinction. Known to many as Mary Lavin's husband, he was content to live in the shadow of her brilliance,' he began. 'But in his own way he was a man of achievement.' Harmon went on to write of what it had meant to Michael Scott to leave the priesthood and of how he had 'with extraordinary patience' taken on the role of stepfather to Mary's daughters who had loved and respected him. 'Only those who have been close to the Lavin-Scott household can appreciate how different it must have been from the orderly life he had known as a Jesuit.' As dean of the School of Irish Studies, he had been respected by faculty and students alike. He had been for many years 'a father figure, kindly, somewhat austere, but someone in whom they could confide. Many kept in touch with him long after they had returned to America.' In conclusion, the tribute read, 'It seems certain that his unquenchable loyalty to the slip of a girl he met in UCD 60 years ago and who was at his bedside on the afternoon of his death will be remembered forever.'

A further view of Michael's life and death was drawn by Gerard Windsor, who had first seen Michael Scott when Michael was headmaster at St Ignatius Preparatory School in Sydney. Windsor had written an article, titled 'A Biography of Michael Scott', which appeared in the 'New Writing' section of the *Adelaide Review*, sometime after Michael's death, and Dr Gillen had sent the article on to Mary Lavin. According to the author, he was aware of the fame of the woman for whom Michael Scott had left the Jesuit Order and he felt sure that a biography of her would be written. 'Most likely it will be done by an American, and a woman,' he wrote, since she was born in the States and lived there during the early years of her life. But he thought that Michael would be unlikely to get the same attention. 'His *curriculum vitae* is solid, but unlikely to, let's say, win him inclusion in the *Australian Dictionary of Biography*.'

Windsor's first encounter with Michael Scott had been in the early 1950s when Windsor was somewhere between the ages of five and eight. He had gone to the headmaster's office in desperation to say that his lunch had not been put in his satchel. He described the headmaster, Fr Scott, as a 'grave, bespectacled, heavy eyebrowed man, but with the points of a smile, an adult smile, warm but also withheld, flickering in his eyes'. Fr Scott, with a look of sympathy, had taken him to the kitchen and seen to it that he was given a sandwich and had saved him from what was for the child stark tragedy.

In March 1968, when the writer was in Canberra studying for the priesthood, a letter was read to the students saying that Fr Michael Macdonald Scott had, after forty years, been released from his vows, had left the Society and Australia and was in a Benedictine monastery in Belgium. Windsor pointed out that that was 'the age of departures', but seldom were men leaving who had been in the Society for forty years. According to him, the fact that there was to be an interim period, when Fr Scott would be a member of a Benedictine monastery, cushioned somewhat the shock experienced by the whole Jesuit community. 'Such a step meant that there was no public denial of the religious life.'

Later, he read that Michael Scott had married a writer but Mary's name had meant nothing to him. In 1972, when he was a post-graduate student in twentieth-century Irish literature at the University of Sydney, he read her collections for the first time. He noted that *The Great Wave*, 1961, was dedicated to M. S. and *In the Middle of the Fields*, 1967, to Michael Scott, SJ. He then read *Happiness*, which came out the year the Scotts were married. Reading the title story, he went on, he was 'thrown, then laughing, at the technical cheekiness of it'. His further reaction was embarrassment at what seemed to him the 'give-away intimacy of this story'. Mary's portraying so fully the love of the priest for the widow bothered him. He did not feel that she was actually 'betraying' Michael and to call it 'exposing' him would be too strong as well. 'But the duration and the degree of the intimacy that she described . . . was he really ready to have it so spelt out?' He agreed that theirs was a great love story and he could find nothing 'indecorous' in 'Happiness', but, he was troubled. 'What was dedication? Could one vow displace an earlier, and no dark shadow fall like a question across both loyalties?'

On 18 June 1973 Windsor saw Michael at the Sidney Nolan retrospective exhibition at the Royal Dublin Society in Ballsbridge. He was there with Mary. Windsor recognized her from the photos on her books. She was walking ahead of her husband, talking in an animated fashion. To Windsor, Michael appeared to be looking for someone with 'the air of a man for whom this stance was a ploy to avoid taking part in something where he does not feel quite at home'. He went over to speak to Michael, feeling awkward because he had never called him anything but 'Father'. Michael did not recognize him at first but then they talked and Windsor later recorded their conversation.

According to Windsor, Michael had said that he loved Bective but that they spent most of their time in the Mews because Mary's youngest daughter was at UCD in her last year. He was looking forward to retirement and spending as much time as possible at the Abbey Farm. He said he hated city life and Windsor got the impression that perhaps he 'didn't like Ireland all that much'. He had been lucky to get his job at the School of Irish Studies at the age of sixty-three, and in Ireland where 'you had no chance at all unless you knew people'. He hadn't been home since he had left Australia five years earlier because Mary refused to fly. It was very stimulating living with a writer, he said.

On 16 June 1993 the author visited Caroline Walsh in her office at *The Irish Times*. He spoke with her about the Abbey Farm and she told him that the farm had been sold. In the conversation, she referred to Michael as 'my stepfather, my beloved stepfather' and she spoke about his funeral. As Windsor recalled, she had said:

When he died Mick was really just another elderly parishioner to the parish priest. Didn't really know him. It was to be just a quiet ordinary funeral. I was in the porch about to go in and this taxi drew up. Out jumped Frank Martin [Father F. X. Martin, the leader of the Wood Quay fight] with vestments over his arm. 'I just heard on the radio. I rushed over. I have to do the Mass.' I was about to go in again, and there was another priest, running. 'I've been sent by the Jesuit Provincial,' he said. 'I have to say the Mass.' They all spoke. Everyone spoke. The Jesuit said that Mick had come, late, to make his home in Ireland and he had been loved by all who knew him. But, this Jesuit said, long before that, Mick had been a cherished member of another family, the Society of Jesus, and he had never really ceased to belong to that family.

'That was when the tears really came to my eyes,' Caroline said.

For a time after Mick's death in December 1990, Mary went to pieces and, as a matter of fact, cut herself off from people. A letter from the Medlicotts expressing their sorrow had gone unanswered for a time but finally she wrote. She was 'sad' to have lost touch but, she told them, the greatest sadness in her life had come upon her and she doubted if she would ever be able to write again. 'I have grown quite suddenly so old.'

By the end of April 1991, however, she was able to inform Dr Gillen that she seemed 'to be coping reasonably well now, in spite of how ghastly I feel'. She was spending considerable time sorting through Mick's personal papers and trying to handle the vast amount of business correspondence, she told him, and, although she had been thinking of him, she had found it too difficult to write. 'You knew too much and too little at the same time about Mick and me for me to attempt a real letter.' In his reply, written shortly thereafter, he wrote that her comment, so apt, had caused him to review his association with them both. He believed that he at last saw their relationship more clearly. 'The way I understand [it] now makes me feel that I'm past idealising or denigrating it, to understanding something of what it must have meant to both of you to be together when he died.'

Mary's correspondence at that juncture indicates that she was coping remarkably well under the circumstances. A letter to Fred Hanna of the Fred Hanna Ltd bookstore tells him that she has employed secretarial help and asks him to send her *Seven Winters* by Elizabeth Bowen and also *Irish Coins and Medals*. His invoice indicates that he sent her both.

Mary took the trouble also, that April, to answer a letter from a high-school girl in the States, Stephanie McIntyre, who had written her a thoughtful letter about the short story 'The Living'. Mary's reply shows how clearly she was thinking about her work. McIntyre, among other things, raised questions as to the ending of the story and indicated that she did not quite understand it. Mary read the story again, noted very sound minor changes that she would have liked to make in the ending, and then wrote: 'At one time I thought that if someone did not understand a story, the story was a failure. Lately I do not think so. If the author fully understands what he is doing he need not worry about the reader.'

In mid-April Mary received a letter which gave her a great deal of pleasure. Fr P. J. L'Estrange, the rector of Newman College, University of Melbourne, wrote to inform her that he had arranged a Requiem Mass for Michael to be held in the chapel at Newman on the 22 April. He had invited Fr Brian Fleming, who had been Michael's dean at Newman, to 'preach the homily'. He had also invited as many as possible of the students who had been there during 'Michael's Rectorate', as well as 'members of the College Council who served with him, his relatives, and some of the many artists whom he knew and assisted'. Friends and representatives from Aquinas College were also planning on joining them. His letter concluded: 'I am sure you will be close to us in spirit, and hope you experience from afar something of our support for you and the love which so many held for Michael.'

Mary replied immediately to express her delight. When they were first married and living in Bective, she told him, so many of the Jesuits from Australia had stopped by when she was the only one there to receive them that she had 'almost felt I was a J myself'. She concluded by thanking him 'more than I can say for the love you have held for him. I once asked him was he sad at having left you all – the J's I mean – and he said, "They were my brothers, Mary."' It was not until a few years later when, with Elizabeth's help, Mary was attempting to thank those to whom Michael Scott had meant so much, that another letter was written to Fr

L'Estrange. She was writing at her mother's request, Elizabeth wrote, to thank him for sending them the Newman College Collection of Art document. From it they had not only learned more of Michael's life but also were able 'to witness at first hand some of the work in another area of experience' for which he was responsible. She believed Fr L'Estrange would be pleased to know that Michael had kept up his interest in church art and part of his library had been presented to the Ecumenical Centre in Dublin.

Elizabeth went on to write that she had met Michael in the late 1950s, but not until he finally came to Ireland to stay had she come to know his personality and true character. In fact, 'so close did the family become that we, my sisters and myself, responded to him both as a father and as the grandfather he was to our children'. The memory of Michael Scott was not fading, she assured him. 'My mother talks readily about Mick, and has not forgotten what he meant in any respect, both to her personally and to us as a family . . . We all miss him, of course, as did you in the Jesuit order.' They all had grown used to having him by Mary's side and now they were attempting to grow used to doing without him. 'That you also will understand.'

Mary had added a postscript to Elizabeth's letter. 'It's terrible to depend on someone writing for you, not one line of this letter written by Elizabeth is warm enough. I talk to him continually and sometimes I think it's real. I'd like to write more, but it's a miracle to write this much.'

Fr L'Estrange's earlier letter giving Mary details of his plans for a Requiem Mass had touched Mary deeply and she had mentioned to Dr Gillen that she hoped he had been one of those who attended. He had replied that he was. He had been moved 'when the best of Catholicism and the best of the J's brought out the love we all felt for Michael'. They had spoken of how distressed they were when he had left Newman for Mary and her girls. That had been, Dr Gillen acknowledged, the way he had felt and now, when at last he could understand, he grew angry with himself. He had been sure that Michael, who had never had anyone to worry about except himself, would want to return to Melbourne 'to polish all his nice bronze statues, paintings and things, and be with all the people who loved him from a respectful distance'.

There was, after the service in the chapel, a celebratory gathering but Dr Gillen could not bear to stay for it. Michael was the nearest thing to a father he had ever had, he wrote Mary. Both had lost their fathers at the same time in their lives: one more link in the chain of their relationship. It had meant so much to him to have Michael's friendship. Mick's faith in him had given him the courage he had needed badly to sustain him during his years of study and internship and had strengthened his will to go on, even when going on wasn't easy. He added that he was pleased and grateful that Mary's daughters were keeping in touch with him. Because he had shared the family with Michael for so many years, he felt a part of it and their letters made him feel that he mattered to them as they did to him. He had often thought that Mary's children had influenced Mick's desire to marry. Whenever he spoke of them, they were his children and their pains were his and he so loved them. Their trials and tribulations were life to him. 'I remember him devastated by Valdi's operation, worried about Lizzie's bits and pieces and Caroline – that little devil – made him think she so needed a father and he convinced himself that he had to be it. He did so love her for letting him.'

Once Mary had said to Dr Gillen that Mick had always remained a priest. It was a thought that Elizabeth echoed a few years after Michael Scott's death:

I think Mick was a true priest, even when he was laicised. He was both priest and husband, which makes the tragedy of his not having married Mary in earlier times all the greater. I don't think Mick ever regretted his choice to become a priest, nor his choice to leave and marry, as the need was greater for him on both occasions.

For two years Mary made every effort to adjust to life without Mick, and her daughters, her sons-in-law, and her grandchildren gave her all the support within their power. She tried attending an occasional meeting but with only moderate success. Her friend Desmond O'Grady, then living in Cork, was in the habit of coming to Dublin every six months for Aosdána meetings. On one of his visits during that period, Mary had lunch and attended a meeting with him. He was distressed to witness the lack of clarity in her thinking and her inability to concentrate. But she had not lost her ability to view and to question her own circumstances. One night, alone in her apartment and jotting down random thoughts, she wrote:

> Watching the Academy awards I suddenly knew why I am so sad about Mick. I'm sad for him because I want him to enjoy so many things he enjoyed. I also suddenly realised that the reason I was so upset and behaved so badly (but I paid dearly for it) was because I entered into his world whereas I should have brought him into mine which I (but for how long!) have got back into.

She continued to be honoured, but often was unable to attend the awards ceremonies. A month after her eighty-first birthday on American Independence Day, a tribute was paid her as part of the Kells Heritage Festival in County Meath but Mary was not present. She was, however, able to participate when she was named Saoi (wise one) by Aosdana and presented with the gold Torc, a necklace. It was Aosdana's highest honour. The presentation was made by Ireland's president, Mary Robinson. Mary's acquaintance with President Robinson went back a great many years, for the president's mother and Mary had been classmates at Loreto. According to reports, President Robinson, noted for long speeches, was in the habit of concluding them with a phrase in Irish. On this occasion, Mary Lavin, sitting on the platform, was obviously becoming tired during the lengthy speech and, when the Irish words were spoken, was distinctly heard to say, 'Thank God.'

Throughout the year after Mick died, Elizabeth wrote lengthy letters to her mother from Brussels and went over to Sandymount from time to time for as long a visit as possible. She tried not to foist her worries upon her mother but she was not always successful. Consequently, her letters did not spare Mary details of the Peavoys' problems. Money was at the root of one of them. Diarmuid, after difficulties with his superiors, had finally resigned from his position with LOMÉ and there were many months of worry and financial difficulties. But there were many other family matters which concerned both Mary and Elizabeth. For example, there had been a recurrence of Valdi's breast cancer and Elizabeth, commenting on it in a letter to Mary, wrote: 'Anyway we are now back where we started, worrying about Valdi. That, as I said to you, is family life for you.'

It can be inferred from references to Mary's replies that Mary was in complete possession of her faculties, very much interested in all the family's concerns, and was, as always, offering advice. There are in Elizabeth's letters such comments as 'You were right, Mother', and 'Tadhg's injury did make a man of him just as you said it would.' Mary was even giving thought to, as she called it, 'revitalizing' her will, she wrote to Elizabeth.

Elizabeth's identification with her mother was always complete and unmistakable. Another letter – date indistinct – reported that she had gone on holiday in Brittany with her three boys. She drew the parallel with the period after William Walsh died when they had all gone to St Briac, and she commented on the anxiety of being on her own at a great distance from both Brussels and Ireland. That distance, she remarked, 'is not an easy distance for anyone of our keen sensibilities to face single-handed'.

A postscript to one of Elizabeth's letters, though obscure, should be noted. 'Nobody,' she wrote, 'not even complete invalids, talk about never having a drink again – that is utter nonsense – you can tackle Damien [their family physician] on this point.'

But despite the family's efforts, Mary's depression after Mick died failed to lift. Her feeling of despair and futility was a result of more than just his death. That was the culminating factor: Eliza's death in the late 1970s; Valdi's breast cancer, diagnosed in the early 1980s; the selling of the Mews and the need to become accustomed to apartment-dwelling; and a succession of illnesses for both of them. And, finally, the Abbey Farm, so much a part of Mary's life, had been sold.

That decade was winter at its deepest for Mary Lavin. She had survived the death of her first husband and, after what was really a brief period, had made a life for herself and for her three small children. But from the time William Walsh died, Michael Scott had been there: someone who needed her as much as she needed him. His death had left her 'rudderless', as Eoghan Peavoy expressed it. She was no longer young and her health was poor. There didn't seem to be any great need to struggle.

CHAPTER 14

In 1992 the Peavoys returned to Dublin permanently. Diarmuid's resignation from his position in Brussels had been accepted and, after a period when the family were not sure what the next move would be, he was offered a position by RTÉ. Only after they returned home and were settled in did Elizabeth begin to realize that, for herself and her family, it had been an achievement to survive all those years of travel and growing apart from Mick and Mary. It had also been profitable, for the Peavoys had grown together as a family and she had matured.

There could not have been a better time for their return. Mary needed them. For a brief period during the preceding two years, she had been in a hospital which specialized in psychiatric care. When she was discharged, the family was told that she could not live alone. Nevertheless, an attempt was made for her to resume life in the apartment. It was unsuccessful. Not long afterwards, though she resisted the idea, she was persuaded to enter the Newtownpark Nursing Home.

As nursing homes go, this one, situated in a park-like area in Blackrock, was exceptional. It did not give the appearance of an institution but rather of an elegant private home. The front entrance of the main building led into a very large, bright, cheerful lobby where residents sat about, some in wheelchairs, well dressed and chatting with each other. Mary had a room near the end of a fairly long corridor leading off the lobby. It was not a very large room but it was nicely furnished with a lounge chair, a chair for visitors and a single bed. The very well-trained Newtownpark staff made every effort to make Mary's life as pleasant as possible, but their task was not an easy one. She made no attempt to socialize with the other residents nor did she respond to the efforts of the nurses to cheer her up though they tried and were genuinely distressed about their failure. She seemed resentful of her fate. Her attitude could have been interpreted as arrogance or perhaps anger. It may have been closer to anguish.

Two years after entering the nursing home, Mary fell and broke her hip. She was hospitalized and an operation performed successfully but she was for some time in the hospital recovering. When she returned to Newtownpark, she was welcomed by the others and greeted as something of a heroine. After all, recovering from a hip operation at her age was considered a remarkable feat. Mary, always happy to be centre-stage, enjoyed the attention and her attitude towards her fellow patients softened a bit.

Perhaps it was pride, but Mary was not eager to have visitors. She once said that those friends she loved the most were the ones she was the most reluctant to see. It was as if she thought that this was not a fitting end for an eminent author: a recipient of so much praise. 'This is not really Mary Lavin,' she began saying to friends. And it was not difficult for them to understand exactly what she meant. Whatever the reason, she was irascible – at least at first – when friends, and even family, called. There were times when visitors came a long distance to see her and were ordered out of the room. 'I don't want to see you,' she would say. Des MacMahon noted this behaviour when he visited her. He reproved her for turning people away but, for the most part, he was extremely patient with her. Had he not seen evidences of that kind of behaviour by Mary to a modified degree as far back as he could remember, he would have attributed it to her unwillingness to have people see her in a nursing home setting. But, according to Des, Mary's mood changes were not new. 'Way back, as long as I knew her, she could be difficult with people, even people who were close to her whom you thought she loved.' The Medlicotts too had witnessed this behaviour on Mary's part when, sometime

315

after the Storrs period, they had gone to hear her give a reading at Smith College in Massachusetts. When, after the reading, they went forward to speak with her, their reception was more than cold and they had been at a loss to interpret it.

Elizabeth, as reported in the *Sunday Independent*, 28 May 1995, gave her interpretation of her mother's feelings at that juncture. 'You are looking at a highly successful, articulate, inspired woman – a genius really – with a vital force which is being strained, sucked out of her by the tragic happenings in her life. Mother felt much worse about things than you or I would feel. And she had absolutely no way of fighting back.'

Mary had always impressed upon her daughters the importance of surrounding oneself with beautiful objects. At the farm there had always been a Waterford vase with white roses in it on the dining room table. She might save an attractive box though she had long since forgotten what it had contained. Elizabeth thought that Mary considered those objects to be a tie to the greater beauty of life or nature or the outside world. Significantly, when speaking of her mother's love of beautiful things, she said, 'like Mrs Bird,' and added, 'it would have been nurtured in her'.

It distressed Elizabeth to see her mother without any sign of beauty around her towards the end of her life. In the nursing home there were no paintings on her walls, no evidence of either academic prowess or literature or those things that she had considered so vital. The only personal items in her room were Mick's desk chair and a desk that Elizabeth had bought in an 'on-the-street shop – a carry-away your furniture shop', as she called it. 'But I can tell you one thing,' Elizabeth said proudly, 'she adapted very well to that pattern of having to do without her things.' Resignation might have been a better appraisal than adaptation, however. For days Mary had insisted that Des remove the desk Elizabeth had bought – it had to go, she said – but then Elizabeth overheard Mary asking her nurse to polish it.

All during those days, family members visited Mary faithfully. Caroline, by then an associate editor at *The Irish Times* and a busy, highly respected journalist, had a regular day for visiting once a week. Mary's reception of her girls varied greatly. Often, with Elizabeth and Valdi, she would complain that they had neglected to come when they had promised or when she had expected they would. Her complaints seemed to have very little basis in fact for either one or the other visited her almost daily. Elizabeth, when she visited, often insisted upon Mary putting on her coat and coming out in the car with her. It was difficult to persuade Mary to do so but Elizabeth persisted with her valiant attempts to bring Mary back into society. And, in fact, people often came over to welcome her and to tell her how good it was to see her and she seemed pleased.

The pattern on these excursions was to go to a craft shop and restaurant a short distance from the city – the Avoca Handweavers – and walk through the shop, with Elizabeth trying to interest Mary in what was going on about her. Mary's only reaction was to protest loudly. However, in spite of herself, she responded when, on these trips, Elizabeth pointed out familiar scenes and talked a little about past experiences in the area. On one occasion, they stopped to sit on a bench near the ocean and were joined by an acquaintance. There were signs of the old Mary when the friend said: 'Are you cold, Mary?' and the reply was a haughty 'Don't call me Mary.' But a moment later she said, very quietly, 'I'm cold in my heart.'

During those hours when Elizabeth sat quietly in her mother's room, Mary, with very little encouragement, would talk about Nora. She wasn't really a bad mother, Mary once said. She talked, too, a great deal about Mick but, Elizabeth noted, very little about William Walsh. It seemed to Elizabeth that Mary was talking to her almost as if she were talking to herself. As a matter of fact, at one time she said to Elizabeth, 'Oh, you don't count.' And Elizabeth had no difficulty in understanding what she meant.

The visits were not easy for any of Mary's daughters but, in varying degrees, they were successful in making them seem matter-of-fact and casual. Sometimes there were signs of the relationship as it had been in the past when they laughed easily and often together at their own expense. One day Mary's condition took a turn for the worst and Elizabeth and Valdi rushed to her side, sure it was the end. Later they told Mary all the details, adding 'You had a dry run, Mud.' And Mary chuckled.

Each of the girls assumed a different role during those trying days. Valdi became the one Mary depended upon for practical matters. As Elizabeth phrased it, 'Valdi called the shots.' She took charge of all money matters and she was responsible for hiring outside help when it was necessary. All expenditures were checked with Valdi. But the dependency was taking its toll. Valdi was finding the situation almost impossible to handle. To witness her mother's illness and to see her gradually fading, and to have her own illness to contend with, was at times beyond her. The expression she used often as she witnessed her mother's condition was, 'I'm not going to take this on board.'

Visits from her sons-in-law and grandchildren produced quite a different reaction in Mary from those of her daughters, possibly because she expected less. It was with them that Mary was most like her old self. Both Eoghan and Adam Peavoy reported that she enquired about their classes at UCD, asked questions about their special interests, and appeared keen to hear their answers. Kathleen MacMahon, however, found seeing her grandmother in the Home traumatic, though she did go to visit. Mary seldom asked her about her school work but, when she learned that Kathleen was majoring in English at UCD, she enquired about her classes and her professors.

Des MacMahon visited Mary regularly and, in the last years, quite often, even though it distressed him. 'There wasn't a lot of conversation,' he said, 'certainly no sustained conversation.' They talked about family matters and Mary might reminisce a bit about the past and about Bective. She continued to insist that she should not have sold it and that Des had made her sell it. He didn't contradict her. It seemed to him that, to a great extent, her life and her personality had disintegrated in her later years, and it was a great pity. As he interpreted it, Mary was unable to cope with getting old. 'It was all profoundly sad,' he said. 'Nevertheless, and certainly in the last few months, there was a kind of a warmth between us on my visits to her and I thought maybe I gave her some comfort – I hope I did.'

Diarmuid Peavoy, now a senior journalist with RTÉ, also visited Mary regularly. They talked about his children: their plans were always of interest to her. He believed she looked forward to his visits and he enjoyed them as well. As Diarmuid said, she repeated her stories but she told them so well that he didn't mind. He felt that for some time now he and Mary had understood each other. 'I knew where Mary was coming from,' Diarmuid said. His admiration for what she had accomplished in her life was boundless. As one who knew from experience how all-absorbing writing could be, he had always been amazed at the way Mary could divorce her work from the mundane world. He had seen her write all day and then make no mention of it but go on with the life around her and participate in it fully.

The son-in-law who visited her the most frequently was James Ryan. Newtownpark Comprehensive School where he taught was not very far from the nursing home and it was easy for James to stop in often. They discussed writing and at one point Mary, with her uncanny ability to see beneath the surface, had turned to him and asked if he were writing a novel. He had denied it, but by that time he was. Actually, James had not thought of writing a book, fiction or otherwise, prior to the birth of his children. Shortly after the birth of his second child Alice in 1986, however, he began to write his novel. He told no one, not even Caroline. Only when he was ready to submit it to a publisher did she learn of it. When he speculated on why he had kept his creative writing a secret, he came to the conclusion that it was because he was surrounded by achievers: and matriarchal achievers at that.

How much was James influenced by his association with Mary Lavin? It is hard to say. He realized that spending so much time in a literary atmosphere before and after his marriage to Caroline must have had a great influence upon him, at the very least subconsciously. Basically, however, he thought that the influence was indirect. Caroline had edited collections of short stories and he recalled that there would be a huge pile of manuscripts alongside their bed. She would go through them 'with amazing speed' and would know immediately which were worth considering and which were not, and she talked about why. He learned from her what not to do – what made a story good. As he said, he was influenced by Mary second-hand. And yet she must have supplied some direct inspiration as well. Even in the years before his marriage, she had discussed books and talked about her own work and work habits, about the guidelines she followed, and about technique in general. In any event, what James accomplished was remarkable. When his novel, *Home from England,* was finished, he sent it off, unsolicited, to the publishing director of Phoenix House in London, Maggie McKernan. He had heard her name mentioned as the editor of a Booker Prize winner, Ben Okri. Convinced that it was the work of an experienced writer who was using a pseudonym, she took it immediately. She had not made a mistake. The book, published in 1995, was widely reviewed and critically acclaimed. Even the *Times Literary Supplement* called it 'brilliant', and added, 'it is hard to believe that this is Ryan's first novel'.

James had an enquiring and analytical mind. Mary had told him that he was the psychologist in the family and he thought that was her way of saying that he shared her interest in, as he put it, 'excavating', and had the patience and the interest in the minutiae of what people said or did.

Mary's past life intrigued James, and while visiting in the nursing home he thought a great deal about it. There had been so many different kinds of love in it, all of them deep. For her father, there had been unquestioning love: and, James thought, perhaps she should have questioned more. For William Walsh. there had been a deep and caring love. For Michael Scott, there had been – from the time she first saw him at UCD – a love so steadfast and enduring that it survived all the years of their separation and his priesthood. James felt sure Michael Scott had seen the symptoms of her decline early on but, no matter how distressing it was to see them, his memory of what she had been far outweighed them.

The same year that Mary entered Newtownpark, and in honour of her eightieth birthday, RTÉ filmed a documentary of Mary called *An Arrow in Flight*. As noted earlier, Mary had used that expression in explaining how short stories were structured. A section of the documentary was devoted to an extended excerpt from 'The Cuckoo Spit', which had been televised by RTÉ in 1984. In it the fine Irish actress Siobhan McKenna, now deceased, was cast as Mary Lavin and her performance was outstanding. It was easy to believe that she was Mary. Some critics felt that the excerpt was too long and, though the section is extremely well done, it is a valid criticism. The documentary is, however, a gripping portrayal of its subject and a fitting tribute to her.

The film was produced by Cian Ó hÉigeartaigh of the RTÉ staff. For some time, he had thought that someone should do a programme about Mary and a year or two previously he had pursued the idea. When he approached Mary, however, Michael Scott had just died and she was too depressed to consider cooperating. Later, it was Nuala O'Faolain, with whom he had been working on various programmes, who had told him that Mary was well enough to be interviewed and who convinced him that the time was ripe for the making of the documentary. Accordingly, he talked with Mary, who agreed to be interviewed at the Home. Sitting in her lounge chair, she was relaxed and smiling and seemed quite well.

Ó hÉigeartaigh was well suited to the task of making the film for he appreciated Mary's work and had a thorough knowledge of it. His only regret was that the film had not been made ten years earlier when Mary herself could have talked about her work. He was sure that much could be learned from the technique of her writing: from the way she shaped her stories. As it was, she seemed to want to talk only about her personal life, and he had to rely on what other people had to say about her work.

Ó hÉigeartaigh was puzzled as to why, when people had at last begun to come to grips with women's writing in Ireland, the work of the country's most distinguished woman writer, for well over a hundred years he believed, had 'just vanished off the shelves'. He knew that she had stopped writing new work sometime in the 1980s but, even a few years earlier, it had not been easy to obtain a Lavin collection. It was, he felt, 'a great shame' because the quality of her work was so high.

Appearing in the film are Thomas Kilroy, Maurice Harmon, Nuala O'Faolain, Eavan Boland and Caroline Walsh. The opening scene shows Nuala O'Faolain addressing a good-sized gathering at a public meeting organized to honour Mary and her work. She shares with the audience her recollections of Mary Lavin, this writer who would arise at dawn, 'put a breadboard over her knee' and work on her stories, and her account is both poignant and amusing. She talks about what it meant to her to visit the Mews and what it meant to many aspiring young writers as well. Those were the days when 'you only had one coat and it was always wet,' she said.

Early on in the film, Mary Lavin is shown at her desk in the Sandymount apartment, pencil in hand, seemingly crossing out something: surely a typical scene. For those viewing the documentary, her delight in talking about Michael Scott is unconcealed. They wrote to each other almost daily after William Walsh's death, she said. Coyly, she informs her audience that when he phoned her to say he was leaving the priesthood to marry her, she was 'half resentful'. As a widow, she 'had a great time', and she intimates that she was not sure she wanted to change her status.

As an illustration of how completely Michael Scott had followed the strictures of church doctrine, she cites an occasion when she suggested that she might take a thousand pounds out of her savings and send it to him so that he could come over to Ireland for a visit. He told her not to do that for, if she did, he would have to turn it over to the church.

With obvious amusement, Mary relates an incident which took place in the early days of their relationship. When Michael was preparing to leave Dublin after graduation from UCD, he asked her if she would write to him. When she said yes, he asked his bishop for permission to reply to her and it was granted. 'Wasn't he a lovely man to give me permission?' Mick said to Mary. Her reply: 'A lovely man? Why, he was a right bastard. He knew that, if he didn't grant permission, you would have come out!'

A friend, after viewing the documentary, asked Elizabeth how she reacted to her mother's use of the word 'bastard'. Her reply was that she found it most amusing. Caroline, on the other hand, when asked the same question, said it was shocking, unlike her mother, and possibly should not have been left in. For Caroline it was most important that her mother be recognized as the outstanding person she was and, to her, decorum was a necessary requisite. Caroline had learned well her lesson as to what was fitting and proper from her mother. Years later, when one of her sons-in-law wanted to take a picture of Mary standing near the sink in the Abbey Farm kitchen, Mary put her foot down. No picture of her was to be taken against that background. Presumably Caroline would have understood, and even Elizabeth indicated that she had agreed with her mother.

During Elizabeth's frequent visits to the nursing home, she made an attempt to revive in Mary some interest in her work, or at least some awakening of pride in her accomplishments. Several times she took collections of Mary's stories out to her but always Mary waved them away impatiently. She refused to allow Elizabeth to bring anything to the nursing home which revived memories of her writing days. But 1995 changed that attitude temporarily.

While Elizabeth was still in Brussels, and after the final work was done on selections for Volume III and on *A Family Likeness*, Mary had begun to go over some of her stories and to make changes with an eye to bringing out another collection. When, in 1992, Elizabeth had resettled in Ireland, she found that the final selections and editing for that collection – it would be Volume IV – had still not been done. Mary's condition being what it was, she saw that it was up to her to finish what Mary had started. A great many marginal notations had already been made and Elizabeth, determined to make the collection exactly what Mary would have wanted it to be, set to work deciphering her mother's almost illegible handwriting. It would have been well-nigh impossible, she said, if she had not got a 'sudden illumination. It was uncanny to say the least. I always knew exactly what the changes were to be, no dilemma in making them out. I almost felt someone was watching me to make the task easier. I had no agonizing to decide what to put down. I knew all along what the story line should be.'

The end result was *In a Café*, a collection brought out in May 1995 by Town House and Country House, a Dublin publishing firm. Elizabeth had succeeded in encompassing a good cross-section of her mother's work. Of the sixteen stories she chose, six had appeared as early as the 1940s: 'The Girders', 'A Cup of Tea', 'The Joy-Ride', 'A Story with A Pattern', 'The Widow's Son' and 'The Will'; 'A Gentle Soul', 'Chamois Gloves', 'The Convert' and 'The Little Prince' were all published in the 1950s; 'In the Middle of the Fields', 'In a Café' and 'Lemonade' appeared in the 1960s; and 'Tom' and 'Trastevere' were published in the 1970s. The latest one – 'A Family Likeness' – appeared in 1981. The stories incorporate the changes made by Mary after their first publication but these changes are relatively minor ones.

When Elizabeth was choosing 'The Will' for incorporation in the collection, she saw that Mary had been compressing it further for her final version and she thought 'My God, why is she doing this, taking some of her valuable writing away?' But then she realized that, in a story with a 'slender' theme like 'The Will', Mary felt that it should not be 'held up to the light'. Elizabeth could see that cutting it down had improved it. Mary's instincts could, she saw, be trusted.

The foreword for *In a Café* was written by Thomas Kilroy. It was fitting that he, Mary's friend since the Mews days and a bit earlier, should be the one to do it. He empathized with Mary and he understood her work. He saw her 'addiction' to telling stories as part of her make-up: part of her love of and curiosity about those around her. As he put it, telling their stories 'is as natural for her as chatting in Grafton Street or in the Mews . . . as natural as a glass of water'.

Mary had told Tom Kilroy early on that she was of the opinion that her stories developed out of an opening sentence. He proved her point by listing several instances from the stories in *Tales from Bective Bridge*: 'Sarah had a bit of a bad name', from 'Sarah'; 'She was one of the most beautiful women they had ever seen and so they hated her', from 'A Fable'; and 'The cat decided Miss Holland', from 'Miss Holland'. As he wrote, 'The hook is in place from the word go.'

Once Tom Kilroy asked Mary which of her stories she considered to be the 'finest expression of her art'. Her choice was 'The Will', one of the stories selected for the new collection and, as indicated, written as early as the 1940s. Reading it afresh, he could readily see why. In it, as in 'The Little Prince', 'Frail Vessel' and 'The Becker Wives', she delved into 'a particular Irish setting: small town, genteel, familial, under threat from the forces of life's anarchy'. He believed that no other Irish writer had done it as well.

In his preface Kilroy did not neglect to mention Mary's ability to use her stories to portray various aspects of her religion as she saw it. As he pointed out cogently, 'She has written with generosity about Irish Catholicism, but with her own implacable eye on its worst deformations.' He listed 'The Chamois Gloves', 'The Convert' – both in this collection – and 'The Great Wave'. 'There is a great range in these stories and they are clearly the work of a spiritual, if iconoclastic, writer.' His own favourites, he wrote, are the widow stories: quite natural since it was during that period that she came into his life. He described his own identification with those stories as well as what Mary Lavin had achieved in them.

> I know the people who walk in them as I know kin, although everything here is fiction. In these stories she has looked into herself, but never in a limited, solipsistic way. Everything is shaped, subjected to a high degree of formal construction. To effect this kind of distancing upon one's own experience requires an immense inner strength on the part of the writer.

One of the widow stories he especially liked was 'In the Middle of the Fields', which appeared in the *New Yorker* fairly early in her widowhood and which is the first story in the new collection. He considered its opening sentence a good example of her 'mature style': 'Like a rock in the sea, she was islanded by fields, the heavy grass washing about the house, and the cattle wading in it as in water.' It is, as he wrote, a simple story but, for him, in that story 'Mary Lavin the writer and Mary Lavin the person that I know have become one.'

A preamble to the collection was written by Elizabeth. She began with, 'I have never judged her writing from without, nor have I ever found her reputation to be intimidating. Thus I bring the enthusiasm of a daughter to the lifetime gifts of a writer, wholly undepleted.' She traced her mother's life through her stories, deploring the fact that, though she and her mother had walked 'along the river Arno in Florence, or through the pedestrianised Roman thorough-fares', they had never seemed to have enough time. 'In a way,' she wrote in summary, 'getting this book together has been . . . a chance for me to perambulate with my mother down along the walkways of her mind. Not to race, but to take the journey quietly at our own pace.'

The launching of *In a Café* took place at the Newtown-park Nursing Home with Mary's daughters and their families there to greet her guests. The publisher was there too with copies of Mary's latest collection, and it was very definitely Mary's. 'Mother had done all the work. It was all done before she went to the nursing home,' Elizabeth wrote in her *Sunday Independent* article. When it came time for the opening of the champagne, one of the grandsons was instructed to open the bottles where his grandmother could witness it. Mary's girls were determined to make the occasion as happy as it could possibly be.

The whole scene seemed to have a revitalizing effect upon Mary. During the months following the launching of *In a Café*, however, she grew very tired, very weak, and painfully thin. Her attitude towards those around her was more restrained – not quite as irascible. It was almost as though she had at last come to accept her fate. At one time – it is impossible to know exactly how much earlier – Mary had marked a passage on death in *Howard's End*, the book mentioned earlier. It read: 'It is thus, if there is any rule, that we ought to die – neither as victim nor as fanatic, but as the seafarer who can greet with an equal eye the deep that he is entering, and the shore that he must leave.'

Not long before Mary's death, Diarmuid visited her. It was difficult to witness how weak and cold she was. She would ask for a cup of tea and then not finish it. She slept a great deal and was scarcely mobile. He felt that she had lost the will to live and he looked back longingly on that period some four years earlier when he and his family had returned to Dublin. Then they would take Mary out for a drive and a walk on the beach and he had marvelled at her vitality.

It surprised no one that one day Mary said to Valdi, 'I can't go on like this.' Elizabeth, hearing this, had thought of Mary's 'Happiness'. There is, in the conclusion of 'Happiness', a deathbed scene. The mother, seemingly struggling against the knowledge that she was dying, had said 'beseechingly' that she could not face it. And one of the daughters had taken her face 'between her palms as tenderly as if it were the face of a child', and 'blurted out the truth'.

'It's all right, Mother. You don't *have* to face it! It's over! You've finished with this world, Mother,' she said, and, confident that her tidings were joyous, her voice was strong.
Mother . . . let out a sigh, and, closing her eyes, she sank back, and this time her head sank so deep into the pillow that it would have been dented had it been a pillow of stone.

In the autumn, the family began to feel that Mary 'would not see Christmas'. She was sleeping a great deal and though she still maintained an interest in family matters – or at least appeared to do so – her attention span was clearly narrowing.

On a Monday morning, 25 March 1996, Mary Lavin died. She was eighty-three. 'It's terrible that we weren't with her,' Elizabeth said, 'but the staff were around her and she died peacefully, they told us.' Her girls had had a long period to prepare for this but somehow it did not help.

On Tuesday evening Mary's body was removed to the Star of the Sea Church in Sandymount. More than 300 people, led by Mary's daughters, her sons-in-law and her grandchildren, joined the cortège. Among them were representatives of every branch of the arts, as well as academics, journalists, members of the legal profession, the clergy and industry. Close friends as well as those who had come merely to pay homage: all were present.

A funeral Mass was held the following day in Dunderry Church, Navan, County Meath. At the service the Taoiseach, John Bruton, spoke. 'Her life was characterised by gentleness and her work by an ability to make the ordinary extraordinary. She took run-of-the-mill people and turned their lives into ones of great sympathy and humanity,' he said. 'She would not have been able to draw so much good out of the world if she was not such a good person herself. She was a neighbour and a friend and somebody whom I liked very much indeed.'

Tom Hayes, the film maker who had played an important part in the preparation of the documentary, *An Arrow in Flight*, spoke of Mary as 'an earthy, tough, glowing woman, a passionate person with a great thirst for life. She knew the many secrets of the heart for her life was all about living.' For him, he said, 'she never grew old. She sometimes grew difficult, but the sudden recollection of some quirky incident would bring that wicked smile back to play about her lips, and all was well again.'

Paddy Rahill and John Daly carried Mary's coffin out of the church. For Mary the Rahills, who still lived on the farm in a cottage, were family. John Daly, Mary's good friend and neighbour, had worked with Mick in the garden and in the fields up until the time the Abbey Farm was sold.

At the graveside the playwright Tom MacIntyre, one of the many writers at the funeral whom Mary had befriended, spoke of how Mary had 'opened his eyes to the world'.

President Mary Robinson, visiting South Africa at the time of Mary's death, was deeply saddened when the news reached her. Mary Lavin had made a remarkable contribution to Irish literature, she stated. 'Mary was held in great esteem by people both in Ireland and abroad and her sad departure will be a profound loss to Irish writing.'

The news of Mary's death was on the front page of *The Irish Times*, with Eileen Battersby, the paper's book critic, referring to Mary's stories as 'among the finest written this century because she understood the fine balance of sympathy, intelligence, humanity and, above all, honesty'.

It was, however, the London *Times* obituary, with no byline, that conveyed something of the lustre of Mary Lavin's personality. The account read, in part:

> Her skill as a storyteller seemed a part of her make-up as a person. Watching the world with her button-bright eyes, she had a restless curiosity about people, whether close friends or merely passers-by in the street. She drew her inspiration from the well of character rather than the sea of experience, plumbing the secret depths of personality.

Obituaries appeared in the *Scotsman*, the *Daily Telegraph* in London, the *Herald* in Glasgow, and in the *Independent* as well as *The Irish Times* during the week following Mary's death, and some contained perceptive observations about her work. 'Subtle, lucid and shrewdly observed, her themes range from harsh to gentle, combining sense of sorrow with hints of mystery,' the *Scotsman* obituary read.

In Dublin W. J. McCormack wrote in the *Irish*

Independent that, in his opinion, Mary's years in the States 'provided her with a poise which was both artistic and personal: it gave her an awareness of externality, of distant places, and this in turn informed the provincial towns and farms of her best'. She had been 'confronted by the distinctly male genre of the short story, a literary form so intensely worked by James Joyce . . . The other two masters of the short story – Sean O'Faolain and Frank O'Connor – had virtually established copyright on what an Irish story should be. The formula which, with whatever injustice to individual writers and stories, came to be recognised by readers, never fitted Mary Lavin's work and she never succumbed to its allure.'

McCormack's viewpoint on the Dunsany connection is unique. 'Tradition has it that she broke through with the aid of Lord Dunsany, a minor writer whose ancestral estates included the part of County Meath in which she settled,' and he went on to say:

> But in retrospect it is hard to believe that she needed patronage, even harder to think of her as sponsored by one of the oldest families in Ireland. Hers was a middle-class milieu, solidly located below Dunsany Castle and even below Bowen's Court, equally distant from and above the back streets and townlands of O'Faolain and O'Connor in their classic phase.

The day after Mary died, an article by the novelist William Trevor was carried in the *Guardian* and headed 'Ireland's Acute Observer'. In it Trevor wrote: 'Elizabeth Bowen described the modern storyteller's task as revealing the hidden significance of "the small event", and in this Lavin succeeded superbly well.' He went on to quote Lord Dunsany, who had written that her stories were about people who led ordinary lives, 'who many might suppose have no story to tell in their experience; and when she tells these stories there may be some whose ears, attuned to the modern thriller, may suppose they are not stories at all . . . All that seemed "tiny and unimportant" was grist to her mill: she was already cultivating a genius for beadily seeking out what the less observant left behind.'

Nearly fifty years have gone by since Lord Dunsany wrote those words and as Trevor wrote, 'it has been demonstrated that stories which at first glance seem to be "not stories at all" are among the best there are. During all that time, Lavin was at the forefront of establishing a place for them, and of ensuring that what began with Chekhov did not wither.'

Trevor called Ireland 'a fruitful breeding ground for short-story writers. Individual stories are remembered and talked about, as novels are elsewhere.' And 'that predilection Lavin helped to conserve, while finding a place for elements of the antique form in the second half of the 20th century. In much of what she wrote there is a faint echo of the oral tradition, cunningly utilised.' He went on:

> Lavin's stories eschew self-importance and that shrillness which is the bane of the form. They are subtle without making a palaver about it, beautifully told, no pat endings, no slickness; and as in life, nothing is resolved . . . The harshness and gentleness that mingle so often in the Irish character is repeatedly, acutely, observed. A sense of sorrow often lingers, as does the whiff of mystery. And such shadows are never just there by chance: take any aspect of a Mary Lavin story and you'll find it contributes to the mechanics of the whole.

Trevor's conclusion credited Mary Lavin with 'extracting from the depths of the unremarkable a universal truth . . . As a person, she was both humble and certain, complicated and simple – an apt reflection of her role as an artist. The short story of today owes her a very great debt.'

The novelist Maeve Binchy, in her 'Maeve's Week' column in *The Irish Times* of 30 March 1996, wrote of her great affection for Mary Lavin. There had been 'no shortage of memories and stories' at Mary Lavin's funeral, she wrote. 'Everyone had a tale to tell.' She then told hers. What she wrote captured Mary so completely that – like Trevor – it warrants quoting lavishly.

Her memories of Mary began when she was a teacher at Pembroke School and two of her pupils were Elizabeth and Caroline Walsh, Mary's daughters. In the staffroom, the teachers always said that their mother 'was a dream to deal with'. Those were the days 'long before the age of parent/teacher associations or open days so we knew the mothers because they delivered and collected their children, or they came to thank us or make enquiries or to complain or worry'. For the most part the mothers were 'nice', though they didn't understand their children at all. 'The mothers of demons often thought they were angels, the mothers of nice, dreamy, idealistic children thought they were vixens. But as teachers we thought that just went with the territory. We understood the girls, but their parents mainly hadn't a clue.' The parents the teachers loved were the 'enthusiastic parents. And Mary Lavin was that in spades.'

> She used to call in at the school in her flowing black clothes, briefcase clenched in her hand, and tell us we were all wonderful. I can still remember the smiles around the little table in the tiniest staff room in the world when she had paid a visit . . . A visit from Mary Lavin was like a vitamin shot. We marched off to our classrooms full of enthusiasm, knowing that it was, after all, the most important job in the whole world.

Binchy tried to remember exactly what it was that Mary would say but was unsuccessful because 'it was mainly the mood of the thing that was so strong. But whenever we saw her come into the building there was a sense of cheer.' Mary remembered all their names and 'any little funny story we had told in class she repeated as if it were the latest pearl from Peter Ustinov'.

One of Binchy's sentences underlined an outstanding Lavin trait: 'She had a great sense of wonder about things,' she wrote. Mary would repeat something that one of the teachers had said in class: it had made her look up a book on the subject, she would say. And then she would loan it to the teacher.

> We loved being lent books by her. It never seemed like she was trying to widen our horizons, or deepen what she could well have identified as a somewhat shallow grasp of things. No, it sounded as if we were all ongoing partners in the business of educating children. We would adjust the halo and read whatever she gave us with huge gratitude.

Mary Clarke, the teacher of Irish and one of Binchy's friends, never tired of repeating Mary's words of praise. She was, she said, always going to remember what 'Ireland's greatest living writer at the time' had said.

Binchy and her good friend Mary Clarke had also on occasion been invited to parties in the Mews, 'where there would be strong drink and liberal chat and late hours, but Mary Lavin had her children so well trained that not a word of this ever leaked out to the pupils. No tales were ever told that Miss Clarke and Miss Binchy might have been boisterous in civilian life.'

What Mary Lavin had to say about being a writer seemed to Binchy to be 'terrific advice for any writer', and she found the way that Mary 'demystified' it 'endearing'. Mary had said that going to the National Library to write was for her like going to an office and 'if she was late she would run down Kildare Street as anyone would run if they were going to be late for a job'. You could 'never be sure of inspiration but you should be sitting down quietly with your pen and paper ready in case it did strike rather than be asleep or having coffee with friends'.

Mary made the teachers feel as if she considered their job more difficult than hers:

> I can see her now, her hands clasped with admiration. 'I don't know how you do it, I really don't. Dozens of them day after day, hour after hour. And you're so patient with all of them. You never lose your tempers, you should all be canonised.' . . . And if you met her socially she would introduce you with awe as a Teacher, just as you might introduce an Explorer or a Lion Tamer. 'You know they aren't paid nearly enough when you think what they do,' she would say about us. 'What kind of a society are we at all that we don't rate teachers as the highest of the high? The Greeks used to think that the teachers were the most important members of the tribe, the Jews use the word rabbi, signifying a position of huge importance in the community. What can be wrong with our values that we don't feel the same?'

Binchy admitted that Mary was not alone as a 'supportive parent'. There were others who were appreciative and who 'knew we weren't sadists who had it in for their daughters and lived a life of short hours and long holidays'. But, she added,

> Mary Lavin was special, not just because she was famous or an amazing extrovert but because she genuinely did seem to believe that we were special . . . In years to come when Mary Lavin is remembered in history books and in literary criticism, I don't want people to forget that she was also a benign, enthusi-

335

astic parent loved and remembered by a generation of school teachers whose true worth she was able to recognise and acknowledge.

Surely Mary would have been pleased to note that Binchy did not fail to write that it was not necessary to show any 'particular favouritism' for her girls. 'They were fine and continued to be fine.' And Mary would have smiled at this addition. 'I have even forgiven Caroline for changing her status entirely and moving from being a little girl in my classroom in Pembroke Road to being my boss as features editor of *The Irish Times*.'

Mary Lavin's grave is in St Mary's cemetery in Navan, County Meath, in the family plot where Nora and Tom Lavin, William Walsh and Michael Scott are buried. On the existing stone which marks the graves, the family added a simple inscription: 'And Mary, daughter of Thomas Lavin', and then a line from one of Mary's poems: 'Let me come inland always'. That touching poem merits quoting in its entirety:

Let me come inland always
To the uneventful plains
Where cattle break a pathway
Through the slender rains.

Let me come inland always
Where beeches freely scatter
Green light dappled deeper
Where the leaves are doubled.

Let me come inland always
Where every wind that passes
Tries in vain to rob the grasses
Of their green philosophy.
Let me come inland always

Where spring hedges hold the rose
And down the wildly tossing fields
The hawthorn galleon blows.

Let me come inland always
Where the silence is so great
The lonely bark of the farmer's dog
Can deckle edge the night.

Let me come inland always
Where you can hardly notice
Time winding his windlass
And only the trees grow old.

Let me come inland always
For fear that I should see
The gold sand shore that brings
Such thoughts of the past to me.

I fear those long blonde beaches
As I fear the shores of the past
Lest looking down their reaches
I should see with slanted mast
The keeled up happiness of days
That once sailed free.

In the summer of 1996 Radio Telefís Éireann carried this poem in their *Selected Favourites* programme as well as in the *Island and the Seashore* programme.

One day, not too long after Mary died, Valdi and Elizabeth visited her grave. Valdi wrote an article about that day for the *Meath Chronicle*, entitled, 'Cemetery Sunday in Navan'. 'I had never been to Cemetery Sunday before,' Valdi wrote, 'but I will always be there in the future.' As she approached her mother's grave, she saw Elizabeth sitting on the kerb by it, 'like a little girl with her lovely grey hair and pretty face'. Valdi looked about her and noted that there was nobody standing by some of the graves and she thought of all those years when 'we did not go and stand' even though her grandfather, her grandmother, her father and her stepfather were all buried there. Would anyone stand for them, she wondered? As she drove back to Dublin, 'How Great Thou Art', the hymn that had played over the loudspeakers at the cemetery, echoed in her mind.

A month after Mary's death, her family sent a card of thanks for their expressions of sympathy to Mary's friends and admirers which contained a quotation from Mary's story 'Happiness':

> If anything ever happens to me, children, suddenly, I mean, or when you are not near me, or I cannot speak to you, I want you to promise you won't feel bad. There's no need! Just remember that I had a happy life – and that if I had to choose my kind of heaven I'd take it on this earth with you again, no matter how much you might annoy me!

Time and time again Mary Lavin had said that, even though only when she was writing was she convinced that all was right with the world, her children always came first. It seems fitting, therefore, that that quotation – Mary's own words, as she wrote them in that story so many years earlier – should conclude this chronicle of her life.

NOTES

Because of the character of the source material, it seemed inadvisable to use note numbers in the text. I have, however, mentioned sources therein, where it was possible to do so without interrupting the flow of the narrative.

Three critical studies of Mary Lavin's work have been used extensively throughout: Zack Bowen, *Mary Lavin*; Richard F. Peterson, *Mary Lavin*; A. A. Kelly, *Mary Lavin, Quiet Rebel*. The Mary Lavin Special Issue of the *Irish University Review*, Autumn 1979, vol. 9, no. 2, has also been invaluable as a source of reference material. Other sources used throughout are, for the most part, listed in the notes for Chapter 1.

Some of Mary Lavin's papers have been deposited in the Special Collections or Rare Books sections of Southern Illinois University, Carbondale; New York State University at Binghamton; Boston University; and University College Dublin. The bulk of Mary Lavin's papers, however, are still in the possession of the family in Dublin. I have had full access to them and have used material from them throughout the manuscript.

It may be assumed that the information concerned with people and events, unless otherwise indicated, is from correspondence between Mary Lavin and her daughters and from the author's conversations, correspondence and interviews with them as well as with other family members, friends and colleagues.

CHAPTER 1

Material from the following radio interviews was used throughout and has, wherever possible, been cited in the text: *John Bowman's Saturday 8.30*, 5 and 19 August 1995; the *Arts Show*, 30 April 1995. The conversation with the poet Eavan Boland took place in the 5 August 1995 interview.

A true copy of the marriage certificate of Mary's parents (5 July 1911) and her birth certificate (10 June 1912) were obtained from the Town Clerk of Walpole, Massachusetts. Facts about the town of East Walpole were supplied by Elizabeth Cottrell, Vice-President of the Walpole Historical Society, and Sister Esther Brady, a resident of East Walpole, who recalled that her father often had a drink with Tom Lavin.

Description of the Bird estate, as well as of members of the Bird family and of Bective House, is from an unpublished memoir, *A New Englander*, by Eleanor Stewart Heiser, and dedicated to Anna Child Bird. The memoir is used in later chapters as well.

Because so many of Mary Lavin's stories are semi-autobiographical, her collections, listed separately, were used throughout the book. Her story 'Tom' was used heavily in this chapter, as noted in the text. 'Lemonade' appeared first in her 1961 collection, *The Great Wave and Other Stories*, but is used in later collections as well.

Other sources used in this chapter and throughout were 'Mary Lavin', from *A Portrait of the Artist as a Young Girl*; transcript of a discussion on 10 November 1967 with students at Merrimack College, North Andover, Massachusetts, written by Catherine Murphy and titled 'Mary Lavin: An Interview', and Lavin's 'Afterword'. Both the Murphy interview and the Mary Lavin 'Afterword', are from the special edition of the *Irish University Review*. A transcript of an interview with Robert Stevens, English Department, North Texas State University, summer 1981 is from the Rare Books section of the UCD library.

Some of the information about Mary Lavin at Loreto was in 'Past Pupils Reminisce: Mary Lavin' from *Loreto College, St Stephen's Green*, a brochure, 1988.

An interview with Mary Lavin's cousin Eileen O'Toole on 27 April 1994 proved very valuable for family background and is used in other chapters as well. The only recollection Eileen had of Mary Lavin visiting them in Dublin was of a rather chubby little girl, about ten, lying on the bed and bouncing a ball off the wall beside her. Eileen and her husband Augustine had never, they said, heard Mary Lavin's mother called anything but Lolo.

Mary Lavin's correspondence with the director of the Strokestown Heritage Centre, July 1989, indicates she was still attempting to trace her father's ancestry without success.

Chapter 2
Taped interviews with Zack Bowen in 1972 were made available by the Rare Books section of the University of New York at Binghamton library. Cassette of the documentary, *An Arrow in Flight*, made by Irish television in honour of Mary Lavin's eightieth birthday, was supplied by Cian Ó hÉigeartaigh of RTÉ.

The following interviews supplied information for this chapter and for succeeding chapters as well: Professor Lorna Reynolds, 13 April 1994; Benedict Kiely, 21 April 1994; Mervyn Wall, 26 April 1994, and the Hon. Edward Plunkett at Dunsany Castle, 6 October 1996. Other sources: Terence Brown, *Ireland: A Social and Cultural History, 1922-1985*; Declan Kiberd, *Inventing Ireland*; Mary Lavin, 'Preface', *Selected Stories* ; Lord Dunsany, 'Preface', *Tales from Bective Bridge*; V. S. Pritchett, 1971 introduction to *Collected Stories*; letters from Lord and Lady Dunsany, housed in Special Collections, Glenn G. Bartle Library, State University of New York at Binghamton; *Bird's Neponsett Review*, vol. xv, 1927; James Stern article in *Irish Press*, 5 October 1978.

Facts about Michael MacDonald Scott are from his curriculum vitae, now in the UCD library. The Eleanor Gay interview with Mary Lavin in 1957, source unknown, contained the information on success of some of Lavin's classmates at University College Dublin. It was not until the 1960s that UCD moved from its St Stephen's Green location to Belfield, on the outskirts of Dublin's centre.

The quotation from Declan Kiberd in this chapter can be found in his *Inventing Ireland* (580). The quotation from Terence Brown is in *Ireland* (141).

CHAPTER 3

Material on William Walsh is from an interview with Michael Walshe, William Walsh's nephew, on 25 April 1994, and telephone conversations with Florence Walsh, his niece, in October 1997 (like William Walsh, the Florence Walsh branch of the family dropped the 'e' from its name); an article by William Walsh, 'Young Ladies and Little Boys: Boyhood in a Dublin Convent', *Commonweal*, 26 April 1957; an article by William Walsh headed 'Youth of World Meets in Quest for Peace', no date; and Patrick Shanley's 'Reminiscences' as well as interviews with him during September 1995 and October 1996. Another source was the author's correspondence with the late Augustine Martin, October 1994, and his article: 'A Skeleton Key to the Stories of Mary Lavin', *Studies*, Winter 1963.

Jack B. Yeats' letters are dated 7 January 1947 and 9 November 1950.

CHAPTER 4

The letter to Mrs Bird from Mary Lavin is dated 25 October 1945. The letter to Mrs Bird from William Walsh is dated 2 February 1946. Both were sent from Bective House.

Selected Stories (Macmillan 1959) is not to be confused with a collection, also called *Selected Stories*, which was brought out by Penguin in 1981. The latter collection has a Preface by Mary Lavin. There she states that, when she was invited by Penguin to make her own selection, she decided to make it as representative as possible of her whole body of work by choosing the title story in each of her other collections. *Tales from Bective Bridge*, naturally, had to be the exception. In that case she simply chose at random: her choice was 'Lilacs'.

Zack Bowen, in his study of Mary Lavin, writes: 'Given Mary Lavin's lifelong concern with practicalities, money problems, responsibilities, and the effects of death, her vision of reality is harsh and closely circumscribed by an acute awareness of social class, and society's sanctions and rules.' (23)

Edward Weeks of the *Atlantic Monthly*, in his *Writers and Friends* (120), writes: 'From Ireland Mary Lavin sent a long narrative, "At Sallygap", the haunting dreams of an Irish fiddler written with that lyrical dialogue and pathos characteristic of her work. ("At Sallygap" became the title story of Mary's first book and so attracted Eudora [Welty] that the three of us years later spent a happy day together at Mary's snow-white cottage beside the river Boyne in County Meath.)'

During Mary Lavin's years as a writer for the *New Yorker*, her editor was Rachel MacKenzie. William Maxwell, for forty years a fiction editor at the *New Yorker*, wrote to the author on 27 March 1997 recounting one of his memories of Mary Lavin: 'She [Lavin] was, needless to say, charming and amusing and a delightful conversationalist. I heard her read once at the 92nd Street Y with John Updike. The audience was so dazzled by Updike that they rather failed to appreciate her story, which was first rate.'

Shortly before Mary Lavin's eighty-third birthday, Desmond O'Grady wrote to her to offer his congratulations and to express the hope that she might celebrate many more 'with all your familiar gusto and joy in life so characteristic of you'. He wrote, too, of the days when he visited the Mews and the Abbey Farm. 'Those were romantic days for all of us who were beginning to write and who had you as a superb example of discipline of work and clarity of expression.' For him, he wrote, she 'exemplified the timeless comportment of "whatever you do, do it well and with grace".'

The quotation from Robert Caswell is from the *Kilkenny Magazine*, Double Number Spring 1965, 'The Human Heart's Vagaries' (69).

CHAPTER 5

Details of Michael MacDonald Scott's background are in Christopher Marshall, *A Deep Sonorous Thing: The Newman College Collection of Art* (Newman College, University of Melbourne, 1993), and in correspondence with Fr P. J. L'Estrange, Rector, Newman College; Gerard Windsor, 'A Biography for Michael Scott', *New Writing* in the *Adelaide Review*, no date; and a brochure issued by the School of Irish Studies. Correspondence and a telephone interview with Dr Robert S. Gillen, Adelaide, South Australia, added considerably to the picture. Information from these sources is also used in subsequent chapters.

The Mews material is from the author's interview with architect Sam Stephenson, 16 September 1995; and with Nuala O'Faolain, 15 April 1994.

In her autobiographical *Are You Somebody?* Nuala O'Faolain writes:

> I remember Dublin as dark and dramatic then, at the end of the 1950's, the streets drifting with smoke and rain . . . Pubs and cafés were thrilling, because light and warmth spilled from them. The students moved like guerrillas around the centre of the city, hardly visible. They walked everywhere. They borrowed each other's coats. They lent each other books, and ate egg-and-onion sandwiches and chips with mince sauce and if they had money, at three o'clock potato cakes came on the menu in Bewley's. You ate them slowly, a whole pat of butter on each one, sometimes accompanied by the snuffles of Myles na Gopaleen, toying with a white pudding on toast at the next table. (55-56)

Telephone interviews and correspondence with Elizabeth Cullinan, Desmond O'Grady and Thomas Kilroy, as well as correspondence with Tom MacIntyre added further information.

The material concerned with Elizabeth Cullinan and with

Anne Francis Cavanaugh is from 'A Bouquet for Mary', the *Irish Literary Supplement*, Autumn 1996, 4-5, also used in later chapters.

A telephone conversation with Elizabeth Cullinan and correspondence with her further substantiated the fact that the characters Isabel and Cecilia and their mother Maura in 'Maura's Friends' were based on Valdi, Elizabeth and Mary Lavin.

Joan and John Cahill now live in Phoenix, Arizona. They were interviewed by the author while they were on holiday in Dublin in October 1996.

The Hortense Calisher story is from the 'Introduction' to Susan Cahill's *Women and Fiction* (xv).

Caroline Walsh's article on the Bective area appeared in *The Irish Times* on 20 June 1978.

CHAPTER 6

Marion Fitzgerald interview, *Evening Press*, 9 December 1963 and Bríd Mahon interview, *Sunday Press*, 21 April 1968, were used in this and subsequent chapters. A. A. Kelly's Chapter 3, 'Religious Conventions', provided some information on Mary Lavin's attitude towards religion.

Information about the death of Dermot Bouchier-Hayes is in miscellanous notes, not yet catalogued in 1996, in the Rare Books section of the UCD library.

CHAPTER 7

Information on Mary Lavin's two periods at the University of Connecticut at Storrs is from the author's interviews with Professor Alex Medlicott, Mary Lavin's colleague, 19 November 1994, from extensive correspondence with him, and also from his interview with Mary Lavin in 1977 at the Abbey Farm.

The article by M. Kelly Lynch on George Brandon Saul in *Eire Ireland: A Journal of Irish Studies*, Winter 1994 (169-181) not only delves fully into his career and personality but also includes a comprehensive list of his writings.

The information about the FitzGerald-Lavin connection is from correspondence between the author and Dr Garret FitzGerald dated 15 October, 15 December, 18 December 1995 and 24 January 1996. Kathleen and Leo, Nora Lavin's sister and brother, to whom her letter in this chapter was addressed, were the two Mahons who had stayed on to manage the family business in Athenry.

CHAPTER 8

Information pertaining to the Lavin-Scott marriage and Michael Scott's work on his family history is from an exchange of letters between the author and Dr Robert Gillen between March and June 1995, an exchange of letters between Michael Scott and Dr Robert Gillen in 1982 and 1988, and a letter from Dr Robert Gillen to Mary Lavin, 16 May 1991. These letters were used in subsequent chapters as well.

A letter dated 6 June 1995 from Dr Gillen to the author states that Mary Lavin's work did not 'catch on' in Australia.

Also used: Caroline Walsh correspondence with Alex Medlicott; interview with Maura and Maurice Harmon, 26 November 1993; V. S. Pritchett's *Dublin: A Portrait*; and Kiberd's *Inventing Ireland* (409).

Material on the School of Irish Studies is from its brochure issued for the 1977–78 school year.

The letter from Mary Lavin to Michael Scott which was never sent was dated 24 October 1971. In it, details in connection with the supervision of the Abbey Farm indicate what a crucial role Michael Scott played in it.

CHAPTER 9

Two of the four Jack B. Yeats paintings which Mary Lavin owned were sold in 1980: *The Old Ale House* and *The Man in the Shooting Gallery*.

Facts concerned with women writers are from Janet

Madden-Simpson's *Woman's Part*, and Caroline Walsh's *Virgins and Hyacinths*. Kiberd's *Inventing Ireland* also comments on this subject.

The source for the information on translations of Lavin stories as well as other honours was Janet E. Dunleavy, 'Mary Lavin', *Dictionary of Literary Biography*, vol. 15, 1983 and, as indicated, family correspondence.

Cultural Relations Committee and Aosdana material can be found in both Kiberd and Brown. The quotation from Kiberd is in *Inventing Ireland* (409).

The quoted paragraph from Seamus Heaney is from a letter to the author dated 3 December 1996.

CHAPTER 10

Mary Lavin's opinions on *New Yorker* stories were voiced by her during a Liam Nolan interview on RTÉ radio in 1972, parts of which are quoted in one of the Bowman radio interviews cited in the Chapter 1 notes. About writing for the *New Yorker*, she said further that she did not know how to appeal to people who read it mainly for 'The Talk of the Town' or the cartoons.

Facts for the Wood Quay story are from 'The Wood Quay Saga: Bulldozers and a National Monument' by F. X. Martin, OSA, published in the *Belvederian*, 1979, as well as from correspondence between Fr Martin and the author during December 1996.

The details concerning Mary Lavin's appearance at Harvard following the death of Elizabeth Bishop are from Anne Frances Cavanaugh's portion of 'A Bouquet for Mary', the article in the Iris*h Literary Supplement*, Autumn 1996.

CHAPTER 11

Details about James Ryan's friendship with Mary Lavin and his marriage to Caroline Walsh at Trinity College Chapel in October 1981, as well as the material on dinners at the Abbey Farm, are from an interview with him on 19

September 1995.

Facts about Mary Lavin's physical condition are from Michael Scott's letters to Dr Robert Gillen, 7 December 1982 and 14 May 1987, and from Mary Lavin's letters to Elizabeth Walsh Peavoy.

The Lavin poem was carried in A. A. Kelly's critical study as an example of Mary Lavin's ironic approach to religion (14–15).

Mary Lavin's analysis of drinking is from Alex Medlicott's 1977 interview with the Scotts at the Abbey Farm.

In 1977 Elizabeth Walsh Peavoy attended a writers' workshop in Galway. She wrote to her mother that Anthony Cronin, moderator of the course on creative writing, had said that, studying her stories, he believed she was 'established' along her own lines as a writer. 'The Irish Girl', referred to in this chapter, appeared in the *Irish Press*, no date.

At one point, before Diarmuid Peavoy accepted the Brussels position, there was some talk of his taking a position which would entail separation from his family for two years. Mary Lavin voiced her opinion of that in a letter to Elizabeth. 'Are you mad? In today's world your marriage wouldn't last a quarter of that time.'

CHAPTER 12
Details of visits of grandchildren to the Abbey Farm are from an interview with Kathleen MacMahon, Valentine's oldest child, on 16 April 1994. Eoghan Peavoy's memories are from his essay, written in August 1994 after his graduation from UCD.

The date of the Desmond MacMahon interview was 10 October 1996.

CHAPTER 13
Details about Michael Scott's injury, his physical condition in general, and the memorial service are from the author's correspondence with Dr Robert Gillen during March, April

and June 1995, and from an exchange of letters between Michael Scott and Dr Gillen in 1987 and 1988. Dr Gillen also supplied the Windsor article, used extensively in this chapter. Further details are from Mary Lavin's letters to Dr Gillen, 8 September 1988 and 30 April 1991.

Gerard Windsor writes that Michael Scott was the first Jesuit he had ever met, his first headmaster, and 'an old boy of the school he later attended'.

Mary Lavin's letter to Fred Hanna is dated 22 April 1991; the letter from Stephanie McIntyre, 19 March 1991, and the Lavin reply 24 April 1991; Fr L'Estrange's letter is dated 11 April 1991 and her reply 22 April 1991.

The letter written by Elizabeth Peavoy on Mary Lavin's behalf to Fr L'Estrange in Australia is dated 9 March 1994.

CHAPTER 14

The James Ryan interview was used extensively in this chapter, as was the documentary done by RTÉ, Tom Kilroy's 'Foreword' to *In a Café*, and the preamble by Elizabeth Walsh Peavoy.

So many of the condolence notes received were spur of the moment. The poet Paul Durcan, a selection of whose poetry received the Patrick Kavanagh Award for Poetry in 1974, wrote to Elizabeth Walsh Peavoy from the Dublin airport on his way to Paris. A few hours earlier at an Aosdana meeting the proceedings had been interrupted, and he had listened to an announcement of Mary Lavin's death. 'We stood in silence,' he wrote. 'Now I am sitting in silence and in Paris I will walk in silence with Mary before me lighting the way. I turn the pages to the year 1963 and behold her yet again lighting my way amidst all that dark.' Elizabeth recalled him, a youngish man – he was only nineteen at the time – whom Mary had 'given shelter' when he had left home. 'I can never forget her kindness,' he wrote.

Mary Lavin's Works

Collections of Short Stories

Tales from Bective Bridge. Boston: Little, Brown, 1942; London: Michael Joseph, 1943; London: Readers Union, 1945; Stuttgart: Tauchnitz, 1952; revised and reissued, Dublin: Poolbeg Press, 1978; reissued, Dublin: Town House and Country House, 1996. Contains: 'Sarah', 'Brother Boniface', 'Lilacs', 'At Sallygap', 'Love is for Lovers', 'Say Could that Lad Be I?', 'A Fable', 'Miss Holland', 'The Dead Soldier', 'The Green Grave and the Black Grave'.

The Long Ago and Other Stories. London: Michael Joseph, 1944. Contains: 'The Will', 'A Cup of Tea', 'The Cemetery in the Demesne', 'Grief', 'The Haymaking', 'The Bunch of Grapes', 'Sunday Brings Sunday', 'The Long Ago', 'The Inspector's Wife', 'The Young Girls', 'The Nun's Mother', 'A Wet Day'.

The Becker Wives and Other Stories. London: Michael Joseph, 1946; New York: New American Library, 1971. Contains: 'The Becker Wives', 'The Joy Ride', 'A Happy Death', 'Magenta'.

At Sallygap and Other Stories. Boston: Little, Brown, 1947. Contains: 'At Sallygap', 'The Nun's Mother', 'The Will', 'The Haymaking', 'The Green Grave and the Black Grave', 'Sarah', 'The Sand Castle', 'A Wet Day', 'Brother Boniface', 'Love is for Lovers', 'A Cup of Tea', 'A Happy Death'.

A Single Lady and Other Stories. London: Michael Joseph, 1951. Contains: 'A Single Lady', 'The Sand Castle', 'Posy', 'A Story with a Pattern', 'The Small Bequest', 'The Convert', 'A Woman Friend', 'The Widow's Son', 'The Pastor of Six Mile Bush', 'A Gentle Soul', 'A Visit to the Cemetery'.

The Patriot Son and Other Stories. London: Michael Joseph,
1956. Contains: 'The Patriot Son', 'Scylla and Charybdis',
'Chamois Gloves', 'An Old Boot', 'Limbo', 'A Tragedy',
'A Glimpse of Katey', 'The Long Holidays', 'An Akoulina
of the Irish Midlands', 'Frail Vessel', 'My Vocation', 'The
Little Prince'.

Selected Stories. New York: Macmillan, 1959. Contains: 'The
Will', 'Chamois Gloves', 'Asigh', 'Posy', 'The Cemetery
in the Demesne', 'The Little Prince', 'My Vocation', 'The
Small Bequest', 'A Woman Friend', 'Brigid', 'A Wet Day',
'A Happy Death'.

The Great Wave and Other Stories. London and New York:
Macmillan, 1961. Contains: 'The Great Wave', 'The
Mouse', 'Second-Hand', 'In a Café', 'Lemonade', 'What's
Wrong with Aubretia?', 'The Villas', 'Bridal Sheets', 'My
Molly', 'Loving Memory', 'The Yellow Beret', 'The
Living'.

The Stories of Mary Lavin, Vol. I. London: Constable, 1st ed.
1964; 2nd ed. 1970. Contains: 'Frail Vessel', 'The
Cemetery in the Demesne', 'A Gentle Soul', 'A Single
Lady', 'The Sand Castle', 'Posy', 'The Convert', 'The
Widow's Son', 'A Visit to the Cemetery', 'The Dead
Soldier', 'The Will', 'A Cup of Tea', 'The Bunch of
Grape', 'The Young Girls', 'A Happy Death', 'The Patriot
Son', 'Chamois Gloves', 'Limbo', 'A Tragedy', 'My
Vocation', 'The Little Prince', 'The Great Wave', 'In a
Café'.

In the Middle of the Fields and Other Stories. London:
Constable, 1967; New York: Macmillan, 1969. Contains:
'In the Middle of the Fields', 'The Lucky Pair', 'Heart of
Gold', 'The Cuckoo Spit', 'One Summer', 'The Mock
Auction'.

Happiness and Other Stories. London: Constable, 1969;
Boston: Houghton Mifflin, 1970. Contains: 'Happiness',
'The New Gardener', 'One Evening', 'A Pure Accident',
'The Lost Child'.

Collected Stories. Boston: Houghton Mifflin, 1971. Contains: 'The Green Grave and the Black Grave', 'At Sallygap', 'The Cemetery in the Demesne', 'Sunday Brings Sunday', 'The Long Ago', 'The Young Girls', 'A Happy Death', 'The Sand Castle', 'The Small Bequest', 'A Visit to the Cemetery', 'A Tragedy', 'The Long Holidays', 'My Vocation', 'Frail Vessel', 'Brigid', 'The Great Wave', 'The Mouse', 'The Living', 'In the Middle of the Fields', 'The Cuckoo Spit', 'Happiness', 'The New Gardener'.

A Memory and other Stories. London: Constable, 1972; Boston: Houghton Mifflin, 1973. Contains: 'Tomb of An Ancestor', 'Trastevere', 'Asigh', 'Villa Violetta', 'A Memory'.

The Stories of Mary Lavin, Vol. II. London: Constable, 1974. Contains: 'The Green Grave and the Black Grave', 'Sarah', 'At Sallygap', 'The Nun's Mother', 'Brother Boniface', 'Say Could That Lad Be I?', ' Sunday Brings Sunday', 'The Long Ago', 'A Wet Day', 'Brigid', 'The Small Bequest', 'A Woman Friend', 'The Long Holidays', 'An Akoulina of the Irish Midlands', 'My Molly', 'The Living', 'Bridal Sheets', 'The Mouse', 'Loving Memory', 'The Yellow Beret', 'The Becker Wives', 'A Likely Story'.

The Shrine and Other Stories. London: Constable, 1977. Contains: 'The Shrine', 'Tom', 'The Mug of Water', 'Senility', 'Eterna'.

Selected Stories. New York: Penguin Books, 1981. Contains: 'Lilacs', 'The Long Ago', 'The Becker Wives', 'A Single Lady', 'A Likely Story', 'The Patriot Son', 'The Great Wave', 'In the Middle of the Fields', 'Happiness', 'A Memory', 'The Shrine'.

The Stories of Mary Lavin, Vol. III. London: Constable, 1985. Contains: 'Lilacs', 'Happiness', 'The New Gardener', 'Lemonade', 'In the Middle of the Fields', 'The Lucky Pair', 'Heart of Gold', 'The Cuckoo Spit', 'One Summer', 'The Mock Auction', 'One Evening', 'A Pure Accident', 'The Lost Child'.

A Family Likeness and Other Stories. London: Constable, 1985. Contains: 'A Family Likeness', 'A Walk on the Cliff', 'A Marriage', 'The Face of Hate', 'A Bevy of Aunts', 'A House To Let'.

In a Café. Dublin: Town House and Country House, 1995. Contains: 'In the Middle of the Fields', 'A Family Likeness', 'Lemonade', 'Tom', 'The Girders', 'A Cup of Tea', 'A Gentle Soul', 'Chamois Gloves', 'The Joy-Ride', 'The Convert', 'In a Café', 'A Story with a Pattern', 'The Widow's Son', 'The Will', 'The Little Prince', 'Trastevere'.

NOVELS

The House in Clewe Street. London: Michael Joseph, 1945; Boston: Little, Brown, 1946; Harmondsworth: Penguin, 1949.

Mary O'Grady. London: Michael Joseph, 1950; Boston: Little, Brown, 1950.

MISCELLANEOUS

A Likely Story. New York: Macmillan, 1957; Dublin: Dolmen, 1967. (Children's)

The Second-Best Children in the World. London: Longman, 1972; Boston: Houghton Mifflin, 1972. (Children's)

'Let Me Come Inland Always' (poem), *Dublin Magazine*, 15, January–March 1940, 1–2.

'Poem', *Dublin Magazine*, 15, January–March 1940, 2.

'Preface', *Selected Stories*. New York: Macmillan, 1959, v-viii.

'The Fields Will Never Leave You' (essay), *Country Beautiful*, 2, no. 1, September 1962, 18–20.

'Introduction', *Tales from Bective Bridge*. Dublin: Poolbeg Press, 1978, 5–7.

BIBLIOGRAPHY

BOOKS

Adams, Michael. *Censorship: The Irish Experience.* University, Ala.: The University of Alabama Press, 1968.

Bowen, Zack. *Mary Lavin.* Lewisburg: Bucknell University Press, Irish Writers Series, 1975.

Bowen, Elizabeth. *The Heat of the Day.* New York: Alfred A. Knopf, 1949.

Brown, Terence. *Ireland: A Social and Cultural History, 1922–1985.* London: Fontana Press, 1985.

Cullinan, Elizabeth. *The Time of Adam.* Boston: Houghton Mifflin, 1971.

_____. *A Change of Scene.* New York: Norton, 1982.

Fallis, Richard. *The Irish Renaissance: An Introduction to Anglo-Irish Literature.* Dublin: Gill and Macmillan, 1977.

FitzGerald, Garret. *Towards a New Ireland.* Dublin: Torc Books, Gill and Macmillan, 1973.

Glendinning, Victoria. *Elizabeth Bowen: Portrait of A Writer.* London: Weidenfeld and Nicolson, 1977.

Harmon, Maurice. *Sean O'Faolain: A Life.* London: Constable, 1994.

Kelly, A. A. *Mary Lavin, Quiet Rebel: A Study of Her Short Stories.* Dublin: Wolfhound Press, 1980.

Kiberd, Declan. *Inventing Ireland.* Cambridge, MA: Harvard University Press, 1995.

Lee, J. J. (ed.). *Ireland: 1945–1970.* Dublin: Gill and Macmillan, 1979.

Mahoney, Rosemary. *Whoredom in Kimmage: Irish Women Coming of Age.* Boston: Houghton Mifflin, 1993.

Murphy, John A. *Ireland in the Twentieth Century.* Dublin: Gill and Macmillan, 1975.

O'Brien, Kate. *The Land of Spices.* Preface by Lorna Reynolds. Dublin: Arlen House, 1982.

O'Connor, Frank. *A Short History of Irish Literature: A Backward Look.* New York: Capricorn Books, 1968.

_____. *Stories by Frank O'Connor.* New York: Vintage Books, 1956.

O'Faolain, Nuala. *Are You Somebody?* Dublin: New Island Books, 1996.

O'Faolain, Sean. *The Irish.* London: Penguin, 1969.

Peterson, Richard F. *Mary Lavin.* Boston: Twayne Publishers, 1978.

Plunkett, James. *Collected Short Stories.* Dublin: Poolbeg Press, 1977.

Pritchett, V. S. *Dublin: A Portrait.* Photographs by Evelyn Hofer. New York: Harper and Row, 1967.

Rose, Catherine. *The Female Experience: The Story of the Woman Movement in Ireland.* Dublin: Arlen House, 1975.

Ryan, James. *Home from England.* London: Phoenix House, 1995.

Shannon, Elizabeth. *Up in the Park: The Diary of the Wife of the American Ambassador to Ireland, 1977-1981,* New York: Atheneum, 1983.

Sheehy, Maurice (ed.). *Michael/Frank: Studies on Frank O'Connor.* New York: Alfred A. Knopf, 1969.

Strong, L. A. G. *Personal Remarks.* New York: Liveright Publishing Corporation, 1953.

Wall, Mervyn. *Leaves for the Burning.* Dublin: Millington, 1973.

Weeks, Edward. *Writers and Friends.* Boston: Little, Brown and Company, 1981.

ANTHOLOGIES AND ESSAYS

Great Irish Short Stories. Edited and with an introduction by Vivian Mercier. New York: Dell Publishing Company, 1964. Contains Mary Lavin's 'Brigid' and 'The Nun's Mother'.

Irish Women: Image and Achievement. ed. Eiléan Ní Chuilleanáin. Dublin: Arlen House, 1985. Essays.

Michael/Frank: Studies on Frank O'Connor. ed. Maurice Sheehy. New York: Alfred A. Knopf, 1969.

Modern Irish Short Stories. Selected and with an introduction by Frank O'Connor. London: Oxford University Press. First published in the World's Classics in 1957 and reprinted in 1959, 1962, 1964, 1966, 1968, 1970 and 1974. Contains Mary Lavin's 'The Will' and 'A Wet Day'.

The Portable Irish Reader. Selected and edited by Diarmuid Russell. New York: The Viking Press, 1946. Contains Mary Lavin's 'Lilacs'.

A Portrait of the Artist As a Young Girl. ed. John Quinn. 'Foreword' by Seamus Heaney. London: Mandarin Paperback with Radio Telefis Éireann, 1986. Edited versions of interviews conducted by John Quinn.

Virgins and Hyacinths: An Attic Press Book of Fiction. ed. Caroline Walsh. Dublin: Attic Press, 1993.

Woman's Part: An Anthology of Short Fiction by and About Irish Women, 1890-1960. Selected and introduced by Janet Madden-Simpson. Dublin: Arlen House, 1984. Contains Mary Lavin's 'Frail Vessel'.

Women and Fiction: Short Stories by and About Women. ed. Susan Cahill. New York: A Mentor Book, 1975. Contains Mary Lavin's 'In a Café'.

ARTICLES, REVIEWS

Anon. 'A Moralist of the Heart'. *The Irish Times,* 6 June 1992.

Anon. 'Double Tribute to Mary Lavin'. *RTÉ Guide,* 49, 6 December 1974, 10.

Bryson, Mary E. 'Dublin Letters: John Eglinton and *The Dial,* 1921-1929'. *Eire-Ireland,* Winter 1994, 132–148.

Caswell, Robert W. 'Irish Political Reality and Mary Lavin's *Tales from Bective Bridge'. Eire-Ireland,* 3, Spring 1968, 48–60.

_____. 'The Human Heart's Vagaries'. *Kilkenny Magazine,* Double Number, Spring 1965, 69–89.

Cullinan, Elizabeth. 'Nora's Friends'. *New Yorker*, 29 August 1970, 26–32.

Dunleavy, Janet E. 'The Making of Mary Lavin's "Happiness".' *Irish University Review*, vol. 9, 2, Autumn 1979, 225–231.

_____. 'Mary Lavin'. *Dictionary of Literary Biography*, 15, 1983, 261–69.

Dunsany, Lord. 'A Preface'. *Tales from Bective Bridge*. Boston: Little, Brown, 1942.

Fitzgerald, Marion. 'Talking to Mary Lavin'. *Evening Press*, 9 December 1963.

Harmon, Maurice. 'Courageous Chronicler of the Vagaries of the Human Heart'. *The Irish Times*, 26 March 1996.

Hicks, Granville. 'Tale of Three Lands'. *Saturday Review*, 13 June 1959.

Jordan, Heather B. 'A Particular Flair, A Hound's Nose, A Keen Scent: Sean O'Faolain's Editorship of *The Bell*'. *Eire-Ireland*, Winter 1994, 149–60.

Kenneally, James J. 'Sexism, the Church, Irish Women'. *Eire-Ireland*, Autumn 1986, 3–16.

Kiely, Benedict. 'Mary and Elizabeth'. *The Irish Times*, 4 November 1978. Review of Lavin's *Tales from Bective Bridge* and Bowen's *Irish Stories*.

_____. 'The Greatness of Mary Lavin'. *The Irish Times*, 21 October 1972. Review of *A Memory and Other Stories*, *The Second-Best Children in the World* and *The Becker Wives*.

_____. 'An Addiction to Truth'. *Sunday Independent*, 12 January 1986. *A Family Likeness and Other Stories* reviewed.

Kilroy, Thomas. 'A Complex Heart'. *The Irish Times*, 20 May 1995.

Liddy, James. 'How We Stood Our Rounds: Bohemian Dublin in the Sixties'. *Eire-Ireland*, Spring 1995, 7–16.

Lynch, M. Kelly. 'George Brandon Saul, 1901–1986: An Appreciation and a Selected Checklist'. *Eire-Ireland*,

Winter 1994, 169–181.

Mahon, Bríd. 'The Quiet Authoress'. *Sunday Press*, 21 April 1968.

Martin, Augustine. 'A Skeleton Key to the Stories of Mary Lavin'. *Studies*, Winter 1963.

Martin, Fr F. X., OSA. 'Wood Quay: A Modern Viking Saga', from 'The Wood Quay Saga, November 1977–January 1979: Bulldozers and a National Monument', *Belvederian*, 1979.

Murphy, Catherine. 'Mary Lavin: An Interview'. *Irish University Review*: Mary Lavin Special Issue, Autumn 1979, 207–224.

O'Connor, Frank. 'The Girl at the Gaol Gate'. *Review of English Literature*, I, April 1960, 25–33.

Peavoy, Elizabeth Walsh. 'Voyage Round My Mother'. *Sunday Independent*, 28 May 1995.

Pritchett, V. S. 'Introduction'. *Collected Stories*. Boston: Houghton Mifflin, 1971.

Reynolds, Lorna. 'Mary Lavin: An Appreciation'. *Hibernia*, 15 May 1970, 15.

Scott, Bonnie Kime. 'Mary Lavin and the Life of the Mind'. *Irish University Review*: Mary Lavin Special Issue, Autumn 1979, 262–78.

Sheridan, Niall, 'Writer in Profile: Mary Lavin'. *RTÉ Guide*, 15 November 1968.

Stern, James, 'Home Thoughts'. *Irish Press*, 5 October 1978. Review of *Tales from Bective Bridge*.

Walsh, Caroline. 'Once You Belong, You Belong'. *The Irish Times*, 20 June 1978.

Windsor, Gerard, 'A Biography for Michael Scott'. *New Writing, Adelaide Review* (monthly newspaper), no date.

INDEX

As always, I feel it is the most peaceful place I know. I love its strange combination of total privacy . . . so far from the road and any sight or sound of passing traffic and yet providing vistas and a far-distant horizon. I have had great happiness and peace and contentment (and occasionally a little of the other!) here and shall miss it more than I can say.

There was no doubt in Mick's mind that Mary was heartbroken at the thought of giving the farm up. For her it meant her father, the Dunsanys, her life with William Walsh, and the children growing up there. And yet he knew none of those factors was sufficient to keep her happy there for lengthy periods. She had to get away from it from time to time. It was, as he wrote to Dr Gillen, 'a love-hate relationship'. She was lonely there. She had to be with people, to have lengthy conversations, to gossip, and at the farm she had 'no one to talk to or at except myself and I am not as good a listener as I once was!'

Mick was right about Mary's feelings, of course, and as soon as the decision was made she began having regrets. 'My heart is broken for Bective & I cannot understand how I let them persuade me to sell it except that I was I suppose very very ill.' She seemed to derive some solace from passing the blame for the decision to sell on to Des MacMahon. In fact, it had been obvious to all of the family that it was no longer practicable to keep the farm. That decision had not been Des's but, once it was made, it had indeed been Des who had looked after the details and organized the auction for the sale. Mary's ambivalence was obvious to him. For a few years before the farm was to be sold, she would say she hated the place though it was obvious that she loved it. It was his opinion that she had mixed feelings about a great many things, however. Selling the farm apparently was only one of them.

Unlike Mary, Mick was content in the Sandymount

apartment as well as at the farm. He realized that it was a bit claustrophobic and that he and Mary were indeed too much 'in each other's pockets'. His hope was that they could realize enough from the sale of the farm to get a larger flat with a study for each of them and with a small garden. Meanwhile, he was spending as much time as possible at the farm, getting lawns mown, fences mended and the roadside hedges trimmed. There was a great deal of work to be done to get everything in order for prospective buyers and he was enjoying himself enormously. Mary had refused to join him and to take advantage of the joys of Bective for the time remaining. She had gone off on a holiday with an old school and university friend but Mick had no doubt at all that she would soon come racing back. She had only been gone two days and already word from her indicated that she was bored to death.

There is a letter from her to Elizabeth, dated 23 May, no year, which must have been written around that time. She wrote that she seemed always to be waiting for something bad to happen as it does in her stories. As examples, she mentioned, 'A Memory', 'A Marriage' and, she added, perhaps 'Senility'. She wished that she could learn not to plague herself in advance. Here she was, unhappy at the thought of Mick's leaving her alone to take a trip to Australia, when his plans to go had not yet been made. And for some time she had worried about Mick's dying and Bective's being sold. Now Mick had a great many things wrong with him and Bective was 'as good as gone'. Since Mick was two years her senior, she had to face the fact that when he was gone she would once more be alone as she had been when William Walsh died. But she was very aware that this time – and she brooded about it – she would not have the girls around her to fill her life.

She had once said to Mick that they both had a visible question mark over their lives while other people had an invisible one over theirs. She imagined that Mick was worried